PACIFIC ISLANDS REGIONAL INTEGRATION AND GOVERNANCE

PACIFIC ISLANDS REGIONAL INTEGRATION AND GOVERNANCE

SATISH CHAND ed.

ANU
E PRESS

Asia Pacific Press at
The Australian National University

ANU

E PRESS

Co-published by ANU E Press and Asia Pacific Press
The Australian National Unversity
Canberra ACT 0200
Ph: 61-2-6125 4700 Fax: 61-2-6257 2886
Email: books@asiapacificpress.com
Website: http://www.asiapacificpress.com

National Library of Australia Cataloguing-in-Publication entry

Pacific Island Regional Integration and Governance

Bibliography.
Includes index.
ISBN 0 7315 3739 4.

1. Regionalism - Pacific Area. 2. Economic policy - Pacific Area. 3. Pacific Area - Economic integration. 4. Pacific Area - Foreign economic relations. I. Chand, Satish.

337.196

Editors: Polly Hemming, Jenny Bourne—Asia Pacific Press
Cover design: Annie di Nallo

CONTENTS

TABLES

APPENDIX TABLES

FIGURES

ABBREVIATIONS USED IN TABLES

n.a.	not applicable
..	not available
-	zero
.	insignificant

ABBREVIATIONS

AGOA	African Growth and Opportunity Act
ACP	African, Caribbean and Pacific
ATPSM	Agricultural Trade Policy Simulation Model
ABARE	Australian Bureau of Agricultural and Resource Economics
ACIAR	Australian Centre for International Agricultural Research
BOAC	British Overseas Airways Corporation
CBI	Caribbean Basin Initiative
CARICOM	Caribbean Community and Common Market
CER	Closer Economic Relations
CFA	Compact of Free Association
CGE	computable general equilibrium
CPIA	Country Policy and Institutional Assessment
EPA	Economic Partnership Agreement
EIU	Economist Intelligence Unit
EU	European Union
EC	European Community
ELAC	excess local area content
FAO	Food and Agriculture Organization

FDI	foreign direct investment
FIC	Forum island country
FTA	free trade agreement
GATT	General Agreement on Tariffs and Trade
GPT	Generalised Preferential Tariff
GSP	Generalised System of Preferences
GDP	gross domestic product
ICAO	International Civil Aviation Organization
IFPRI	International Food Policy Research Institute
MFN	most-favoured nation
MALIAT	Multilateral Agreement on the Liberalization of International Air Transportation
NAFTA	North American Free Trade Agreement
PACER	Pacific Agreement on Closer Economic Relations
PDMC	Pacific Developing Member Country
PICTA	Pacific Island Countries Trade Agreement
PIASA	Pacific Islands Air Services Agreement
PRTS	Pacific Regional Transport Study
RTA	regional trading arrangement
SPARTECA	South Pacific Regional Trade and Economic Cooperation Agreement
SPEC	South Pacific Bureau of Economic Cooperation
UNCTAD	United Nations Conference on Trade and Development
WTO	World Trade Organization

CONTRIBUTORS

Vinaye Ancharaz is a lecturer in the Department of Economics and Statistics, Faculty of Social Studies and Humanities at the University of Mauritius.

David Barber is a Governance Adviser with AusAID.

Lino Briguglio is Head of the Economics Department at the University of Malta, Director of the Islands and Small States Institute at the Foundation for International Studies and Director of the Malta University Centre.

Satish Chand is Director of the Pacific Policy Project and a Senior Lecturer in International and Development Economics in the Asia Pacific School of Economics and Government at The Australian National University.

Gordon Cordina is an Assistant Lecturer in Resource Economics. He has worked as an economist at the Central Bank of Malta and later was head of the Research Department.

Ron Duncan is Executive Director of the Pacific Institute of Advanced Studies in Development and Governance at the University of the South Pacific. Previously, he was Director of the Asia Pacific School of Economics and Management at the Australian National University.

Nadia Farrugia is an economist and a part-time economics lecturer at the University of Malta.

Christopher Findlay is Head of the School of Economics at the University of Adelaide. He is also Vice-Chair of the Australian Committee for Pacific Economic Cooperation (AUSPECC).

Peter Forsyth is Deputy Director of the Tourism Research Unit and Professor in the Department of Economics at Monash University.

Greg Fry is Hedley Bull Fellow in the Department of International Relations and Director of Studies of the Graduate Studies in International Affairs at The Australian National University. Before taking up his present appointment he was a lecturer in the Department of Political Science.

Quentin Grafton is Professor of International and Development Economics, Asia Pacific School of Economics and Government, The Australian National University.

John King is an aviation consultant and Managing Director of Aviation and Tourism Management, Pty Ltd.

Tom Kompas is Director, Graduate Program in International and Development Economics at the Asia Pacific School of Economics and Government. He is Associate Editor of *Australian Journal of Agricultural Resource Economics.*

Theodore Levantis is an economic modeller with the Australian Bureau of Agricultural and Resource Economics.

Luca Monge Roffarello is an economic expert at the Trade Negotiations and Commercial Diplomacy Branch, UNCTAD.

Hannah Parris is currently completing a PhD at the Asia Pacific School of Economics and Government at The Australian National University. Prior to this, Ms Parris worked as a climate change and natural resource management policy analyst for the Australian Government.

Phillip T. Powell is Associate Clinical Professor of Business Economics & Public Policy and Healthcare Academy Director, Indiana University.

Robert Scollay is Associate Professor & Director of the APEC Study Centre at the University of Auckland. He is currently coordinator of the PECC Trade Forum, a network of trade experts from countries around the Pacific Rim.

Sanjeev Sobhee is Head of the Economics and Statistics Department at the Univeristy of Mauritius.

Michael Swidinsky is an economist in the Multilateral Trade Policy Division of Agriculture and Agri-Food Canada.

Ray Trewin is Research Program Manager for the Agricultural Development Policy Program at the Australian Centre for International Agricultural Research. Dr Trewin has held senior positions in ABARE and the Department of Primary Industries and Energy's Australian Fisheries Service.

David Vanzetti is a Visiting Fellow with the Asia Pacific School of Economics and Government at The Australian National University. He has held senior trade positions with the United Nations Conference on Trade and Development (UNCTAD) in Geneva.

Stephanie Vella is an economist and a part-time economics lecturer at the University of Malta.

Alan Winters is Director of the World Bank's Development Research Group. Professor Winters is also a Research Fellow and former Program Director of the Centre for Economic Policy Research in London and has previously worked in the Universities of Cambridge, Bristol, Wales and Birmingham, and as Economist, Division Chief and Research Manager in the World Bank.

ACKNOWLEDGMENTS

This book grew out of a conference on Pacific regional integration held by the Australian National University in June 2005. The organisers of the conference would like to acknowledge the support of the Australian government's international development agency, the Australian Agency for International Development for intellectual input and financial support for the conference and for the publication of this book.

The contributors would like thank the staff of Asia Pacific Press at The Australian National University for their assistance in bringing together the contributions made at the conference into this volume.

1

PACIFIC ISLAND REGIONAL INTEGRATION AND GOVERNANCE: AN OVERVIEW

Satish Chand

The geographic clustering of several small Pacific island countries (PICs) in the immediate neighbourhood of Australia and New Zealand has supported a degree of regional identity. The Pacific islands, moreover, have long remained sheltered from the pressures of global commerce, and particularly from the competitive pressures of the rapidly growing Asian economies located to the north. In the case of Pacific island nations, even the closest neighbour could be located some several hundred kilometres away by sea, with its attendant high costs of transportation. Local industries, therefore, have enjoyed a significant degree of 'natural' protection. Furthermore, a number of the local PIC-based industries have enjoyed regulatory advantages through a combination of high domestic tariffs and preferential access into industrial country markets. The natural and policy-induced barriers to trade, however, are falling rapidly, with this trend likely to continue for the foreseeable future. Transportation and communication costs have been falling due to technological progress, while the regulatory barriers are receding as global trade is liberalised. These developments are exerting pressures for change within several Pacific island countries. The adjustment, if well managed, has the potential to offer significant economic gains to the individual countries and to the region collectively.

The forces for regionalism, that is increased trade intensity between neighbouring states, has persisted over history but these forces are likely to be even stronger in the future. Large fixed costs of trade, including those pertaining to communication and shipping, have meant that neighbouring states have a greater tendency to trade amongst themselves than with economies located afar. Globalisation, constituting an increasing volume of trade and investment flows between sovereign states, however, is having its impact on the most isolated of the economies. The handicap of geographic distances is diminishing given rapidly falling communications and transportation costs. The expanding spatial horizons of international trade and commerce are creating their own challenges as much as presenting new opportunities for growth amongst hitherto isolated and thus sheltered island economies of the Pacific.

Regionalism offers the opportunity to reap the benefits of scale. The Pacific islands countries, as a group, face cost disadvantages due to their small local markets and isolation from the major markets. The large distances by sea raise transportation costs in comparison to similar distances by land, so falling transportation and communication costs present the opportunity to the Pacific island countries as a group to integrate their markets in order to tap into the gains from a larger and more deeply integrated market. The highly fragmented markets have to date raised the costs of local industries and particularly those with inherently large economies of scale. The problems of small markets were long recognised and have been responsible for the establishment of several regional institutions including a regional airline, a regional university, a regional shipping service, and separate regional institutions to manage the maritime environment, air safety, and the fisheries stocks. The emergence of international security concerns, including the threats of drug trafficking, people smuggling, and international terrorism, all provide even greater impetus for regional governance.

The benefits of economies of scale extend to the provision of regional public goods such as environmental protection, air and marine safety, sustainable management of deep-water fisheries, and more lately the control of cross-border crimes. An institutional architecture that provides for regional public goods such as regional security has several merits, including the advantages of scale leading to greater cost efficiencies and the ability to integrate information flows across national jurisdictions. Given the geographic proximity of the Pacific island countries to Australia and New Zealand, such advantages are likely to flow on to the wider Pacific region and the global community more generally. Recent concerns with regional security have drawn Australia and New Zealand closer to the Pacific islands countries, particularly in addressing security threats within the region. The Pacific Plan signed by the 16 leaders of the Pacific Forum at its 2005 meeting, as an example, has an economic and security agenda. Greater fluidity in information flows across the Pacific, moreover, could lead to closer cultural, economic, and social ties between the communities, thus consolidating a regional identity.

The ongoing process of deeper regional integration within the Pacific island countries will raise the competitive pressures faced by domestic industry from abroad. These pressures will create the demand for more efficient delivery of public services. The Pacific island countries could thus be pressured into pooling regional resources to reach economies of scale in the supply of goods and services enjoying significant economies of scale. The individual Pacific island country that continues to face the cost disadvantages of size and isolation could end up facing large out-migration, leading to a hollowing out of domestic industry as the most productive labour and capital gravitate towards the metropolis in the surrounding industrialised countries. This is not necessarily an undesirable outcome, particularly when it could lead to a situation of large remittance flows back to the Pacific island countries. Such flows could sustain a small resident population within the Pacific island countries and possibly attract retirees from elsewhere. Remittances and retirees could, in a deeply integrated region, sustain far-flung communities without the need for donor support

The Pacific island countries have lagged behind the Caribbean and Mediterranean small island states in their experimentation with regional integration and pooled governance. The Caribbean states, for example, have invested in a common currency while the Mediterranean states of Malta and Cyprus have adopted the Euro and have now joined the European Community. The Indian Ocean state of Mauritius, in contrast, has adopted a unilateral stance towards liberal trade and has its own currency. The Caribbean Community provides a model for the Pacific island countries to consider assessing how they might maximise their gains from the recently endorsed Pacific Island Countries Trade Agreement (PICTA). Mauritius, in contrast, offers an alternative path in the form of unilateral liberalisation. The Pacific island countries have the advantage of backwardness in that they can draw lessons from the experience of other small states.

The twelve chapters in this edited volume are the product of a conference held at the Australian National University in June 2005 that brought together experts from around the world to consider specific issues pertaining to regional integration and governance within small states. The papers collectively address the challenges posed to small states by the quickened pace of globalisation. The lessons learnt from the experiences of small states are then used to draw policy lessons for the Pacific island countries. The issues addressed in this volume are far from being either exhaustive in their coverage or conclusive in their findings; the aim here has been to wet the appetite of the interested reader and to encourage greater research on this subject.

While the individual chapters are written as standalone pieces, the volume has been structured in four parts; namely, the context, governance, case studies, and a contrarian view. Chapters 2, 3 and 4 provide the context in terms of the policy challenges facing small island states from globalisation; chapters 5, 6 and 7 provide the institutional settings and the potential for pooled regional governance; chapters 8 to 11 are specific case studies drawn from the PICs; and chapter 12 is a contrarian view on the appropriateness of regionalism in the Pacific.

Chapter 2 by Alan Winters sets the context for Pacific-specific analysis on regionalism and governance. Alan, drawing on an earlier joint study with Pedro Martins, shows that the costs of manufacturing activity for small economies are considerably larger than those for larger economies. This finding is of little surprise, but then leads to the stark conclusion that small isolated states would not be able to sustain a manufacturing sector under liberal global trade. Trade protection, as argued by Winters, is damaging since it only exacerbates the problems of smallness. Donor-funded industry subsidies such as those offered by trade preferences could be, but are not necessarily, welfare enhancing. The moral case for aid on the handicaps of size is also discounted since small states on the whole are not income-poor. Regionalism, by permitting the 'scaling-up' of small fragmented economies, and international labour mobility provide the most pragmatic options for welfare-enhancing reforms. Chapter 3 by Briguglio et al. provides a conceptual framework to measuring economic resilience. Economic resilience is distinguished from economic vulnerability—the latter is inherited, while the former constitute policy actions taken to mitigate the adverse consequences of the inherited handicaps of size and isolation. Chapter 4 uses a partial equilibrium model to assess the impact of WTO-sponsored agricultural trade liberalisation on small, island developing economies. The authors find that the large gains from such liberalisation are inequitably distributed, and more pertinent to this volume, that small states are net losers from liberalisation of global agricultural trade.

Chapter 5 provides the Pacific context, particularly with respect to past attempts at pooling resources in industries facing large economies of scale advantages. Greg Fry notes that the Australian government's recent push for greater pooling of regional resources is not all that new. He provides several examples of regional institutions created in the early to mid-nineteenth century by the colonial administration with a view to pooling regional resources for greater cost efficiency. Fry contrasts 'regional integration' that is inwardly focused with 'collective diplomacy' that has an outward focus and is motivated by the pursuit of collective foreign policy objectives. Ron Duncan in Chapter 6 considers the prospect of a common currency for the Pacific Island region. Ron argues that capital market integration is something the Pacific island countries cannot do without, thus the choice for PIC policymakers is between monetary independence and exchange rate stability. He makes a strong case for the latter. Chapter 7 builds on the notion of vulnerability, arguing that the rising pace of globalisation increases the economic vulnerability of small states. The authors use the case of Mauritius to provide evidence in support of the proposition that government size increases with openness to international trade. They argue that larger governments are needed as a buffer against the adverse effects of globalisation.

The four case studies, each covered in chapters 8 to 11, are instructive on the challenges of, and opportunities presented by, increased regional trade. Robert Scollay in chapter 8 notes the asymmetry in exports vis-à-vis imports between the Pacific island countries as a group and Australia and New Zealand. While Australia and New Zealand account for some 30–55 per cent of total PIC imports, the Pacific island countries collectively account for less than 2 per cent of total exports from Australia and New Zealand. The major exports from the Pacific island countries into Australia and New Zealand are PNG minerals, Fiji garments, and Samoan automotive (wire harness) parts: the last two are due to preferential trading arrangements and thus under threat due to preference erosion. Future trade losses to the Pacific island countries will be compounded by the formation of new preferential trading arrangements with Asia and between Australia and the United States that exclude the Pacific island countries. Parris and Grafton in chapter 9 note that some 40 per cent of the global tuna catch is from the PICs' exclusive economic zones. The common pool nature of this resource calls for joint management but this is absent given poor governance and inferior institutions. The discussant to this paper raises an interesting concept of 'tuna mining'. Chapter 10 considers the case of air transport, an industry that enjoys significant scale economies and network externalities but one that has experienced serious problems within the Pacific islands countries lately. The authors highlight the inherent problems of low densities and policies that have impeded competition within PIC aviation. Chapter 11 is a case study of preference erosion in the case of Fiji sugar. Preferences, as shown by this case study, can induce the development of an inefficient industry that is then left exposed to serious adjustments following their withdrawal. Policies in the form of lump-sum transfers equivalent in value to the preferential rents and marginal cost pricing is recommended to induce adjustment to a subsidy-free trading environment.

The last chapter offers a contrarian view on regional integration in the Pacific. Phil Powell argues that integration amongst the individual Pacific island countries is possible only after the nation state has matured. He argues that current proposals for deeper regional integration within the Pacific are, thus, premature. This view is not without controversy, however.

2

Policy challenges for small economies in a globalising world

L. Alan Winters

This chapter is a sequel to work I conducted recently with Pedro Martins on the costs of doing business in small economies (Winters and Martins 2004, 2005). Somewhat to my surprise, this research, based on specially collected data, showed that, *ceteris paribus*, manufacturing and tourism faced significantly higher business costs in small isolated economies than elsewhere. It would be absurd to proclaim the estimates we produced to be unassailable, but their size and the fairly thorough review they received in the November 2004 issue of the *World Trade Review* leave me convinced that they are qualitatively correct.

The next question, therefore, is what should we—and they—do about these excess costs? That is the issue taken up in this chapter. It discusses international trade policy, industrial policy, governance and government for small isolated economies, and trade preferences, aid and migration as responses by the international community. There appear to me to be no easy solutions for the small countries themselves, but there certainly are helpful steps that many could take on trade policy and governance. For the world community, I do not see how we can avoid ultimately talking about migration.

THE COSTS OF SMALL SIZE

The starting point for this study is the results of Winters and Martins' (2004, 2005) studies showing that the private costs of manufacturing activity are considerably higher for small economies than for larger ones.

Their work collates data on business costs in 92 economies drawn from four distinct sources. The largest contribution is from the Economist Intelligence Unit (EIU) which surveys 54 medium-sized and large countries twice a year. The remaining surveys were commissioned by the Commonwealth Secretariat for the Winters and Martins study from three regional organisations covering various (mostly small) economies: Imani Capricorn in Africa, the Caribbean Community in the Caribbean and the Pacific Islands Forum in the Pacific. All these surveys date from mid 2002. The questions covered transport costs on exports and imports, the costs of utilities, the wages of different types of labour, taxes and rents as continuous variables, plus labour shortages, utility reliability and policy regimes on a categorical basis.

Having collected the data, Winters and Martins test empirically for the existence of relationships between the different business costs and country size (population, and occasionally aggregate GDP). As well as descriptive statistics, they run simple linear regressions (OLS) on size and other appropriate variables for the continuous variables, and ordered logit equations for the categorical variables in which respondents classify their country in one of several categories. Given the regression results, they calculate the cost disadvantage for four specimen countries, chosen to represent micro (12,000 inhabitants), very small (200,000), 'threshold' (1.6 million) and small economies (4 million) relative to their median country, which has approximately 10 million inhabitants.[1]

The population values used for these representative countries correspond to Anguilla, Vanuatu, Botswana, Singapore and Hungary, respectively. These calculations suggest that there are significant penalties to small size in most of the costs analysed (Table 2.1). In a second exercise, Winters and Martins (2004) aggregate the cost disadvantage factors to estimate the competitive disadvantages of small economies in three example industries (electronic assembly, clothing and tourism) in which small countries seem likely to have comparative advantage and hence export potential. Using data on the importance of particular costs in the overall cost of supplying exports to the world market (production and transportation costs), they weight together the cost disadvantage factors to calculate the excess costs of exports from small economies. These are presented in Table 2.2.

Given the uncertainties of the data it seems that small countries (of which the exemplar is Singapore, population 4 million) are not severely handicapped in comparison with Winters and Martins' fictional median country and neither is the threshold country. However, it is equally clear that for the very small or micro countries (Vanuatu, population 200,000; and Anguilla, population 12,000), the size disadvantages are huge. Moreover, if these cost premia can not be passed onto customers (that is, if small economies have to sell their goods and services at world prices), the small economy can only export if some part of the production process is willing to bear the costs by accepting lower returns than it would reap in the median economy. When Winters and Martins convert the cost inflation factors into such income penalties, they are huge for very small and micro economies. In most cases the data suggest that capital

Table 2.1   Summary of cost disadvantages
(% deviation of costs from those in the median economy)

Area of cost	Micro	Very Small	Threshold	Small
Airfreight average[a]	31.8	4.1	−1.8	−1.7
Seafreight average	219.6	70.5	20.5	9.1
Unskilled wages average	60.1	31.6	13.6	6.6
Semi-skilled wages average	22.4	12.1	5.8	2.6
Skilled wages average	38.0	20.3	8.9	4.3
Telephone average (marginal costs)	98.5	47.2	19.1	9.0
Electricity (marginal costs)	93.1	47.0	19.7	9.4
Water (marginal costs)	-	-	-	-
Fuel average	53.8	28.3	12.3	5.9
Personal air travel average	115.7	56.8	23.3	11.0
Land rent average	−3.5	−17.2	−14.2	−8.9

Note: [a] 'Average' denotes that the reported estimate is the mean of several measures of the costs concerned.
Source: Central case from Winters, L.A. and Martins, P.M.G., 2004. 'When comparative advantage is not enough: business costs in small remote economies', *World Trade Review*, 3(3):347–83.

Table 2.2   Cost inflation factors (% by which target country costs of supplying exports exceed median country costs)

Industry	Micro	Very small	Threshold	Small
Electronic assembly	36.4	14.3	5.0	2.7
Clothing	36.3	14.3	5.1	2.7
Hotels and tourism	57.5	28.5	11.9	6.2

Source: Winters, L.A. and Martins, P.M.G., 2004. 'When comparative advantage is not enough: business costs in small remote economies', *World Trade Review*, 3(3):347–83.

would earn negative returns if it were invested in a micro economy and had to bear all the cost of the inefficiencies itself. Similarly, even if wages were zero in a micro economy, total costs in manufacturing would still exceed world prices.

Finally, Winters and Martins present some data to see if small states have worse policies than other countries, using variables such as bank interest rates, corporate tax rates and import and export duties. These show no strong evidence of size effects. Interest rates seem to be lower in small economies, but there is compelling proof of neither higher tax rates for business nor higher import/export duties than in larger economies.

TRADE POLICY

A first reaction to the high costs faced by manufacturing in small, isolated economies is that, in order to compensate for these extra costs and for the costs of international trading, these countries need the right to protect their industries.[2] This is completely misguided. The problem is not that imports can get in too easily but the very opposite. Adding barriers to trade will exacerbate, not relieve, problems of smallness. Even where local industries could be successfully established behind tariff walls, there is nothing in the observation of transaction costs or genuine 'excess costs' of inputs to suggest that such an approach would be economically beneficial. Simple theory has long shown that following comparative advantage maximises real income. The costs identified by Winters and Martins do not change this—they merely show that for some countries comparative advantage may entail no trade and that for some, possibly the same, countries, maximum income might not be adequate.

A related response has been to suggest subsidising business activities, or perhaps investment, in order to overcome the cost disadvantages of smallness. There are many arguments in the policymaking literature for subsidising business in an economy. I do not generally agree with them, but, even if I did, smallness adds nothing to them. If you would not subsidise business in a large economy, neither should you do so in an equivalent small one, for precisely the reasons outlined in the previous paragraph. Smallness does not generally introduce marginal distortions that need to be countervailed, but an overall feasibility constraint. If income is insufficient when you maximise it, it will certainly be insufficient when you do not; and in the absence of the market failures usually adduced to justify industrial policy, subsidising manufacturing puts you in the latter category.

It is useful to make these points graphically. First, transactions costs with the rest of the world affect the offer curve that a small open economy faces. In Figure 2.1, if the rest of the world will trade at prices P'QP', the broken line, a small country (which has to pay its own transactions costs) faces an offer curve of PQP, the solid line, where Q represents the point of no trade. PQP lies below P'QP' everywhere except Q. Regardless in which direction the country trades, it has to finance the transactions costs on both legs of the journey. Assuming that for each good these costs are the same in both directions and that, without loss of generality, they have to be paid in Y, we can derive PQP as follows.

Suppose the slope of P'QP' is p, so that one X trades for p units of Y. Consider a trade that swaps one X for pY on world markets and that transactions costs are a units of Y per Y traded and b units of Y per X traded ($a, b < 1$). If our country exports X, the supposed trade would take the world to point A, but because we have to pay $(ap+b)$ units of Y for transport, etc., our country achieves

Figure 2.1   The transaction-cost modified offer curve

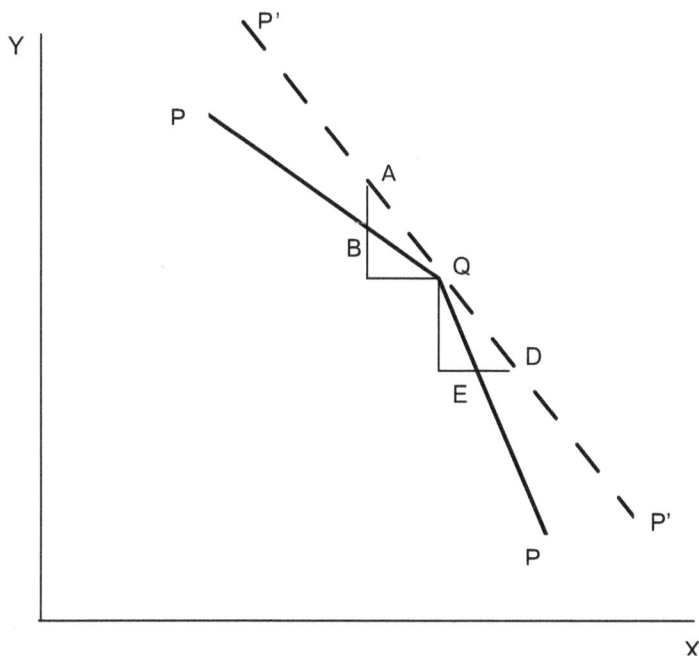

only point B with $1-(a+bp)$ units of Y. Now suppose that we export pY to place the rest of the world at D, we still have to find $(ap+b)$ again, and supposing that this is deducted from imports of X we receive only $1-(a+b/p)$ units of X, that is, we achieve point E.

Given PQP we can derive the consumption possibility frontier (CC) for our small country by sliding it along FF the production possibility frontier in Figure 2.2, and tracing the northeasterly-most points. Figure 2.2 shows three possible locations for PQP corresponding to three regimes. With production at Q_1 we have comparative advantage in X and export it to consume at, say, C_1. With production at Q_3, the opposite applies—we export Y to consume at, say, C_3. Along the middle range, in which the slope of FF lies between those of the branches of PQP we do not trade, and hence consume at the production point. (Because PQP has linear segments there is no virtue in producing to the left of Q_1—the consumption locus would lie inside that shown. If PQP were continuous and concave, that would not apply, but then we would not be a small country for the world price ratio would be changing as our country's trade changed).

Given CC we can find the optimal consumption and production pair using a (well-behaved) social welfare function. Note that at all along CC the marginal rates of transformation and substitution (the slopes of FF and the corresponding piece of CC, respectively) are equal, so that there is no case for trade intervention or for production subsidies or taxes. For example, if free trade took us to Q_1, a production subsidy on Y would move us to the left and the consumption locus would lie unambiguously inside the CC shown. For standard reasons, a tariff would be even worse, for it would move the consumption locus inwards and choose a non-optimal point along it.

Similarly, consider starting at Q_2. A production subsidy to either X or Y would move us towards Q_3 or Q_1, respectively, but would not normally induce any trade because an indifference map preferring Q_2 to all other points on CC would prefer consuming at Q_3 to all points along the segment Q_3C_3. An export subsidy, however, could move us to a point along that segment but again, fairly obviously from the figure, that would be even worse than settling at Q_3.

The discussion so far presumes that FF is the true social production possibility frontier. That is, although our small economy may face inefficiencies in the transformation of primary factors into final goods and services deriving from its small scale, these do not represent *domestic* distortions. Thus while, for example, inefficiencies in power generation may make electricity more expensive

Figure 2.2   The consumption possibility locus with transaction costs

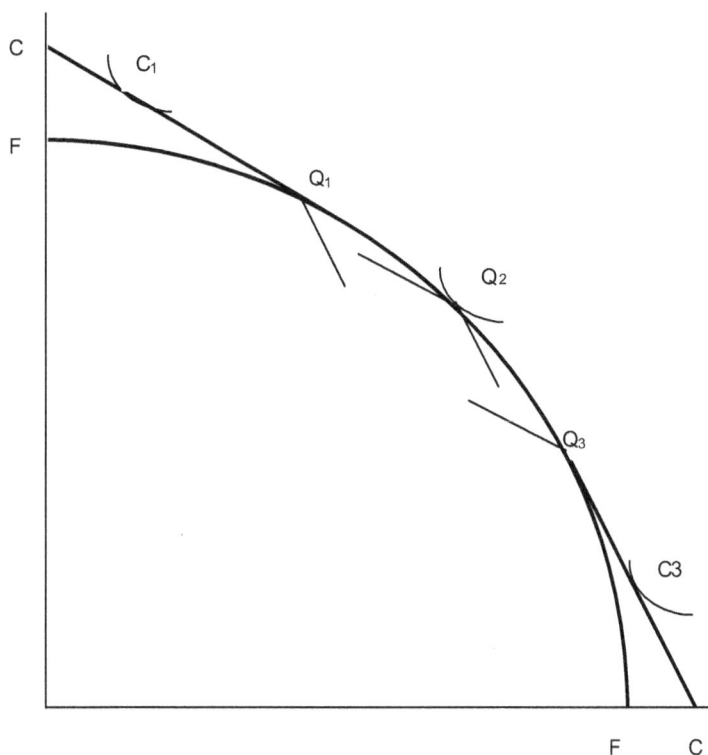

than in the median country, we assume that they are both unavoidable and apply equally to all production sectors. If these conditions are not met, an appropriate policy intervention could push FF (and hence CC) outwards— but precisely how would depend on the factor and/or electricity intensity of sectors and the nature of the intersectoral inequality to be corrected. Under these circumstances, standard second-best theory means that if the fundamental distortions cannot/will not be addressed directly, then a production or trade intervention could be welfare-enhancing.

The introduction of transactions costs does not fundamentally change the standard welfare analysis. Thus, if inefficiencies in electricity production lead to the under-production of, say, X, policies that boost the output of X—subsidies or tariffs—*could* be desirable. The proposition is not that *any* subsidy or tariff would help, however, only that there may be levels that do so. As with large economies, the challenge is finding the distortion and introducing an intervention at the socially optimal level. In small societies this may be even more difficult than in larger ones because of the difficulties of finding disinterested parties and the generally greater power of special interests in small economies (see below). Moreover, the fact remains that addressing the distortion directly is first best, and that if the 'excess costs' are actually non-distortionary, policy interventions will be harmful. For example, if power is unavoidably expensive, small countries do not have comparative advantage in energy-intensive manufacturing. Subsidising such manufacturing to compensate for high power costs would be bad economics—it would increase the use of relatively costly inputs and divert other factors from better uses elsewhere in the economy.

What cost disadvantages in small countries are distortions and what are just 'natural' handicaps? Scale effects in utilities are natural, but the market power emerging from having few suppliers may be distortionary. In these cases, however, subsidising the use of monopolised inputs is very unattractive from a distributional perspective. Monopolists inflate their incomes by restricting their supply. Subsidising sectors that use their output adds insult to injury by further enhancing their incomes at the expense of taxpayers. Far better is to regulate them more effectively. The same analysis applies to other produced inputs, although for tradable goods (and services such as banking) local monopoly is constrained by the threat of imports even if the latter do face high transactions costs, so the problem is likely to be limited.

The excess transactions costs that small and remote countries face on international trade may well also result from monopoly power—of the liner cartel, for example—but these are essentially given for an individual small economy and so are 'real' for the purposes of domestic policy formulation. Similarly high, possibly unreasonable, risk premia on international borrowing are basically part of a small country's environment.

One area of evident difficulty for small isolated economies is human capital. For very high skills, they will never be satisfactory locations—for example, for nuclear physicists, hot-shot property lawyers and leading baseball players. Thus at this level, their shortage is natural. At lower levels of skill, however, the skill shortages—which emerge very clearly in Winters and Martins' findings—may be endogenous, and hence may represent distortions. I do not think we know enough about this and should log it as an area for future research.

A common response to the costs of small scale is to argue that market size should be increased by regional agreements with neighbours. While the intention is entirely correct, the implementation of such agreements is frequently flawed because they are drawn too narrowly. Specifically, if regional agreements are restricted to trade policy— that is, regional trading arrangements (RTAs), which merely provide mutual trade preferences—they are almost certainly doomed. Where the partner country is large, the small country typically just ends up adopting the partner's internal price structure. To the extent that this equals world prices, well and good, but to the extent that the large country has protection, its distortionary effects are merely visited also on the small country. This could offer income gains by giving to the small country higher prices for its exports, although in asymmetric, large–small, regional agreements access to the most protected markets is frequently withheld. The European Union, for example, controls small partners' access to its agricultural markets and (until recently) textile and clothing markets. It also, however, means that the small country has to pay protection-inflated prices for many of its imports from the large partner (trade diversion) rather than lower world prices.

Where the RTA partner is small, the outcome is almost inevitably economically costly. The polar small-partners model of an RTA—see, for example, Winters (2000) or Panagariya (2000)—generates only losses. Small partners cannot satisfy each others' demands, imports continue from the rest of the world, and since neither their prices nor the tariffs they face change, the internal prices of imports do not change, so there is no scope for (welfare-enhancing) trade creation. Trade diversion, on the other hand, continues unabated. Schiff (2001) has modified the polar model, but the basic message is not fundamentally changed.

The problem with RTAs is not that trade with neighbouring countries is free, but that with other countries is restricted. To enlarge effective market size (and to be able to purchase from the cheapest sources) free trade with neighbours typically comes a poor second to free trade with everyone.

It is worth noting that all this analysis presupposes that the small economy has no particular advantage (location, for example) or niche market. The former essentially gives it a cost advantage in some sectors, while the latter essentially allows it to charge higher prices than its competitors. Such favoured countries will fare well and all small countries should aim to achieve such status. The analysis of this chapter is, however, predicated on the reasonable assumption that not all will, although it certainly does not imply that none will.

POLICY AND GOVERNANCE

Winters and Martins (2004) suggest that small countries do not have significantly worse policies than other countries in the few dimensions that they could measure: tariffs, export subsidies and direct taxes.[3] This is only a partial list of policies and misses entirely all aspects of governance, so it is worth exploring these dimensions further. Unfortunately we do not have any comprehensive and objective datasets on the dimensions we require, but partial sources do not suggest large differences between large and small countries. Briguglio et al. (2005) suggest that over 1999–2003 the mean CPIA (Country Policy and Institutional Assessments) scores for 34 small and 102 larger economies were not far different.[4] Small countries were assessed as relatively stronger on financial stability, banking regulation, transparency and governance, but weaker on product and factor markets.

A second source of policy/governance data is the *Doing Business* surveys (World Bank 2004), which for various business-related costs and facilities compares 14 small economies with 131 larger ones. Again the differences in means are not particularly great.

Despite the similarity of means in these measures, however, the small countries should not be complacent. There are wide variances and in a number of cases we know that small countries perform very badly—for example, the incidence of crime in some Caribbean countries and governmental stability in some Pacific ones. More importantly, it is not difficult to imagine models in which economic activity, especially investment, is more sensitive to governance problems in small economies than in larger ones. For example, small economies offer no advantages in terms of local market opportunities, so there is no offset to any shortcomings in production conditions.[5] Thus, in terms of policy priorities, improvement in governance and in the costs of doing business they must rank fairly highly.

One of the major challenges that small economies face in addressing their problems of governance is the difficulty in small polities of avoiding capture by special interests. In small undiversified economies, interest groups are relatively larger and have to deal with only a small number of opponents. This makes the exercise of influence stemming from social status or current economic power easier, with the result that change becomes much more difficult (this argument is due to James Madison in the Federalist Paper No. X of 1788). In addition, in small economies the costs of favouring special interests cannot be hidden but fall squarely, obviously and relatively heavily, on the other groups. This could make decision-making more transparent and rational but is equally likely to make it divisive and costly. Add to this some natural social segmentation, such as that on ethnic grounds, and the problems can become overwhelming.

A second, politically incorrect but statistically inevitable, challenge for small countries, is leadership. If leaders are selected on merit (in whatever dimension), no matter what the underlying distribution of talent, leaders from small countries are likely to be less able than those from larger ones. It is difficult to quantify the cost of the expected shortfall because we don't have well-defined talent-to-performance or performance-to-outcome functions, but its existence is undeniable.

Alesina and Spolaore (2003) explore the consequences of the size of countries/economies by comparing the benefits of size with the costs of trying to meet the conflicting demands of more sub-populations with different preferences as country size increases. Among the benefits of size they note are

- market size, which is mitigated by openness, the effects of which, in turn, are eroded by the transactions costs of trade explored above. This is discussed in the section 'trade policy'[6]
- the mutual insurance that regions in large economies provide for each other
- defence and strategic advantages
- the fixed costs of government.

Government involves some activities with fixed costs such as foreign representation and policy design, and others with strong economies of scale, such as defence and exercising strategic influence. Large countries can spread these more widely than can smaller ones, and Alesina and Spolaore offer empirical evidence on the extra costs of governments for small countries. They find a significant cross-country correlation between population and the share of government consumption in GDP, suggesting that a 1 per cent increase in population reduces the consumption share by around 0.012 percentage points *ceteris paribus*. The effect is strongest for current expenditures excluding transfers, but is entirely absent for defence.

The only realistic answer to these problems of government cost is to combine with other countries in providing these services—to economise on the costs of economic management and/or statehood. Andriamananjara and Schiff (2001) and Schiff and Winters (2003) argue strongly that by combining various functions of government small states can both economise on costs and, possibly, exert a greater influence on their environments. Such efficiencies are not sufficient to overcome all the disadvantage faced by most small countries—for example, combining the entire population of the organisation of East Caribbean states still leaves the resultant 'state' well within the definition of 'small'. But there is undoubtedly a case for seeking such efficiency gains as part of the answer. I also note that in the cases where smallness appears not to matter—small European nations such as Luxembourg, Liechtenstein and Andorra for example—the secret appears to be to integrate more or less seamlessly with the neighbouring large countries.

The last observation is important for small states. Combining to produce government services does not mean establishing regional authorities and then maintaining local capabilities to influence and monitor those authorities. It means a genuine pooling of sovereignty with no local shadowing—, for example, countries within a country maintain no foreign or security policy establishments. This is no mean step—it is essentially political union—and so it relies on mutual trust and on sound regional institutions which ensure that local imperatives are adequately addressed. To many residents of small countries this may seem a high price to pay, but in fact it is no higher than that 'paid' by, say, the Victorians and Queenslanders in forming Australia or, given the very small sizes involved, Yorkshiremen and Lancastrians combining in England. That it is a 'price' is exactly the point made by Alesina and Spolaore—political independence entails economic costs. This perspective raises the question of whether, if political independence is the fundamental problem for small countries, the 'price' should be paid by their residents or by the rest of the world. If it is paid by the latter, we are essentially subsidising smallness and should expect more of it to occur.

One innovative proposal from Briguglio et al. (2005) is that, even if small countries retain their policymaking, they could subcontract many of the administrative functions of governments, such as issuing driving licenses and paying pensions. This may allow some savings although there may be a trade-off between savings and the choice of contractor. Combining these functions among several small countries would offer some savings (and could be made approximately reciprocal in a mercantilist sense if each function went to a different economy), but would probably be less cost-efficient than subcontracting to a major economy with very large economies of scale. In the latter, the service would be a net import, which would have to be paid for by transaction-cost-intensive exports, but provided that the price of foreign exchange were set properly, comparing prices would allow the right decision to be made.

Finally, under this heading we should note one apparent advantage of governmental fragmentation. The current organisation of world society confers some fixed advantages of statehood which are worth more per head to small than to large economies. These include a vote at the United Nations and the WTO and the right to issue (read 'sell') passports, flags of convenience, banking licences and internet addresses. To be politically incorrect again, these advantages mostly entail either the management of external costs or the creation of public goods which impinge, very roughly, equally on everyone in the world (at least in an expected value sense). Thus it is not clear that allocating such rights equally to each state is optimal. Nonetheless, many small states currently make a living from such sales and if we seek to constrain this by international agreements about banking or shipping standards, we will further increase the pressure to support small state incomes in some other way.

INFRASTRUCTURE, HUMAN CAPITAL AND SERVICE EXPORTS

A second way of addressing the excess cost of manufacturing identified by Winters and Martins is to think in terms of services exports. Among the more successful small economies, niche tourism and financial services are major sources of export earnings. These are less handicapped by the excess costs of physical movement than are goods. Success in these areas clearly requires strong governance performance—especially security and regulatory ability, respectively—but if these conditions pertain they are quite promising. I do not believe, however, that they can address all of the income deficits of small economies.

First, the required capital has to be provided. The risk premia faced by small countries are typically higher than one might expect given their governance and economic circumstances. Partly, this may be ignorance on the part of the lenders, but it also reflects real risk phenomena. Even setting aside the apparent higher vulnerability of small remote economies to physical shocks (World Bank 2000a) the lack of diversity in small economies increases the risk of economic disruption.

Second, even if capital can be provided for infrastructure, many of the cost disadvantages of small economies in Winters and Martins are on current expenditure. For example, even if service exports are independent of transportation disadvantages, imports are not. Considering that ships and planes need to travel back as well as towards a small economy, the savings entailed in service exports may not be that great.

Third, the most favourable case for infrastructure-led salvation is probably communications links. If these are excellent and cheap, the electronic provision of services may become competitive, such as data input, software, tele-services. Even in 'electronic services', however, personal contacts are important (see Chanda 2003), so small remote economies will still be disadvantaged by their high travel costs and long travel times.

Fourth, many service exports require human capital. This not only requires investment but also constant honing, typically through contact with customers and rivals abroad. This, in turn, raises the spectre of migration. Winters and Martin (2004) identify serious shortages of skilled labour in small remote economies both in terms of relatively high wages and reported shortages even among current producers. The reasons for this are not hard to find. Up to a point, the returns to skills are a function of the size of the market that is served, merely in terms of covering the fixed cost of skill acquisition. In addition, there are typically economies of agglomeration for skilled activities such as specialisation, stimulation, and the transfer of knowledge.

While some skilled workers can certainly be retained in small economies, not least because of the more pleasant lifestyle, their productivity is for these reasons unlikely to be of the highest order, and the higher the skill level, the greater the deficit.

The 'brain drain' represents a huge challenge to many small countries. The latest data in Docquier and Marfouk (2005), for example, show that 86 per cent of Guyanese and 83 per cent of Jamaicans with higher education live abroad. These are, of course, countries with governance challenges, but the figures are high even for more successful societies—36 per cent for the Bahamas and 61 per cent for Barbados

Some have suggested using bonds to encourage students (or even workers) to return from abroad in order to recoup the costs of their education to their home small economies. This may make sense in Singapore where skills can be properly rewarded in the domestic economy, but for smaller less successful economies it is likely to amount to little more than the *ex post* private finance of education. That is, people will merely pay the bond in order to leave. Given the enforcement difficulties of such bonds, my own preference in these circumstances would be to provide basic education free of charge—as something one generation provides to another—and have private financing of higher education. The latter would need to be supplemented by higher salaries at home (to fund repayment but made possible by savings in the public funding of universities) and also loans and bursaries for poorer households.

I have argued elsewhere that liberalising the temporary movements of labour within the world economy—mode 4 of the GATS—can generate huge economic gains (Winters et al. 2003a, 2003b). This could be a key factor for very small economies, essentially allowing residents to earn abroad but live and consume at home. Temporary workers from small countries would still be at a disadvantage relative to those from larger ones—they would face higher transport costs, less effective networks for finding jobs and easing migratory strains, and higher consumption costs at home. However, particularly if they had preferential access—such as the guaranteed quotas that New Zealand offers some Pacific islanders—they may be able to 'out compete' other sources of labour. Just as with trade preferences, however, the sustainability of the mobility preferences would be a question-mark.

If temporary mobility is to be a long-term solution, there would need to be considerable trust that the receiving larger country would honour the quotas. It would also require trust that that country would encourage (enforce) the temporariness of the labour contracts and not actively screen temporary migrants for permanent places. If these conditions were met, I believe temporary mobility would indeed be a viable means of maintaining some small economies, including providing the incentives for education.

SUBSIDISING THE SMALL COUNTRY: TRADE PREFERENCES AND AID

The previous section proposed policy approaches to smallness that involved larger countries as well. This section pursues the logic further and considers explicit or implicit subsidies for small countries' trade. It differs from the analysis in the section 'trade policy' in that the subsidy is now paid by the external large country (or world community). Thus, while the same distortion is introduced to our small country as before, it is now partially, fully or over-fully compensated by a transfer from abroad. The net effect could be an improvement in welfare, although it need not be.

The current tariff preferences for small countries' exports allow them to sell at industrial country markets' tariff-inclusive prices rather than at world prices. This source of rent has historically been very important—as, for example, with banana or tuna exports to the European Union (EU) or clothing exports from the Caribbean to the United States. The problems are first that other developing countries have become more hostile to these preferences, as with Latin American challenges to banana preferences and East Asian challenges to those on tuna, and that the more legalistic regime of the WTO makes them harder to defend than they were under the General Agreement on Tariffs and Trade (GATT). Second, as donors discover new favourites, the preferences of the old are eroded. Consider Pakistan's recent advantages under the textile quotas and the way in which the North American Free Trade Agreement (NAFTA) and now African Growth and Opportunity Act (AGOA) reduced the advantages of the Caribbean Basin Initiative (CBI). Third, the benefits of preferences are declining anyway as industrial countries move, or are moved, to liberalise their trade regimes. In all these cases, as Winters and Martins show, very small economies face large income penalties as rents are reduced.

An alternative route could be for industrial countries to subsidise small country trade explicitly—either their exports or their imports, or both. This would require conscious policy shifts in the major capitals and also derogations from WTO agreements. This could have the effect of eventually—with large enough subsidies—turning the offer curve in Figure 2.1 from concave to convex, with the upper leg steeper than the lower one. Provided that the subsidies outweighed the transactions costs, the small economy would always trade and could always do better than under 'costless' but unsubsidised trade. In Figure 2.3, P'QP' is the consumption possibility locus under 'costless' free trade, while with export subsidies the locus would be CDC, where points such as C_1 or C_3 would be chosen (with corresponding production points Q_1 and Q_3, respectively).

An alternative route would be straight income transfers (as recommended by de Vries 1975). Here the money would presumably go to the government, which would distribute it somehow. This would avoid the production distortion entailed in the trade subsidies, saving resources, but would pose even greater problems so far as governance and incentives to produce were concerned. In either case, one of the main issues for the recipients would be the security of such transfers. As I noted above, I believe that they would need to be permanent to cover excess costs on current transactions and so could not be dressed up merely as transitional financing to encourage structural adjustment.[7] Preferences are declining and subsidies are always vulnerable, but unless there were reasonable confidence that they would continue, all manner of short-term rent-seeking behaviour would arise.

A second issue, especially for simple income subsidies (aid) and also for the large remittance flows received by some small remote economies is the cancer of aid-dependence. Perpetual and unconditional income flows appear to be very destructive to the productive economy and eventually to society. There is nothing wrong *per se* in not working or investing if the money keeps flowing, but it appears that at the same time as work habits decline so do various other social habits, especially if traditional societal structures have been undermined. Particularly problematic appears to be youth unemployment and boredom. Hence one observes social malaise not only in dependent island economies of the Pacific, but in the native American reservations in the United States, in pension-dependent societies in South Africa and in some oil states.

Figure 2.3   Consumption locus with externally funded export subsidies

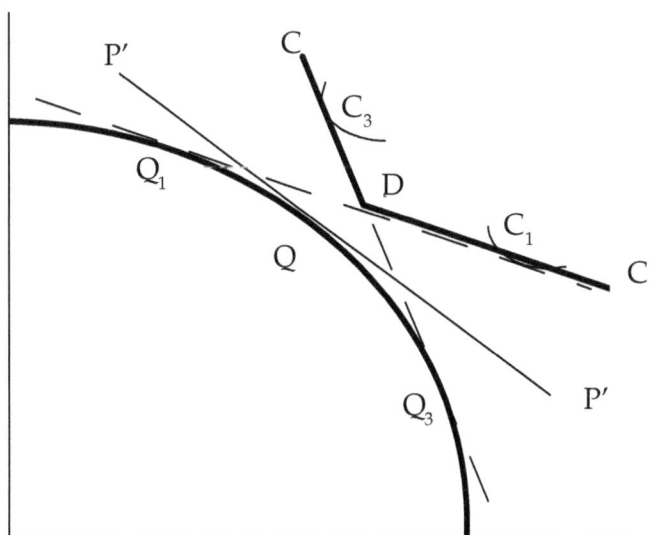

Explicit subsidies to micro and very small economies raise their own very particular political challenges. Specifically, many of the cost disadvantages identified by Winters and Martins must also apply to isolated parts of larger countries. These disadvantaged regions are often subsidised via regional policies, as for example, in the United Kingdom, Europe more generally and China. However, if small economies were permitted to have export subsidies, one would need to argue explicitly why this privilege should not be extended to parts of larger economies, for if it were it would probably fatally undermine subsidies discipline in the WTO. The reason is not hard to formulate, but it may be uncomfortable: within a country, people can move out of uneconomic locations. Ultimately the world must face the possibility that if the current preferences that small countries receive are eroded and their incomes can not be maintained in other ways, many of their inhabitants will seek to move abroad.

CONCLUSION

The preceding observation makes the trade-off for the rest of the world plain. On the other hand, the moral case for international policies to support small remote economies is not overwhelming at present. They are not particularly income-poor by world standards nor particularly stagnant, and once one accounts for their attractions as location and the attractions (to many of us) of smaller societies, they do not seem too badly off. True the developed countries have helped to create their current production structures, and changes in developed country policies have contributed to the concerns about their futures, but this is at most a transitional issue. Moreover, many small economies do not appear to be maximising their prospects for essentially governance-related reasons. Plenty of commentators argue that with sufficient focus small economies could find viable activities and that nothing focuses the mind like the money running out. Thus a case can certainly be made that permanent support for small economies is inappropriate.

On the other hand, I do not believe that all small countries will remain economically viable. Their excess costs are a serious handicap and in an ever more closely integrated and sophisticated world economy their disadvantages are likely to grow. For sure some will thrive by good luck or sound judgment, but left to themselves, others are likely to decline sufficiently that humanitarian imperatives arise, and their problems do become those of the world community.

If we let them get to this stage, economic rescue will be very expensive and population movement will become almost inevitable. Thus it seems to me that if we believe that small economies do not warrant international support we need to be prepared eventually to let their people move elsewhere if incomes fall too low to compensate for the advantages of small society living. Particularly if we limit the relaxation in immigration policy to the micro and very small economies the effects will be very small in aggregate. Around 3.12 million people (0.05 per cent of the world's population) live in countries of below 200,000 population, 6.31 million (0.10 per cent) in those below 400,000 and 28.20 million (0.45 per cent) in those below 1.5 million population.

ACKNOWLEDGMENTS

The findings, interpretations and conclusions expressed in this note are entirely those of the author and do not necessarily reflect the views of the Board of Executive Directors of the World Bank or the governments they represent. I am grateful to Ross Garnaut, workshop members and participants in a seminar at the Australian Treasury for comments on the earlier draft of this paper. They are not responsible for its remaining shortcomings. Thanks are also due to Audrey Kitson-Walters and Zenaida Kranzer for logistical help.

NOTES

[1] 'Threshold' derives from the now fairly standard threshold for defining small economies of 1.5 million people.

[2] On transactions costs, the argument is implicitly that, since high costs curtail exports, policy is required to curtail imports and help producers exploit their domestic markets.

[3] We tried and failed to collect data on VATs and budget deficits.

[4] The Country Policy and Institutional Assessments (CPIA) are assessments by World Bank staff based on a variety of sources and are being published from July 2005 onwards.

[5] Consider how companies persisted with production in China, despite the many instances in which they were unable to protect their assets from local predation. I have not been able to locate any formal tests of the hypothesis that governance matters more for small countries.

[6] Alesina and Spolaore observe that, once global or regional institutions guarantee access to foreign markets, the main cost of smallness is removed and we see greater tendencies towards fragmentation.

[7] Finance to encourage diversification in small economies has not been very successful in the past.

3

CONCEPTUALISING AND MEASURING ECONOMIC RESILIENCE

Lino Briguglio, Gordon Cordina, Nadia Farrugia and Stephanie Vella

Many small states[1] manage to generate a relatively high GDP per capita compared to other developing countries[2] in spite of their high exposure to external economic shocks. This would seem to suggest that there are factors which may offset the disadvantages associated with such vulnerability. This phenomenon is termed by Briguglio (2003) as the 'Singapore Paradox', referring to the fact that Singapore is highly exposed to external shocks, and yet this island state has managed to register high rates of economic growth and high GNP per capita. This reality can be explained in terms of Singapore's ability to build its economic resilience.

Economic vulnerability is well-documented in the literature from both the conceptual and empirical viewpoints (see for example Briguglio 1995, 2003; Crowards 2000; Atkins et al. 2000). Most studies on economic vulnerability provide empirical evidence that small states, particularly island ones, tend to be more economically vulnerable than other groups of countries, due mostly to a high degree of economic openness and a high degree of export concentration. These lead to exposure to exogenous shocks, which could constitute a disadvantage to economic development by magnifying the element of risk in growth processes. Cordina (2004a, 2004b) shows that increased risk can adversely affect economic growth as the negative effects of downside shocks are larger than those of countervailing effects of positive shocks. The high degree of fluctuation in GDP and in export earnings registered by many small states is considered one of the manifestations of such exposure (see Atkins et al. 2000).

THE 'SINGAPORE' PARADOX

As already explained, the 'Singapore Paradox' refers to the seeming contradiction that a country can be highly vulnerable and yet attain high levels of GDP per capita. Briguglio (2003, 2004) explains this in terms of the juxtaposition of economic vulnerability and economic resilience and proposed a methodological approach in this regard. In this approach, economic vulnerability was confined to inherent permanent or quasi-permanent features, while economic resilience was associated with man-made measures, which enable a country to withstand or bounce back from the negative effects of external shocks. Briguglio refers to this type of resilience as 'nurtured'. Cordina (2004a, 2004b) presents a conceptual application of this approach by showing that saving and capital formation in an economy, in response to a situation of vulnerability, can be important sources of resilience.

On the basis of this distinction, Briguglio (2004) identifies four possible scenarios into which countries may be placed according to their vulnerability and resilience characteristics—described as 'best-case', 'worst-case', 'self-made', and 'prodigal son'.

Countries classified as 'self-made' are those with a high degree of inherent economic vulnerability, but which adopt appropriate policies enabling them to cope with or withstand their vulnerability. They take steps to mitigate their inherent vulnerability by building their economic resilience.

Countries falling within the 'prodigal son' category are those with a relatively low degree of inherent economic vulnerability, but which adopt policies that expose them to the adverse effects of exogenous shocks. The analogy with the prodigal son is that these countries, though 'born in a good family', squander their riches.

The 'best-case' scenario applies to countries that are not inherently highly vulnerable and which at the same time adopt resilience-building policies. On the other hand, the 'worst-case' scenario refers to countries that are inherently highly vulnerable and yet adopt policies that exacerbate that vulnerability.

These four scenarios are depicted in Figure 3.1, where the axes measure inherent economic vulnerability and nurtured resilience, respectively. In this scheme, the best situation in economic terms falls in quadrant II. The vulnerable small island states that have adopted resilience-building policies would fall in quadrant I.

Figure 3.1   The four scenarios

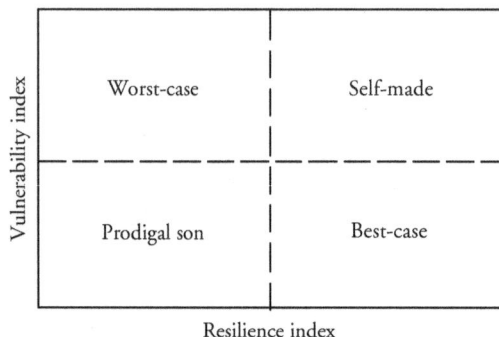

The method of defining vulnerability in terms of inherent features and resilience in terms of policy-induced changes has a number of advantages. First, the vulnerability index would refer to permanent (or quasi-permanent) features over which a country can practically exercise no control and therefore cannot be attributed to bad governance. As such, the index should not differ much over time. In other words, countries scoring highly on the index cannot be accused of inflicting vulnerability on themselves through misguided policy approaches.

Second, the resilience index would refer to what a country can do to mitigate or exacerbate its inherent vulnerability. Scores on this index would, therefore, reflect the appropriateness of policy measures.

Third, the combination of the two indices would indicate the overall risk of being harmed by external shocks due to inherent vulnerability features counterbalanced to different extents by policy measures.

Given these conditions it is highly unlikely that countries will be able to move vertically on this schema, but they will be able to move horizontally. It would thus be possible for countries to switch between the 'worst case' and the 'self-made' classifications, or the 'prodigal son' and the 'best case' classifications by changing their economic policies.

By distinguishing between inherent economic vulnerability and nurtured economic resilience, it is possible to create a methodological framework for assessing the risk of being affected by external shocks (Figure 3.2).

Figure 3.2 shows that risk has two elements, the first is associated with the inherent conditions of the country that is exposed and the second associated with conditions developed to absorb, cope with, or bounce back from, external shocks. The risk of being adversely affected by the shock is therefore the

Figure 3.2   Risks associated with being adversely affected by external shocks

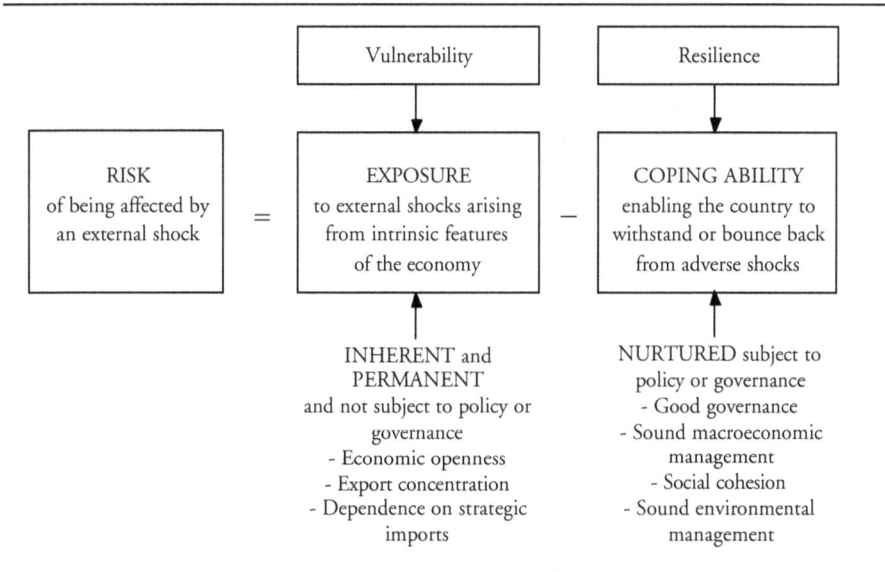

| Vulnerability | Resilience |

RISK
of being affected by
an external shock

=

EXPOSURE
to external shocks arising
from intrinsic features
of the economy

−

COPING ABILITY
enabling the country to
withstand or bounce back
from adverse shocks

INHERENT and
PERMANENT
and not subject to policy or
governance
- Economic openness
- Export concentration
- Dependence on strategic
imports

NURTURED subject to
policy or governance
- Good governance
- Sound macroeconomic
management
- Social cohesion
- Sound environmental
management

combination of the two elements. The negative sign in front of the resilience element indicates that the risk is reduced as resilience builds up.

ECONOMIC VULNERABILITY

Recent work on the economic vulnerability index (see Briguglio 1995, 1997; Briguglio and Galea 2003; Farrugia 2004) is based on the premise that a country's susceptibility to exogenous shocks stems from a number of inherent economic features, including high degrees of economic openness, export concentration and dependence on strategic imports.

Economic openness

Economic openness can be measured as the ratio of international trade to GDP. A high degree of economic openness renders a country susceptible to external economic conditions over which it has no direct control. Economic openness is, to an extent, an inherent feature of an economy, conditioned mainly by a country's ability to produce efficiently the range of goods and services required to satisfy its aggregate demand. If a country's productive base is limited to a narrow range of products, it has to rely on imports to service a substantial part of its needs and on exports to finance its import bill.

It may be argued that openness to international trade is influenced by policy. Practical experience has, however, shown that trade policies tend to influence the composition of a country's external trade flows, rather than their size. It can be further argued that openness to international trade could be a source of strength, in that it may indicate that a country is successfully participating in international markets. This argument, however, does not detract from the fact that, by participating more actively in international trade, a country exposes itself to a larger degree of shocks over which it has relatively little control.[3]

Export concentration

Dependence on a narrow range of exports gives rise to risks associated with lack of diversification, and therefore exacerbates vulnerability associated with economic openness. Again, this condition is to a large extent the result of inherent features in the production base of an economy. Export concentration can be measured by the UNCTAD index of merchandise trade (UNCTAD 2003:section 8), and Briguglio (1997) and Briguglio and Galea (2003) have devised an alternative index which also takes services into account.

Dependence on strategic imports

Another facet of the exposure argument relates to the dependence on strategic imports, which would expose an economy to shocks with regard to the availability and costs of such imports. This variable can be measured as the ratio of the imports of energy, food or industrial supplies to GDP. Again, this condition is inherent in that it depends on country size, resource endowments and possibilities for import-substitution.

All vulnerability indices utilising these variables come to the conclusion that there is a tendency for small states to be more economically vulnerable than other groups of countries.

ECONOMIC RESILIENCE

Economic resilience can be defined in many ways, but here the term is used to refer to the ability to recover from, or adjust to, the negative impacts of external economic shocks.

Usefulness of considering resilience building

The issue of resilience building is important for small states in view of the fact that such states tend to be inherently economically vulnerable, as already explained. In addition, the discussion on resilience sheds light as to why a number of vulnerable small states have managed to do well economically, in spite of (and not because of) being highly exposed to external shocks. Consideration of resilience building also conveys the message that vulnerable states should not be complacent in the face of their economic vulnerability, but could, and should, adopt policy measures that improve their ability to cope with external shocks.

The meaning of economic resilience

Most dictionaries define resilience in terms of the ability to recover quickly from the effect of an adverse incident. This definition originates from the Latin *resilire* 'to leap back'. In economic literature, the term has been used in at least three senses relating to the ability to recover quickly from a shock, withstand the effect of a shock, and avoid the shock altogether.[4]

Ability of an economy to recover quickly. This is associated with the flexibility of an economy, enabling it to bounce back after being adversely affected by a shock. This ability will be severely limited if, for example, there is a chronic tendency for large fiscal deficits or high rates of unemployment. On the other hand, this ability will be enhanced when the economy possesses discretionary policy tools that it can utilise to counteract the effects of negative shocks, such as a strong fiscal position allowing discretionary expenditure or tax cuts to counter the shocks. This type of resilience is therefore associated with 'shock-counteraction'.

Ability to withstand shocks. This suggests that the adverse effect of a shock can be absorbed or neutered, so that the end effect is zero or negligible. This type of resilience occurs when the economy has in place mechanisms to react endogenously to negative shocks to reduce their effects, which we can refer to as 'shock-absorption'. For example, the existence of a flexible, multi-skilled labour force could act as an instrument of shock absorption, as negative external demand shocks affecting a particular sector of economic activity can be relatively easily met by shifting resources to another sector enjoying stronger demand.

Ability of an economy to avoid shocks. In this chapter, this type of resilience is considered to be inherent, and can be considered the obverse of economic vulnerability.

THE CONSTRUCTION OF A RESILIENCE INDEX

Underlying difficulties

In this section, we present the results of an attempt to construct a composite index of economic resilience. Some words of caution are warranted at this stage. The choice of variables as components of the index is somewhat subjective. Care was taken, however, to base the choice on a set of desirable criteria related to: appropriate coverage, simplicity and ease of comprehension, affordability, suitability for international comparisons and transparency. A more detailed consideration of these criteria is given in Briguglio (2003).

In addition, the summing of the components of the index also involves subjective choices, principally in selecting a weighting procedure. There is considerable debate in the literature on composite indices on this issue. Again, these questions are discussed in Briguglio (2003) and are not elaborated upon here.

The compilation of the index encountered a number of problems with regard to data collection, the most important of which were associated with lack or shortage of data and non-homogenous definitions across countries. Briguglio (2003) considers these problems, referring to the fact that data problems occur particularly in the case of small states.

Components of the resilience index

It is hypothesised that elements of 'shock-absorbing' and 'shock-counteracting' resilience in an economy can be found in the following areas
- macroeconomic stability
- microeconomic market efficiency
- good governance
- social development.

All of these areas feature variables which are highly influenced by economic policy and which can serve for an economy to build its economic resilience to meet the consequences of adverse shocks.

Macroeconomic stability. Macroeconomic stability relates to the interaction between an economy's aggregate demand and aggregate supply. If aggregate expenditure in an economy moves in equilibrium with aggregate supply, the economy is characterised by internal balance, manifested in a sustainable fiscal position, low price inflation and an unemployment rate close to the natural rate, as well as by external balance, indicated by the international current account position or by the level of external debt. All these variables are highly influenced by economic policy and can act as good indicators of an economy's resilience in facing adverse shocks.

The macroeconomic stability aspect of the resilience index is thus constructed on the basis of three variables, namely
- the fiscal deficit to GDP ratio
- the sum of the unemployment and inflation rates
- the external debt to GDP ratio.

These variables are available for a set of 102 countries spread over a spectrum of stages of development, size and geographical characteristics. The relative data and country ranking results are presented in Table A3.1.

Fiscal deficit. The government budget position is suitable for inclusion in the resilience index because it is the result of fiscal policy, which is one of the main tools available to government, and indicates resilience of a shock-counteracting nature. This is because a healthy fiscal position allows adjustments to taxation and expenditure policies in the face of adverse shocks. The fiscal deficit, standardised as a ratio to GDP, is thus included in the resilience index proposed in this paper.

Inflation and unemployment. Price inflation and unemployment are also considered suitable indicators of resilience and at the same time they potentially provide information additional to that contained in the fiscal deficit variable. This is because price inflation and unemployment are strongly influenced by other types of economic policy, including monetary and supply-side policies. They are associated with resilience, because if an economy already has high levels of unemployment and inflation, it is likely that adverse shocks will impose significant costs. If, on the other hand, the economy has low levels of inflation and unemployment, it can withstand adverse shocks to these variables without excessive welfare costs. In this sense, therefore, unemployment and inflation indicate resilience of a shock-absorbing nature. The sum of these two variables, also known as the Economic Discomfort Index (or Economic Misery Index), is thus included in the resilience index proposed here.

External debt. The adequacy of external policy may be gauged through the inclusion of the external debt to GDP ratio. This is considered a good measure of resilience because a country with a high level of external debt may find it more difficult to mobilise resources to offset the effects of external shocks. Thus, this variable would indicate resilience of a shock-counteracting nature.[5]

It may be surprising to observe that the United States is not among the first 10 placed in the macroeconomic stability index, although it ranks at a relatively high place in 12th position. A number of small states, on the other hand, notably Hong Kong and Singapore, rank high on the index. In this regard, it should be borne in mind that this index is not a measure of economic development but instead represents the ability of the macroeconomy to absorb or counteract adverse economic shocks.

Microeconomic market efficiency. The science of economics views markets, and their efficient operation through the price mechanism, as the best way to allocate resources in the economy. If markets adjust rapidly to achieve equilibrium, then the effects of shocks can be easily absorbed in the economy and the relative adjustments be readily affected. If, on the other hand, market disequilibria tend to persist, especially in the face of adverse shocks, then resources will not be efficiently allocated in the economy, resulting in welfare costs, manifested, for instance, in outflows of capital, unemployed resources and waste or shortages in the goods markets.

As an example, consider the case of financial markets. If, in the face of an adverse shock, markets respond efficiently by increasing interest rates and decreasing asset prices, capital can be retained in the economy such that the adverse shocks are reflected in price variables rather than in the volume of physical investment, which would have an important influence on economic activity. If, on the other hand, prices in the financial markets fail to adjust properly, then it is more likely that capital will leave the economy in the face of an adverse shock, thereby affecting economic activity and employment. Similar considerations may be made for the way in which the labour and product markets equilibrate in the economy. These issues have important implications for resilience of the shock-absorbing type.

Not many indicators of market efficiency are available for a range of countries sufficiently wide for the purposes of this study. Following a search for suitable indicators, it was decided to use data contained in the *Economic Freedom of the World Index* (2005) published by the Fraser Institute. This is a project which commenced in 1986 led by Professor Milton Friedman, Rose Friedman and Michael Walker, and is aimed at measuring the extent to which markets are operating freely, competitively and efficiently in 126 countries. This index uses quantitative/objective data as well as data from independent surveys, and indirectly attempts to assess the effects of 38 government policies on economic freedom.

The index focuses on five major areas, with indicators relating to the size of government, legal structure and security over property rights, access to sound money, freedom to trade internationally, and regulation of credit, labour and business. For the purposes of the microeconomic efficiency component, the indicators selected is regualtion of credit, labour and business. This is chosen on the basis of their relevance to the resilience concept with regard to market efficiency.

Regulation. This component, which measures regulatory restraints that limit the freedom of exchange in credit, labour and product markets, is made up of fifteen indicators. Regulatory conditions in the domestic credit market, which are measured by assessing the extent to which the banking industry is dominated by private firms, whether foreign banks are permitted to compete in the market, the extent to which credit is supplied to the private sector and whether controls on interest rates interfere with the market in credit, measure the degree of interference by government in the financial market, which could preclude the economy from reacting flexibly to shocks.

Similar considerations apply in the case of the labour market, where unemployment benefits that undermine the incentive to accept employment, dismissal regulations, minimum wages, centralised wage setting, extensions of union contracts to nonparticipating parties and conscription, are viewed as the extent of disincentives to work in an economy, which could preclude work effort from allowing a country to recover from adverse shocks. A country would have a higher market efficiency score if it allows market forces to determine wages and establish conditions of dismissal, avoid excessive unemployment benefits that undermine work incentives, and refrain from the use of conscription.

Like the regulation of credit markets and labour markets, the regulation of business activities may inhibit market efficiency. This sub-component is designed to identify the extent to which regulatory restraints and bureaucratic procedures limit competition and the operation of markets. When regulatory activities retard entry into business and increase the cost of producing products, when prices are not market-determined and when governments use their power to extract financial payments and reward some businesses at the expense of others, they have a crowding-out effect on private sector involvement, and reduce the degree of autonomous resilience which freely-operating markets can produce.

The relative data and country ranking results are presented in Table A3.1. The data used in the index covered 2001 through to 2003. Small vulnerable countries can be found across the entire scale of placing in this index. This indicates that such countries are adopting different policy approaches in terms of microeconomic efficiency towards meeting adverse shocks.

Good governance. Good governance is essential for an economic system to function properly and hence, to be resilient. Governance relates to issues such as rule of law and property rights. Without mechanisms of this kind in place, it would be relatively easy for adverse shocks to result in economic and social chaos and unrest. Hence the effects of vulnerability would be magnified. On the other hand, good governance can strengthen an economy's resilience.

The *Economic Freedom of the World Index* (2005) has a component which is focused on legal structure and security of property rights. This is considered useful in the context of the present exercise in deriving an index of good governance. The index covers the following indicators
 • judicial independence
 • impartiality of courts
 • the protection of intellectual property rights
 • military interference in the rule of law
 • political system and the integrity of the legal system.

The relative data and country ranking results for the years 2001–2003 are presented in Table A3.1. The highest rankings on the governance index are the more economically advanced countries, with the first five placings occupied by major industrialised economies. Singapore, which was among the most resilient economies on economic criteria, ranks fifteenth in terms of governance. Vulnerable economies tend to obtain lower rankings on this count, but it still appears to be the case that the vulnerable economies enjoying a higher per capita GDP also tend to have better systems of governance.

Social development. Social development is another essential component of economic resilience. This factor indicates the extent to which social relations in a society are properly developed, enabling an effective functioning of the economic apparatus without the hindrance of civil unrest. Social cohesion can also indicate the extent to which effective social dialogue takes place in an economy, which would in turn enable collaborative approaches to undertaking corrective measures in the face of adverse shocks. It is therefore hypothesised that social development is directly related to social cohesion—although this assertion cannot be tested empirically due to lack of data.

Social development in a country can be measured in a number of ways. Variables relating to income such as its dispersion and the proportion of the population living in poverty, the long term unemployment rate, the proportion of the population with low skills and inadequate employment prospects, and the proportion of the population with low levels of education could be useful indicators. Still another possible approach would be to measure the number and extent of instances of industrial or civil unrest. These approaches are interesting but rather narrow in scope and very difficult to measure across countries.

The index presented in this paper utilises the education and health indicators used to construct the Human Development Index (UNDP 2002, 2003, 2004).

Education. Education, as measured by the adult literacy rate and school enrolment ratios, is considered to be a good indicator of social development. Education is considered to be strongly positively correlated with social advancement and hence, is indicative of a social fabric which is conducive to economic resilience.

Health. Life expectancy at birth, which is the health indicator in the Human Development Index, is considered to be suitable for measuring the health aspects in society. This in turn is likely to be related to medical facilities, housing and degree of proneness to accident or risk of injury. Again, high life expectancy is considered to be conducive to economic resilience.

The relative data and country ranking results for 2000–02 are presented in Table A3.1. The social development index is very strongly correlated with the degree of economic development, with the countries in the first 20 places on the index having an annual per capita GDP of at least US$11,500. Small island states, including those with a high per capita GDP, rank from the twenty-fifth position downwards.

Correlation between the components of the index. The variables discussed above have been found to be positively related to each other, as shown in Table 3.1, but the correlation is somewhat weak, with the exception of good governance and market efficiency.

The question arises therefore as to whether or not the good governance index is redundant, given its high correlation with good governance. As the correlation is not unduly high, it was decided to retain all components in the composite index.

Other determinants of economic resilience. Economic resilience can also be viewed to be determined by a plethora of other factors apart from those mentioned above. It may be argued, for example, that it could be useful to consider the effects of environmental management on economic resilience. The environment can be an important source of vulnerability by giving rise to shocks of an adverse nature, be they rapid events, such as earthquakes, or in the form of a gradual degradation over time. In turn, these would have important repercussions on the economy and society. In this regard, the efforts being undertaken to compile the Environmental Sustainability Index (Esty et al. 2005) are commendable. Data on these factors are however not readily and extensively available across countries of different sizes,[6] such that the utilisation of this index within the present exercise would have significantly reduced the countries covered by the resilience index.

In addition, there is the possibility that incorporating an environmental management index could lead to the problem of redundancy. That is, using indicators that are highly correlated which would add no new information but would render the procedure unnecessarily complex. In the case of environmental management factors, the socioeconomic resilience aspects covered by the variables discussed above are likely to be highly correlated with environmental management, although in the absence of data, this assertion cannot be tested.

The resilience index

The index was computed by taking a simple average of the four components just described, namely
- macroeconomic stability
- microeconomic market efficiency
- good governance
- social development.

Table 3.1   Correlation matrix

Macroeconomic stability	1			
Market efficiency	0.177526	1		
Good governance	0.284266	0.673311	1	
Social development	0.214263	0.385542	0.664492	1

All observations of the components were standardised using the well-known transformation

$$XSij = (Xij - Minj) / (Maxj - Minj)$$

where *XSij* is the value of the standardised observation *i* of variable *j*; *Xij* is the actual value of the same observation; *Minj* and *Maxj* are the minimum and maximum values of variable *j*. This transforms the values of observations in a particular variable array so that they take a range of values from 0 to 1. The results of the averaging of the four components are shown in Appendix 1. The results show that the countries with the highest GDP per capita, are, as expected, those with the highest resilience scores, as shown in Figure 3.3.

The relation between GDP per capita, resilience and vulnerability. An interesting finding is that GDP per capita of the different countries is to a very high extent explained by vulnerability and resilience. Using the OLS (ordinary least squares) method of regression, GDP per capita (standardised as explained above) was regressed on the vulnerability index (as proposed in Briguglio and Galea 2003: See Table 3A.3) and on the resilience index produced in this study. The results are shown in Table 3.2. All variables have been standardised as explained above, so that their values range between 0 and 1.

This result confirms the hypothesis in Briguglio (2004) and Cordina (2004a, 2004b) that the performance of countries depends on their inherent vulnerability and their nurtured resilience. This is not an extraordinary finding, because it validates a very plausible assumption. However the results of the

Figure 3.3   Per capita GDP and economic resilience

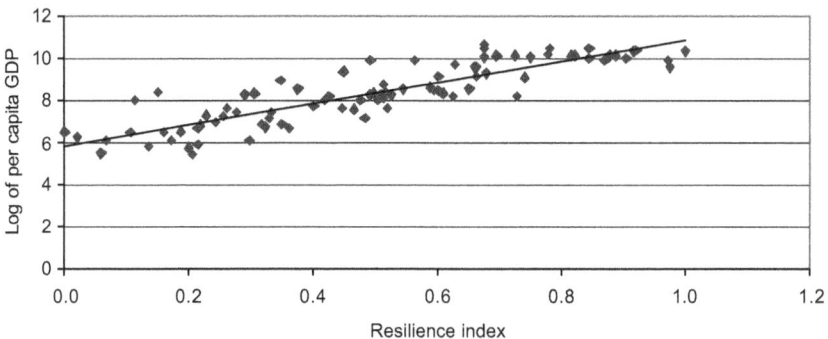

regression exercise have some interesting implications. In particular, the results show that the economic well-being of nations is more dependent on man-made policies rather than on inherent vulnerabilities. The results also confirm that adequate policy approaches can be used to overcome the handicaps posed by vulnerability.

The scenarios

Going back to the scenarios proposed in Figure 3.1, it is possible to place the countries included in the index in the four quadrants shown, using the resilience index proposed in this paper and the vulnerability index presented by Briguglio and Galea (2003). The results are shown in Figure 3.4.

It should be pointed out here that the cut-off values (represented by the dashed lines in Figure 3.4) chosen for the quadrants are the averages of the vulnerability and resilience scores for all countries. This decision is subjective and the classification of countries will change if different cut-off points are chosen. Consequently it was decided to allow a 'border-line' margin of +/-5 per cent for the resilience index (shown by the semi-transparent rectangle) and countries falling within this margin are classified as 'borderline' cases.

Table A3.2 shows which countries have been classified within the different quadrants.

The overall tendencies that can be derived from Table A3.2 are that

- countries which fall in the 'best-case' quadrant include the relatively large countries with a relatively high GDP per capita and relatively low vulnerability scores.
- countries which fall in the 'self-made' quadrant include a number of small states with a high vulnerability score.
- countries which fall in the 'prodigal son' quadrant include relatively large countries and others with a low resilience score.

Table 3.2   Regression results

G =	0.14	+	0.94R	−	0.13V
T stats	(3.4)		(16.8)		−(2.6)

$R^2 = 0.77$
N= 87

Where: G=GDP per capita; R=Resilience Index; and V=Vulnerability Index

- countries which fall in the 'worst case' quadrant include some small countries with relatively high vulnerability and low resilience scores.

THE USES OF THE RESILIENCE INDEX

Supporting decision-making, setting targets and establishing standards

Decision-making by the government and other authorities should lead to action which is systematic and coherent and based on transparent information. The Resilience Index may also be used to set the direction of action and to justify certain priorities. The index could also be useful for setting targets. For example, a country with low resilience scores in certain economic areas may set targets to step up its resilience with regard to that economic variable.

Monitoring and evaluating developments

Indices are of utmost importance to assess whether a given policy or decision is yielding the desired results and to assess whether changes of direction are needed. This is especially so if measured over time. In this way, decisions are not at risk of being taken blindly or based only on hunches and feelings, but would be based on scientific information presented in index format.

Figure 3.4   Economic resilience and economic vulnerability

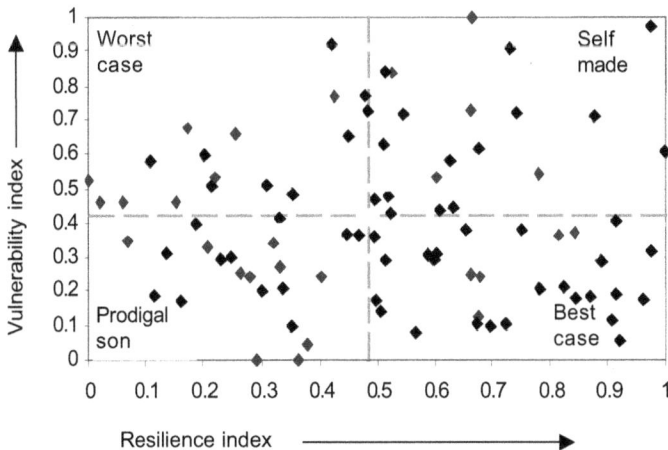

Deriving quantitative estimates

An index summarises complex phenomena, often yielding a single-value measure of the phenomena under consideration. This is useful, if not essential, for donor countries and organisations when making decisions regarding the allocation of financial and technical assistance, or for assigning special status to vulnerable countries.

Dissemination of information and drawing attention to the issue

The resilience index can be used to make the public more aware of certain problems, and to give high profiles to certain trends that can strengthen resilience. In this regard, indices can be used for communication and for alerting stakeholders about issues, including dangers, failures and success stories.

An index is a very good instrument for drawing attention to the issue being investigated. Thus, for example, the exercise of computing an index of resilience may itself make decision-makers aware of the gravity of these problems. Such an exercise may also generate academic discussion and enhance awareness amongst scholars on the issues involved.

Focusing the discussion

Indices can help to develop a common language for discussion. One often finds that persons engaged in debate go off at tangents because of lack of common definitions. In the case of indices, the quantification of its components requires precise definitions, and this could help focus the discussion on matters directly relevant to the issue.

Promoting the idea of integrated action

Composite indices are generally constructed to measure multifaceted realities. This could help to foster an awareness of the interconnections between the components of the index. In the case of economic resilience, for example, it is often not enough, and may even be counterproductive, to take action in one area in isolation from others. The resilience index proposed here could therefore promote the need for an integrated action in this regard.

CONCLUSION

This chapter dealt with conceptual and methodological aspects associated with economic resilience and its measurement. The index developed here covers four areas of economic resilience; namely, macroeconomic stability, microeconomic market efficiency, governance and social cohesion. Each of these areas contains variables considered suitable for gauging the extent to which the policy framework is conducive to absorbing and counteracting the effects of economic shocks.

The results of this exercise can provide an explanation as to why inherently vulnerable countries may register high levels of GNP per capita. It is argued that countries may be economically successful because they are inherently not vulnerable, or because they are resilient in the face of potential vulnerability. The obverse is also true, in that countries may be unsuccessful because they are not sufficiently resilient.

The chapter has also shown that GDP per capita is positively related to economic resilience and negatively related to inherent economic vulnerability. Furthermore, per capita GDP is found to be more sensitive to resilience than to vulnerability.

The index produced in this study is very preliminary, and the work should be considered as still at an early stage of development.

NOTES

[1] In this study, the words 'state' and 'country' are used synonymously. There is no generally agreed definition as to which variable should be used to measure the size of countries and as to what should be the cut-off point between a small country and other countries. Generally speaking, population is used as an indicator of size. In this study, a country with a population of 1.5 million or less is considered to be a small one.

[2] This finding is reported in many studies. See, for example, Briguglio (1995).

[3] Farrugia (2004) elaborated further on these ideas by considering the economic strength of trading partners as a proxy for the probability of shocks to exports.

[4] An analogy relating to an attack of influenza virus may help explain the three senses in which the term 'resilience' has been used. A person exposed to the virus may (a) get infected but recovers quickly; (b) withstand the effect of the virus, possibly by being immunised; and (c) avoid the virus altogether by staying away from infection sources.

[5] It is, however, to be stated that certain countries may have external debt not because of a weak policy framework but due to a highly-developed international financial activity. This is a recognised weakness in the use of this indicator. However the inclusion of other variables related to market efficiency and governance would to an extent 'correct' this weakness, since these variables either exacerbate the effect of external debt in the presence of a weak policy framework or counteract it otherwise.

[6] Esty et al. (2005) do produce some results for a few small states but they were reluctant to include them in the Environmental Sustainability Index.

Table A3.1   Data country and ranking results

Country	Macroecon. stability	Microecon. market efficiency	Social development	Good governance	Resilience index	Country ranking
Albania	0.249866	0.386534	0.765396	0.411278	0.453268	63
Argentina	0.533841	0.258845	0.868035	0.226565	0.471822	59
Australia	0.471526	0.80043	0.98827	0.970713	0.807735	9
Austria	0.692709	0.531446	0.956012	0.927846	0.777003	12
Bangladesh	0.635215	0.304511	0.222874	0.17407	0.334168	81
Barbados	0.631647	0.626714	0.914956	0.721573	0.723723	17
Belgium	0.661383	0.474074	0.982405	0.799757	0.729405	16
Belize	0.186241	0.670694	0.753666	0.607275	0.554469	49
Bolivia	0.46827	0.360133	0.618768	0.173626	0.405199	70
Brazil	0.388055	0.209704	0.721408	0.423359	0.435631	66
Cameroon	0.443272	0.451458	0.231672	0.343852	0.367563	77
Canada	0.632888	0.797511	0.97654	0.910253	0.829298	6
Chile	0.635734	0.561847	0.859238	0.610715	0.666883	28
China	0.653449	0.094953	0.703812	0.468426	0.48016	57
Colombia	0.417252	0.272723	0.753666	0.219628	0.415817	68
Costa Rica	0.608614	0.469847	0.853372	0.623045	0.63872	31
Cote d'Ivoire	0.421575	0.327188	0	0.236807	0.246392	87
Croatia	0.524189	0.516349	0.824047	0.450516	0.578775	40
Cyprus	0.360269	0.406994	0.88563	0.687058	0.584988	38
Czech Republic	0.570785	0.444326	0.856305	0.630779	0.625549	35
Denmark	0.716137	0.682179	0.944282	1	0.83565	5
Dominican Republic	0.656766	0.469506	0.653959	0.304935	0.521291	53
Egypt, Arab Rep.	0.587887	0.150975	0.504399	0.403256	0.411629	69
El Salvador	0.655256	0.484604	0.645161	0.351327	0.534087	52
Estonia	0.634994	0.705067	0.85044	0.673152	0.715913	18
Finland	0.638404	0.670794	0.970674	0.996864	0.819184	7
France	0.49435	0.525839	0.961877	0.743736	0.68145	23
Germany	0.550882	0.348942	0.947214	0.931598	0.694659	20
Greece	0.376219	0.289183	0.929619	0.550436	0.536364	51
Honduras	0.425194	0.38848	0.583578	0.1569	0.388538	72
Hong Kong, China	0.649945	1	0.865103	0.730719	0.811442	8
Hungary	0.435458	0.598013	0.829912	0.656447	0.629957	34
Iceland	0.722204	0.911862	0.967742	0.960131	0.890485	1
India	0.501144	0.309005	0.395894	0.555138	0.440295	65
Indonesia	0.419976	0.06043	0.633431	0.285343	0.349795	79
Iran, Islamic Rep.	0.594709	0	0.630499	0.555373	0.445145	64
Ireland	0.748274	0.631891	0.926686	0.854979	0.790458	11
Israel	0.598613	0.348255	0.932551	0.729831	0.652313	29
Italy	0.563878	0.27718	0.929619	0.668735	0.609853	36
Jamaica	0.403985	0.412831	0.782991	0.467962	0.516942	54
Japan	0.473191	0.530351	0.973607	0.74548	0.680657	24
Jordan	0.388433	0.480286	0.727273	0.637369	0.55834	48
Kenya	0.48918	0.470737	0.29912	0.282871	0.385477	74

Country	Macroecon. stability	Microecon. market efficiency	Social development	Good governance	Resilience index	Country ranking
Kuwait	0.578993	0.655568	0.747801	0.705003	0.671841	27
Latvia	0.522574	0.489853	0.824047	0.554741	0.597804	37
Lithuania	0.548288	0.39104	0.847507	0.470706	0.564385	46
Luxembourg	0.169854	0.751959	0.894428	0.910095	0.681584	22
Madagascar	0.362156	0.266086	0.255132	0.25639	0.284941	85
Malaysia	0.731697	0.493283	0.747801	0.624907	0.649422	30
Malta	0.484228	0.631271	0.870968	0.70835	0.673704	25
Mauritius	0.601564	0.370945	0.70088	0.624736	0.574531	43
Mexico	0.606521	0.281145	0.777126	0.294478	0.489818	56
Morocco	0.495981	0.372758	0.404692	0.566488	0.45998	61
Nepal	0.4917	0.457864	0.260997	0.309663	0.380056	75
Netherlands	0.482792	0.65624	0.979472	0.971333	0.772459	13
New Zealand	0.690428	0.882142	0.973607	0.950714	0.874223	2
Nicaragua	0.023774	0.48574	0.565982	0.18658	0.315519	83
Nigeria	0.471854	0.508743	0.231672	0.219478	0.357937	78
Norway	0.556971	0.549727	0.982405	0.909665	0.749692	14
Pakistan	0.394713	0.414384	0.205279	0.148316	0.290673	84
Panama	0.582466	0.536143	0.806452	0.384237	0.577324	42
Papua New Guinea	0.508531	0.433815	0.290323	0.310375	0.385761	73
Paraguay	0.578202	0.164149	0.730205	0.105776	0.394583	71
Peru	0.568293	0.401304	0.739003	0.315774	0.506094	55
Philippines	0.451332	0.387922	0.771261	0.284718	0.473808	58
Poland	0.56857	0.304017	0.8739	0.520459	0.566737	45
Portugal	0.59533	0.458159	0.914956	0.768367	0.684203	21
Romania	0.38811	0.290391	0.765396	0.408514	0.463103	60
Russian Federation	0.517208	0.092389	0.750733	0.348189	0.42713	67
Senegal	0.403354	0.225306	0.067449	0.342088	0.259549	86
Singapore	1	0.729691	0.876833	0.887539	0.873516	3
Slovak Republic	0.446169	0.445685	0.829912	0.535593	0.56434	47
Slovenia	0.660042	0.307871	0.903226	0.664043	0.633796	33
South Africa	0.576064	0.600028	0.445748	0.663719	0.57139	44
Spain	0.54459	0.556156	0.967742	0.624577	0.673266	26
Sri Lanka	0.318068	0.406613	0.750733	0.355834	0.457812	62
Sweden	0.473626	0.573594	1	0.948877	0.749024	15
Switzerland	0.556796	0.74385	0.950147	0.912063	0.790714	10
Thailand	0.398987	0.473332	0.733138	0.582446	0.546975	50
Trinidad and Tobago	0.640791	0.561979	0.780059	0.557279	0.635027	32
Tunisia	0.510781	0.484403	0.651026	0.682657	0.582217	39
Turkey	0	0.212651	0.674487	0.391459	0.319649	82
Uganda	0.515504	0.424067	0.199413	0.369793	0.377194	76
United Kingdom	0.062219	0.844121	0.970674	0.977112	0.713532	19
United States	0.646397	0.906787	0.944282	0.859822	0.839322	4
Uruguay	0.523452	0.375556	0.8739	0.537029	0.577484	41
Venezuela, RB	0.511099	0.09085	0.777126	0	0.344769	80

Table A3.2   The four scenarios

Country	Resilience Index	Vulnerability Index	Case	Borderline
Barbados	0.741	0.717	Self Made	
Costa Rica	0.609	0.436	Self Made	
Cyprus	0.526	0.840	Self Made	
Estonia	0.729	0.908	Self Made	
Hong Kong, China	0.877	0.713	Self Made	
Iceland	1.000	0.607	Self Made	
Israel	0.630	0.443	Self Made	
Kuwait	0.661	0.731	Self Made	
Latvia	0.546	0.718	Self Made	
Luxembourg	0.676	0.615	Self Made	
Malaysia	0.626	0.587	Self Made	
Malta	0.663	1.000	Self Made	
Norway	0.781	0.543	Self Made	
Singapore	0.974	0.971	Self Made	
Trinidad and Tobago	0.603	0.533	Self Made	
Croatia	0.516	0.480	Self Made	Borderline
Mauritius	0.509	0.632	Self Made	Borderline
Panama	0.514	0.837	Self Made	Borderline
Tunisia	0.521	0.426	Self Made	Borderline
Australia	0.872	0.184	Best Case	
Austria	0.824	0.216	Best Case	
Belgium	0.750	0.384	Best Case	
Canada	0.905	0.117	Best Case	
Chile	0.653	0.379	Best Case	
Czech Republic	0.589	0.309	Best Case	
Denmark	0.915	0.407	Best Case	
Finland	0.889	0.286	Best Case	
France	0.675	0.129	Best Case	
Germany	0.696	0.100	Best Case	
Hungary	0.596	0.294	Best Case	
Ireland	0.845	0.371	Best Case	
Italy	0.564	0.082	Best Case	
Japan	0.674	0.106	Best Case	
Netherlands	0.817	0.364	Best Case	
New Zealand	0.975	0.320	Best Case	
Portugal	0.680	0.242	Best Case	
Slovenia	0.601	0.307	Best Case	
Spain	0.663	0.250	Best Case	
Sweden	0.780	0.208	Best Case	
Switzerland	0.845	0.178	Best Case	
United Kingdom	0.725	0.106	Best Case	
United States	0.921	0.060	Best Case	
South Africa	0.505	0.147	Best Case	Borderline

Country	Resilience Index	Vulnerability Index	Case	Borderline
Uruguay	0.514	0.288	Best Case	Borderline
Cote d'Ivoire	0.000	0.524	Worst Case	
Dominican Republic	0.427	0.768	Worst Case	
Egypt, Arab Rep.	0.257	0.658	Worst Case	
Greece	0.450	0.655	Worst Case	
Honduras	0.221	0.534	Worst Case	
Iran, Islamic Rep.	0.309	0.508	Worst Case	
Jamaica	0.420	0.922	Worst Case	
Kenya	0.216	0.511	Worst Case	
Madagascar	0.060	0.465	Worst Case	
Nicaragua	0.107	0.578	Worst Case	
Nigeria	0.173	0.677	Worst Case	
Papua New Guinea	0.216	0.508	Worst Case	
Philippines	0.353	0.485	Worst Case	
Senegal	0.020	0.464	Worst Case	
Sri Lanka	0.328	0.415	Worst Case	
Uganda	0.203	0.597	Worst Case	
Belize	0.478	0.768	Worst Case	Borderline
Jordan	0.484	0.725	Worst Case	Borderline
Lithuania	0.494	0.466	Worst Case	Borderline
Albania	0.321	0.344	Prodigal Son	
Argentina	0.350	0.100	Prodigal Son	
Bangladesh	0.136	0.313	Prodigal Son	
Bolivia	0.247	0.299	Prodigal Son	
Brazil	0.294	0.001	Prodigal Son	
Cameroon	0.188	0.397	Prodigal Son	
China	0.363	0.000	Prodigal Son	
Colombia	0.263	0.254	Prodigal Son	
El Salvador	0.447	0.362	Prodigal Son	
India	0.301	0.201	Prodigal Son	
Indonesia	0.161	0.174	Prodigal Son	
Mexico	0.378	0.046	Prodigal Son	
Morocco	0.332	0.272	Prodigal Son	
Nepal	0.208	0.327	Prodigal Son	
Pakistan	0.069	0.349	Prodigal Son	
Paraguay	0.230	0.297	Prodigal Son	
Peru	0.403	0.242	Prodigal Son	
Romania	0.336	0.206	Prodigal Son	
Russian Federation	0.281	0.241	Prodigal Son	
Thailand	0.467	0.363	Prodigal Son	
Turkey	0.114	0.182	Prodigal Son	
Venezuela, RB	0.153	0.465	Prodigal Son	
Poland	0.497	0.175	Prodigal Son	Borderline
Slovak Republic	0.494	0.357	Prodigal Son	Borderline

Table A3.3   The Briguglio and Galea vulnerability index

Country	Vulnerability Index	Country Ranking
Albania	0.263	50
Argentina	0.077	81
Australia	0.141	71
Austria	0.166	67
Bangladesh	0.240	53
Barbados	0.549	12
Belgium	0.294	42
Belize	0.588	7
Bolivia	0.229	56
Brazil	0.001	86
Cameroon	0.304	41
Canada	0.089	78
Chile	0.290	43
China	0.000	87
Colombia	0.194	62
Costa Rica	0.334	37
Cote d'Ivoire	0.401	26
Croatia	0.368	31
Cyprus	0.643	5
Czech Republic	0.236	54
Denmark	0.311	40
Dominican Republic	0.588	8
Egypt, Arab Rep.	0.504	15
El Salvador	0.277	47
Estonia	0.695	4
Finland	0.219	60
France	0.099	77
Germany	0.076	82
Greece	0.501	16
Honduras	0.409	24
Hong Kong, China	0.546	13
Hungary	0.225	58
Iceland	0.465	19
India	0.154	70
Indonesia	0.133	75
Iran, Islamic Rep.	0.389	28
Ireland	0.284	44
Israel	0.339	36
Italy	0.062	83
Jamaica	0.706	3
Japan	0.081	79
Jordan	0.555	10
Kenya	0.391	27
Kuwait	0.560	9
Latvia	0.550	11
Lithuania	0.357	32
Luxembourg	0.471	18
Madagascar	0.356	34
Malaysia	0.449	21
Malta	0.765	1

Table A3.3   The Briguglio and Galea vulnerability index

Country	Vulnerability Index	Country ranking
Mauritius	0.484	17
Mexico	0.035	85
Morocco	0.208	61
Nepal	0.250	51
Netherlands	0.279	45
New Zealand	0.245	52
Nicaragua	0.442	22
Nigeria	0.518	14
Norway	0.416	23
Pakistan	0.267	49
Panama	0.640	6
Papua New Guinea	0.389	29
Paraguay	0.227	57
Peru	0.186	64
Philippines	0.371	30
Poland	0.134	74
Portugal	0.185	65
Romania	0.158	69
Russian Federation	0.184	66
Senegal	0.355	35
Singapore	0.743	2
Slovak Republic	0.273	48
Slovenia	0.235	55
South Africa	0.113	76
Spain	0.192	63
Sri Lanka	0.318	39
Sweden	0.159	68
Switzerland	0.136	73
Thailand	0.278	46
Trinidad and Tobago	0.408	25
Tunisia	0.326	38
Turkey	0.140	72
Uganda	0.457	20
United Kingdom	0.081	80
United States	0.046	84
Uruguay	0.221	59
Venezuela, RB	0.356	33

Source: Briguglio, L. and Galea, W., 2003. *Updating the Economic Vulnerability Index*, Occasional Papers on Islands and Small States 2003–4, Islands and Small States Institute, Malta.

4

SINK OR SWIM?
ASSESSING THE IMPACT OF
AGRICULTURAL TRADE LIBERALISATION
ON SMALL ISLAND DEVELOPING STATES

Luca Monge-Roffarello, Michael Swidinsky and David Vanzetti

AGRICULTURAL LIBERALISATION—A DOUBLE-EDGED SWORD

Small island developing states[1] face a number of structural problems that make them less competitive in agricultural trade than many other developing countries. The United Nations, and in particular UNCTAD, has been studying the problems of developing island economies since the 1970s with a view to sensitising the international community to the distinctive needs of these countries, and more recently, to their specific vulnerability (Encontre 1999).[2]

To a greater extent than in most other developing economies—and notably as a result of acute limitations in the resource base and domestic market opportunities available to small island developing states—the magnitude, structure and variability of trade constitutes the most important factors affecting the socioeconomic performance and development capacity of small island developing states. On average, the ratio of merchandise imports to GDP is 47 per cent higher in small island developing economies than in other small economies, while the ratio of their agricultural trade (exports and imports combined) to GDP is the highest among all countries. Whilst larger countries can count on both their domestic and international markets to foster economic growth, small island developing economies have to rely on their export markets as the only avenue for reaping the benefits of economies of scale and capital accumulation (Streeten 1993).

The constraints faced by small island developing economies are well documented.[3] Factors such as small size, insularity and remoteness, and problems associated with the local environment all impose a burden on small island states in achieving efficiency in production (Briguglio 1995). Because of their small land base and population, they have limited ability to exploit economies of scale in agricultural production. Land scarcity, in particular, is a binding constraint on agricultural production, making small island developing economies highly dependent on food imports. They are net agricultural importers and depend on a small number of agricultural exports to pay for their food import bill.

Similarly, small size restricts developing economies' capacity to diversify exports. The need to secure certain scale economies in production, distribution and other economic activities—together with the possibility of taking advantage of some export market opportunities—have, to varying degrees, led small island developing economies to specialise in a narrow range of agricultural products, thus exposing them to the instabilities of world markets.

Insularity and remoteness also give rise to problems associated with transportation of agricultural imports and exports. Small island states tend to import and export fragmented cargoes of agricultural products because they do not have the flexibility and convenience of road transport in handling small shipments, leading to higher shipping costs per unit. Additional costs also arise in instances where indivisible and costly public goods are needed to support agricultural production. Given the limited production involved, this process is bound to be particularly expensive.

Finally, environmental degradation (as well as susceptibility to natural disasters) and resource depletion may have serious implications for the agriculture of small island developing economies. The depletion of arable land from economic development has had a disproportionate effect on agricultural production for these states due to their size. Limited fresh water and poor water management—along with population pressures and an expanding tourism industry—have led to water scarcity, in turn jeopardising agricultural production.

Offsetting these inherent disadvantages, to some extent, are various preferential market access arrangements enjoyed by many small island developing states. These arrangements provide duty free access into specific developed markets such as the EU market for sugar.

Liberalisation is a double-edged sword for small island developing economies. Maintaining and obtaining market access is very important for trade dependent economies. On the other hand, liberalisation also provides additional competition, particularly if preferential access is eroded. While some small island developing economies will swim with the tide of liberalisation, others will need help to adjust. Against this background, the objective of this study is two-fold: first, to examine the pattern of small island developing economies' agricultural trade in the world market; and, second, to provide a quantitative assessment of the likely impacts of continued multilateral agricultural liberalisation on small island developing economies, using UNCTAD's Agricultural Trade Policy Simulation Model (ATPSM).

This chapter looks at the main characteristics of the small island developing economies' agricultural sector, focusing on trade flows and constraints hampering their competitiveness in agriculture. An overview of the preferential trading arrangements available to small island developing economies in their main markets and the actual importance of these schemes for these economies' exports is also provided. Additionally, a quantitative assessment is carried out using the Agricultural Trade Policy Simulation Model of a number of scenarios derived from 'modalities' being discussed in the ongoing WTO negotiations on agriculture. The simulations show the potential impact of liberalisation on prices, exports, government revenues, quota rents and overall welfare. While small island developing economies as a whole may be worse off under certain assumptions, policies to improve their position are examined.

SMALL ISLAND DEVELOPING ECONOMIES AND AGRICULTURAL TRADE

The agricultural sector remains the backbone of the economies of many small island states. It is characterised by a combination of large-scale commercial cash crops and a relatively small sector of food-producing crops for local consumption. The most important food crops grown are starchy staples, such as root and tuber crops, although rapid urbanisation has led to these staples being replaced by imported cereals (FAO 1999a).

Trade patterns

The agricultural trade balance of selected small island developing economies is shown in Table 4.1. The import–export ratio differs greatly between small island developing economies (see Annexes), but as a group, these economies are net agricultural importers—for every US$1 exported, developing island economies import US$1.10. Atlantic Ocean small island developing economies have the highest import-to-export ratio, while Pacific Ocean developing economies are net agricultural exporters.

Table 4.2 provides the top five agricultural import/export products by the degree of product concentration in the agricultural trade of small island developing economies.

Small island developing economies import a wide variety of agricultural products—particularly cereals, meats, dairy products, animal and vegetable fats—which consume 20 per cent of total export earnings. For some small island developing economies, their agricultural import bill exceeds total export revenue. The agricultural import bill of Cape Verde, for example, is 240 per cent of total export revenue; while the import bills of Comoros, Haiti and Tuvalu are 197 per cent, 117 per cent and 109 per cent of export revenue respectively.

Table 4.3 compares the relative importance of agricultural trade in small island developing economies with its importance in other developed, developing, and least developed economies. As exporters, small island developing economies' agricultural exports are concentrated on a number of products, including raw cane sugar, coffee, cocoa and coconut. In many small

Table 4.1   Agricultural trade balance (average for the period 1996–2000)

SIDS regions	Ratio of ag. imports to ag. exports	Share (%) of agricultural		
		imports in total imports	exports in total exports	imports in total exports
Africa	1.4	21	21	29
Caribbean	1.3	16	18	24
Pacific	0.6	18	23	14
All SIDSs	1.2	16	19	23

Notes: Africa: Cape Verde, Comoros, Maldives, Mauritius, the Seychelles, and Sao Tomé and Principe; Caribbean: Antigua and Barbuda, Bahamas, Barbados, Cuba, Dominica, Dominican Republic, Grenada, Haiti, Jamaica, St. Kitts and Nevis, St. Lucia, St. Vincent and the Grenadines, and Trinidad and Tobago; Pacific: Cook Islands, Fiji, Kiribati, Papua New Guinea, Western Samoa, Solomon Islands, Tonga, Tuvalu, and Vanuatu.
Source: FAOStat <http://www.fao.org/waicent/portal/statistics_en.asp>; UNSD Comtrade <http://unstats.un.org/unsd/comtrade>.

Table 4.2　Top five agricultural imports and exports, 1996–2000 (average)

	Import Rank	Product code	Product description	% of total ag. imports	Export rank	Product code	Product description	% of total ag. exports
Africa	1.	04	Dairy produce and birds' eggs	15	1.	170111	Cane sugar	83
	2.	10	Cereals	11	2.	010600	Other live animals	2
	3.	02	Meat and edible meat, meat offal	8	3.	170310	Cane molasses	1
	4.	15	Animal or vegetable fats	10	4.	180100	Cocoa beans, whole or broken	1
	5.	22	Beverages, spirits and vinegar	9	5.	090500	Vanilla	1
			Total	53			Total	89
Caribbean	1.	10	Cereals	20	1.	170111	Cane sugar	35
	2.	04	Dairy produce and birds' eggs	11	2.	240210	Cigars, cheroots and cigarillos	12
	3.	15	Animal or vegetable fats	8	3.	220840	Rum and tafia	11
	4.	22	Beverages, spirits and vinegar	7	4.	080300	Bananas, including plantains	8
	5.	02	Meat and edible meat, meat offal	7	5.	090111	Coffee, not roasted	4
			Total	53			Total	70
Pacific	1.	02	Meat and edible meat, meat offal	24	1.	090111	Coffee, not roasted	24
	2.	04	Dairy produce and birds' eggs	11	2.	170111	Cane sugar	20
	3.	21	Misc. edible preparations	8	3.	151110	Palm oil	18
	4.	15	Animal and vegetable fats	8	4.	120300	Copra	10
	5.	10	Cereals	7	5.	180100	Cocoa beans, whole or broken	8
			Total	57			Total	80
All SIDSs	1.	10	Cereals	18	1.	170111	Cane sugar	37
	2.	04	Dairy produce and birds' eggs	12	2.	240210	Cigars, cheroots and cigarillos	9
	3.	02	Meat and edible meat, meat offal	9	3.	220840	Rum and tafia	8
	4.	15	Animal or vegetable fats	8	4.	090111	Coffee, not roasted	8
	5.	22	Beverages, spirits and vinegar	7	5.	080300	Bananas, including plantains	6
			Total	54			Total	68

Notes: Africa: Cape Verde, Comoros, Maldives, Mauritius, the Seychelles, and Sao Tomé and Principe. Caribbean: Antigua and Barbuda, Bahamas, Barbados, Cuba, Dominica, Dominican Republic, Grenada, Haiti, Jamaica, St. Kitts and Nevis, St. Lucia, St. Vincent and the Grenadines, and Trinidad and Tobago. Pacific: Cook Islands, Federated States of Micronesia, Fiji, Kiribati, Marshall Islands, Nauru, Papua New Guinea, Western Samoa, Solomon Islands, Tonga, Tuvalu, and Vanuatu.
Source: UNSD COMTRADE <http://unstats.un.org/unsd/comtrade>.

Figure 4.1   Small island developing economies—main agricultural exports
as per cent of total agricultural exports, 2000 (per cent)

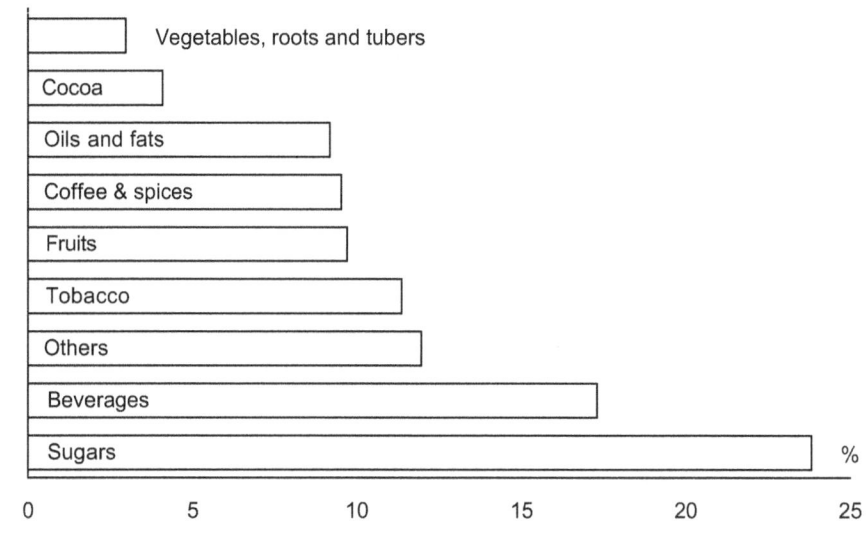

island economies, these few agricultural products are the main source of export earnings (see Figure 4.1). On average, agricultural exports (imports) by small island developing economies account for 24 per cent (14 per cent) of their total merchandise exports (imports), showing a considerably higher dependence on the agricultural sector than the developing economy average. In fact, the trade pattern of small island economies is remarkably similar to that of least developed economies. In the case of Sao Tomé and Principe, over 90 per cent of agricultural export earnings are derived from cocoa alone.

Further increasing their exposure to external shocks, small island developing economies' agricultural exports also show a concentration of destinations. As shown in Table 4.4, the European Union receives more than half of the total small island economies' agricultural exports. Accounting for 87 per cent of their agricultural exports, it is the most important market for African small island developing economies. Pacific small island developing economies (primarily Fiji and Papua New Guinea) export around 65 per cent of their agricultural products to the European Union.

Table 4.3   Importance of agricultural trade, 2000

Country groups	Agricultural exports in total exports %	Agricultural imports in total imports %	Imports/ exports ratio in agriculture	Agricultural exports/GDP (1999)[a] %	Agricultural imports/GDP (1999)[a] %
Developed	6.8	6.5	1.1	1.1	2.9
Developing (exc. LDCs)	7.2	6.7	0.98	2.7	7.0
LDCs	31.4	16.4	1.1	3.7	7.4
SIDS[b]	24.0	14.0	2.5	7.4	14.7

Notes: [a] Data on GDP only available for selected countries. Trade information from UN COMTRADE. GDP data are taken from the World Bank's World Development Indicators.
[b] SIDS for which trade data was available to compile this table include: Bahamas, Barbados, Comoros, Dominica, Fiji, Papua New Guinea, Mauritius, Grenada, Jamaica, Maldives, Saint Vincent and the Grenadines, Saint Lucia, Saint Kitts and Nevis, and Trinidad and Tobago.
Source: UNSD COMTRADE <http://unstats.un.org/unsd/comtrade>.

The United States and Canada are also important markets, though to a much lesser extent than the European Union, receiving 29 per cent of the small island developing economies' agricultural exports. The Caribbean islands sell up to 40 per cent of their agricultural exports to these markets, ranging from 50 per cent in the case of Jamaica to 20 per cent for other smaller Caribbean islands.

Japan captures only 3 per cent of total small island developing economies' agricultural exports, but it has become an important market for the Pacific island economies, absorbing more than 6 per cent of their exports. This figure is substantially greater than the small island developing economies' exports to Australia and New Zealand combined (despite the existence of a regional trade agreement, the South Pacific Regional Trade and Economic Cooperation Agreement, between most Pacific small island developing states and these two countries); Mexico; or the whole of the Southeast Asian region.

Preferential market access for small island developing economies

The high geographical concentration of small island developing economies' exports in the European Union and the United States, coupled with a high level of product specialisation, is probably due to the provision of non-reciprocal preferential market access to their products, stemming from historical trade relationships with these countries.

Preferential market access—in terms of tariff advantages and/or preferential quotas—are important for small island developing economies' agricultural

Table 4.4   Concentration of small island developing economies'
              agricultural trade, 2000 (per cent)

	All SIDS	African SIDS	Caribbean SIDS	Pacific SIDS
European Union	52.1	87.1	41.6	65.0
United States	27.1	5.2	37.6	8.2
Canada	1.6	0.8	2.3	0.1
Japan	3.1	1.8	2.4	5.8
Australia/New Zealand	0.7	0.1	0.3	2.1
Mexico	0.5	0.1	0.8	0.0
Southeast Asia	2.6	2.0	0.3	9.4
Others	12.0	2.8	14.4	9.4
Total	100.0	10.90	65.37	23.73

exporters for two reasons. First, a preferential margin may provide substantial 'quota rents' to small island exporters. Second, preferential margins, where substantial, can compensate for a general lack of price competitiveness of agricultural exports from small island economies *vis-à-vis* low-cost exporters competing in the same markets.

This section provides an overview of preferential market access granted by the Quad countries to small island developing economies' agricultural exports, and the values of such preferences.

European Union. Being the largest market for the small island developing economies' agricultural exports, the European Union grants two preferential trading arrangements that are particularly important for small island developing economies. That is, the EU/ACP Cotonou Partnership Agreement,[4] signed in 2000 between the European Union and 77 African, Caribbean and Pacific States (31 of the 77 ACP countries are small island developing states);[5] and the 'everything but arms' initiative in favour of products originating in least developed economies (10 of the 49 least developed economies are small island developing economies) under the aegis of the EU scheme of Generalised System of Preferences.

The Cotonou Partnership Agreement, which provides for an eight-year rollover of the previous trade preferences granted under Lomé, grants small island developing economies' beneficiaries with duty-free access for most of their agricultural products.[6] For small island developing economies, particularly important are the three protocols on bananas (affecting mostly the Windward Islands), sugar (Fiji, Mauritius, Barbados, Jamaica and Trinidad and Tobago)

Figure 4.2   Small island developing economies—destinations of agricultural exports, 2000

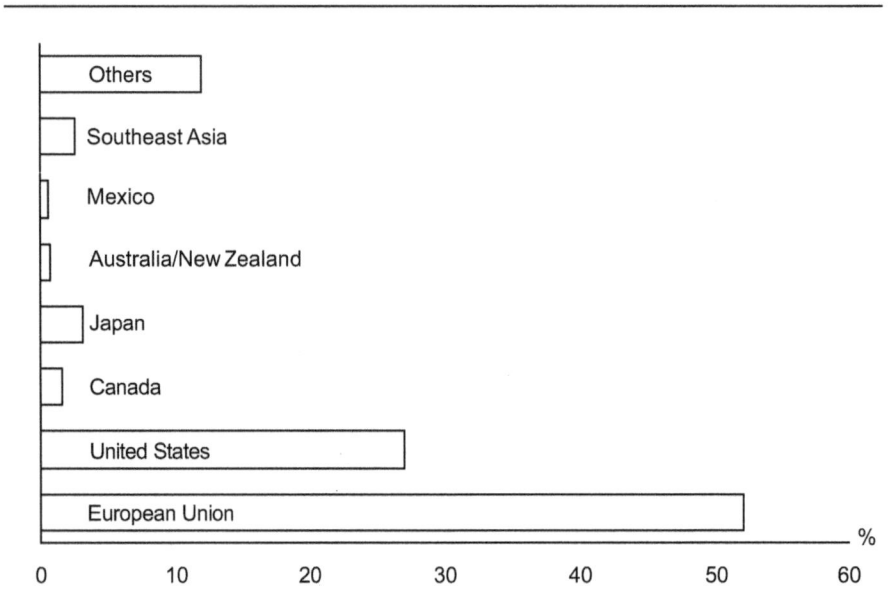

and rum (Caribbean small island developing states)—those products alone account for 69 per cent of small island developing economies' total exports to the European Union.

The Cotonou Agreement creates a considerable level of preferential tariff margin not only over applied most-favoured nation (MFN) rates, but also over most Generalised System of Preferences rates excluding the 'everything but arms' initiative. In 2000, for those products whose average MFN rates were above 20 per cent (accounting for almost half of small island developing economies' exports), small island developing economies' agricultural exports to the European Union received preferential margins of 25 percentage points against MFN rates and 15 percentage points against Generalised System of Preferences rates.

The 'everything but arms' initiative provides least developed economies with a duty-free treatment for all agricultural products (except bananas, rice and sugar until 2007), including very sensitive products such as beef, dairy products, fruit and vegetables (fresh as well as processed), cereals, starch, vegetable oils, confectionery, pasta and alcoholic beverages.[7]

For those least developed small island economies, the 'everything but arms' initiative has now made the EU Generalised System of Preferences a more favourable scheme than the Cotonou preferences in terms of tariff treatment, product coverage and preferential tariff margins. The initiative has also imparted greater stability to 'everything but arms'–Generalised System of Preferences for least developed economies, as the Euopean Union undertook to maintain this special preferential treatment for an unlimited period of time, exempting such treatment from the periodical reviews of the basic Generalised System of Preferences scheme.

United States. The United States recently renewed its Generalised System of Preferences program (applicable until 2006), which provides duty-free access for 5000 tariff line items to over 100 beneficiary countries and territories. The program covers agricultural and fishery products that are not otherwise duty-free, or are subject to tariff quotas/ceilings. An additional 1783 lines are added to the list of eligible products for recipients in least developed economies. The recently approved USA Trade and Development Act of 2000 has expanded the preferences granted to Sub-Saharan Africa under the African Growth and Opportunity Act,[8] as well as to the Caribbean Basin under the Caribbean Basin Trade Partnership Act.

The African Growth and Opportunity Act beneficiary countries (including small island economies such as Cape Verde, Sao Tome and Principe, Mauritius and Seychelles) now receive a 'super Generalised System of Preferences'[9]—duty-free access for a wider range of products than the 'normal' Generalised System of Preferences program.[10]

To 24 beneficiary countries of the Caribbean Basin Initiative,[11]—most of which are small island developing economies—the Caribbean Basin under the Caribbean Basin Trade Partnership Act provides trade preferences similar to those given under the African Growth and Opportunity Act. It also provides North American Free Trade Agreement (NAFTA)-equivalent tariff treatment for certain items previously excluded from duty-free treatment under the Caribbean Basin program (such as canned tuna). The NAFTA-parity is provided with a view to offsetting in part the negative effects in term of trade and investments diversion experienced by these countries since the entry of Mexico into NAFTA.[12]

Under these preferential schemes, approximately 60 per cent of small island developing economies' exports (which include products such as cigars, beer, alcohol and certain food preparations) enjoy preferential margins of 4.2 percentage points on average over corresponding MFN rates. The preferential tariff margin increases as the MFN tariff increases, but these large tariff margins apply only to a small share (6 per cent) of the total small island developing economies' agricultural exports. It was not possible to calculate preferential margins for some 14 per cent of small island developing economies' exports to the United States, largely sugar, as MFN tariffs are given in non-*ad valorem* technical rates and *ad valorem* equivalents could not be calculated.[13]

Canada. Canada provides two distinct preferential market access regimes that are of immediate relevance to small island developing economies' agricultural exports: the Generalised Preferential Tariff (GPT) and the CARIBCAN or Commonwealth Caribbean Countries Tariff. The Generalised Preferential Tariff, which is equivalent to the Generalised System of Preferences, grants reduced tariff rates or duty-free access to 184 beneficiary countries and territories, including all small island developing economies. In addition to the general Generalised Preferential Tariff, least developed economies receive duty-free market access to an additional 570 tariff lines.

The CARIBCAN—a program providing the Commonwealth Carribean with economic and trade development assistance—provides most Caribbean developing economies[14] with duty-free market access for a large number of products, including all agricultural products. However, preferential tariff margins on those products are generally low as corresponding MFN tariffs are already low (duties on more than 53 per cent of small island developing states agricultural exports are already zero). As these exports consist mainly of fresh fruits and vegetables, the Caribbean exporters seem to benefit more from a geographical proximity than from the tariff preferences they receive. Thus, for the majority of agricultural exports (some 94 per cent, including those exports already receiving MFN duty free), small island developing economies receive 'empty preferences', either because of zero MFN duties or because similar preferential treatment is given to other developing countries.

Japan. Trade preferences for small island developing economies (as for other developing economies) are made available under the Japanese Generalised System of Preferences scheme, which was reviewed in 2002 and extended until 31 March 2011.[15] The extent of the product coverage and tariff treatment provided to beneficiary countries varies considerably among agricultural products.

Preferential Generalised System of Preferences tariffs applicable to developing economies range from duty-free to a 20 per cent reduction in MFN duties. Least developed economies enjoy duty-free entry for all products covered under the scheme, plus an additional list of products. Preferences to least developed economies have been improved by increasing the number of tariff items for duty-free and quota-free access specifically available to all 49 least developed economies' exports as long as they request them.[16]

Despite the existence of the Generalised System of Preferences scheme, the overwhelming majority of small island developing economies' agricultural exports enter the Japanese market on a MFN basis—66.3 per cent of small island developing economies' exports, most importantly coffee and copra, enter Japan at zero MFN rates, while for another 31.5 per cent of exports (including sugar, pumpkins and rum), preferences are simply not available. This implies that the impact of further agricultural trade liberalisation, while being rather limited on small island developing economies' preferences, might result in new trade opportunities for all those developing-economy products still affected by high MFN duties.

Liberalisation and the erosion of preferences

Further liberalisation in agriculture will affect the value of preferential market access currently provided to small island developing economies. The impact will depend on a number of factors. First, the impact of the erosion of preferences depends on the initial insurability provided by the preferential treatment *vis-à-vis* competitions with other exporters. In terms of a geographical grouping, further MFN tariff cuts may result in much faster erosion, if not elimination, of preferential tariff margins available to the Caribbean island economies than those to other island developing economies, as the preferences received by the Caribbean small island developing states on some 70 per cent of their exports are empty. However, the impact of the preference erosion on the trade flows of the Caribbean island developing economies would be, on average, less dramatic as they are already exposed to a certain degree of competition with other developing country exporters either on a MFN basis or within a Generalised System of Preferences scheme of an importing country. Conversely, the African small island developing economies enjoy the highest level of preferences in terms of preferential margins and product coverage, and are thus subject to lower levels of preference erosion following MFN tariff cuts. They will, however, lose quota rents by the reduction of outquota tariffs. Further, should these preferences be considerably reduced as a result of the negotiations on agriculture—or be legally challenged by other WTO members[17]—adjustment costs arising from the preference erosion to these preference-dependent countries may be significant, as they have previously been sheltered against world competition.

Second, whether preferential tariffs are 'linked' to, or 'de-linked' from, MFN rates, may result in different impacts upon the values of preferences after a MFN tariff cut. In the case of the African, Carribean and Pacific–EU preferences, there are still a number of products whose preferences are expressed as a percentage of the MFN rate (and thus linked to these rates). If the initial MFN rates are sufficiently high, further MFN cuts would reduce the nominal preferential margins of the African, Carribean and Pacific preference only slightly. Beneficiaries of such preferences are more likely to retain tariff advantages not only over MFN tariffs but also over other preferences providing less extensive degree of market access treatment. This might be the case with various palm products, cigars, fruits and vegetables (such as oranges, onion, garlic, carrots, peaches and cabbages), although small island developing economies' exports of the latter items are currently limited. Where preferences to small island developing economies are de-linked from the corresponding MFN rates as in the case of the US Generalised System of Preferences scheme, the only difference among various preferential schemes is the extent of the product coverage rather than the preferential margins provided. In this case, MFN tariff cuts will inevitably reduce small island developing economies' preferential margins.

Third, the recent initiatives undertaken to provide better market access for least developed economies and countries in the Sub-Saharan African region have yet to fully materialise. As additional and substantial preferential margins for certain small island developing economies are created, the negative impact in terms of preferential margins coming from further trade liberalisation might be somehow mitigated.

Finally, current preferences, although wide, could still be expanded. For example, in the case of the European Union, the African, Carribean and Pacific–EU preferences are quite limited for agricultural and processed products that are subject to the Common Organisation of the Market (listed in the 'Joint Declaration concerning agricultural products')[18] and for products that are subject to specific rules under the Common Agricultural Policy. Many of those sensitive products (namely meat and diary products, cheese, tomatoes, mandarins and some cereals) are subject to a combined tariff which is made up of an *ad valorem* component and a specific-rate component. Preferential market access for those products normally takes the form of an elimination of the *ad valorem* component and a reduced level of a specific-rate component, whose *ad valorem* equivalent can go up as high as 80 per cent.

Similarly, for certain categories of processed agricultural products of the 'Harmonised System' chapter 4 (milk and milk products), 17 (sugar and sugar confectionery), 18 (cocoa and cocoa preparations), 19 (processed foodstuffs), 20 (beverages) and 21 (miscellaneous edible preparations), the European Union maintains a system of a technical tariff which includes the so-called agricultural component. That is, a combination of *ad valorem* and specific duties that may vary according to the presence in different percentages or quantities of certain ingredients such as sugar, starches or glucose and milk fat or proteins contained in the final products. However, it is largely the specific component that constitutes the bulk of the protection and not the *ad valorem* part.

In addition, around 15 products, mainly fruits and vegetables as well as some processed products like fruit juices, are subject to the entry price system.[19] Neither African, Carribean and Pacific nor Generalised System of Preferences beneficiary countries are granted special preferences for the products subject to the entry price system (Article 1 of Annex V of the ACP–EU Partnership Agreement). The Cotonou Agreement foresees amelioration of the African, Carribean and Pacific preferences (Article 1 of Annex V of the ACP–EU Partnership Agreement) during the transitional period, and the European Commission has already tabled a proposal for improving the current market access conditions given to the African, Carribean and Pacific countries.[20]

SURVIVING AGRICULTURAL LIBERALISATION: A QUANTITATIVE ASSESSMENT

It is anticipated that the stalled WTO negotiations on agriculture may eventually result in further reductions, if not elimination, of tariffs and trade-distorting subsidies provided to agricultural products in the world. When this occurs, the distribution of the welfare gains will be uneven among regions, with many losers amongst the winners. A study by Vanzetti and Peters (2003), using the same Agricultural Trade Policy Simulation Model as used here, shows that 110–20 of 161 countries modelled lose from partial global agricultural liberalisation. The study suggests that welfare losses result from rising world prices, loss of quota rents and the absence of significant allocative efficiency gains because the gap between bound and applied tariff rates means that little actual reform is undertaken in many countries. The rising world prices may benefit some countries, depending on whether countries are net importers or exporters of the products for which prices rise.

Agricultural liberalisation raises world prices of temperate agricultural products relative to prices of tropical products, leading to an increase in food import bills for those small island developing economies that import temperate products and export a narrow range of tropical products. At the same time, as MFN tariff cuts reduce the margin of preference, importers are likely to take supplies from low cost countries. For example, assuming exporters of sugar to the European Union are receiving EU prices, any lowering of those prices will make other exporters—such as Brazil—more competitive.

This section examines likely impacts of agricultural trade liberalisation on small island developing states under different liberalisation scenarios, with a view to identifying liberalisation modalities that would at least offset possible negative impacts from liberalisation, if not creating welfare gains.

The Agricultural Trade Policy Simulation Model framework

To assess the potential impacts of agricultural liberalisation on small island developing economies, UNCTAD's Agricultural Trade Policy Simulation Model Version 2.2 is used in this study.[21] The model is a partial equilibrium model that can be used to evaluate agricultural trade policy changes in the main areas covered by the Uruguay Round Agreements Act. These areas include market access, export subsidies and domestic support. The model distinguishes between bound and applied tariffs, as well as between inquota and outquota tariffs on products under tariff rate quotas. It can be used to assess the impact of policy changes on quota rents forgone and received. As quota rents are an important contributor to small island developing economies' agriculture, this feature of the model is desirable in applications discussed here.

Unlike a general equilibrium model, the Agricultural Trade Policy Simulation Model is confined to the agricultural sector and does not account for interactions with other sectors of the economy. As a result, capital and labour used in agricultural production cannot be reallocated across non-agricultural sectors in response to a shock. It is assumed that this limitation will have little bearing on the empirical results since small island developing economies have few alternative sectors for resources to shift into from agriculture.

The Agricultural Trade Policy Simulation Model can simulate and evaluate the various agricultural trade policy changes that may be suggested for or in the WTO negotiations on agriculture, such as

- most-favoured nation (bound or applied) and/or tariff rate quotas inquota tariff cuts
- change in tariff rate quota quantities
- reductions in trade-distorting domestic support (such as market price support)
- reductions in export subsidies
- different percentage changes in all the above policies applied to selected countries or country groups and commodities.

The Agricultural Trade Policy Simulation Model produces five categories of economic estimates: volumes in production, consumption, imports and exports; trade (exports, imports and trade balance); welfare (producer surplus, consumer surplus and net government revenue); prices (domestic and world); and tariff quota rents. The model is applied to 161 countries, including 25 of the 32 small island developing economy members[22] for the 36 agricultural commodities shown in Table 4.5.

The model is both simple and complex. Its simplicity derives from linear demand and supply equations. The complexity follows from the policy detail in the model. For this reason it is necessary to explain in the next section how the model works. The initial data, particularly on the distribution of rents, are examined next.

Quota rents. The Uruguay Round led to the establishment of tariff rate quotas—a two-tier tariff system based on import quotas. Imports below the quota level are levied at rates that are substantially lower than the corresponding out-of-quota (or outquota) MFN tariff rates. During the Uruguay Round, the quota quantities were either set as 3 per cent growing to 5 per cent of the level of domestic consumption observed during the 1986–1988 base period, or they were based on historical trade flows. Not all countries utilise tariff rate quotas—only 43 WTO member countries established the total of over 1370 tariff rate quotas.

The introduction of a two-tier tariff system created a new category of economic effects, the tariff quota rents. A quota rent is the difference between the outquota and inquota tariffs times the value of the quota. This is illustrated in Figure 4.3. Assuming the quota, q, is full and the domestic price reflects the higher outquota tariff, $t2$, exporters with quota can supply goods over the lower tariff, $t1$, and receive the higher domestic price. Once the quota is filled, outquota imports are taxed at the higher tariff rate and no further rents are generated. Clearly, reduction in outquota tariffs reduces the quota rent.

An important issue is the distribution of the rents between exporters, processors, distributors, taxpayers and consumers, on which the effects of liberalisation largely depend. Rents may be captured by the government by auctioning rights to import or export, but often they accrue to other groups depending on the means by which quotas are allocated. There is, however, no one uniform method of administering the tariff rate quotas, thus there is no general rule on how quota rents and tariff revenues will change with trade liberalisation. In this study, it is assumed that, where quotas are based on a historical allocation, all the quota rents go to the exporter. The method of allocation has been tabulated by the WTO (WTO 2002) and incorporated into the Agricultural Trade Policy Simulation Model. This method applies to the markets for sugar and bananas, which account for 99 per cent of the rents captured by small island developing economies. The rents not captured by exporters are assumed to accrue eventually to government revenue in the importing country, instead of being transferred to consumers in the importing countries.

Table 4.5   Commodity coverage in the Agricultural Trade Policy Simulation Model

01100 Bovine meat	05440 Tomatoes
01210 Sheep meat	05700 Non-tropical Fruits
01220 Pig meat	05710 Citrus fruits
01230 Poultry	05730 Bananas
02212 Milk, fresh	05790 Other tropical fruits
02222 Milk, conc.	07110 Coffee green bags
02300 Butter	07120 Coffee roasted
02400 Cheese	07131 Coffee extracts
04100 Wheat	07210 Cocoa beans
04400 Maize	07240 Cocoa butter
04530 Sorghum	07220 Cocoa powder
04300 Barley	07300 Chocolate
04200 Rice	07410 Tea
06100 Sugar	12100 Tobacco leaves
22100 Oil seeds	12210 Cigars
42000 Vegetable oils	12220 Cigarettes
05420 Pulses	12230 Other tobacco - mfr.
05480 Roots & tubers	26300 Cotton linters

To estimate the actual size of a quota rent, it is necessary to have observations of global quotas, bilateral quotas, inquota and outquota tariff rates, world market prices and imports. The size of the global quotas (that is, the total level of imports at the lower tariff level) are obtained from annual notifications made to the WTO by tariff rate quota-using countries, but these notifications do not always provide a breakdown of quotas among different exporting countries. The model uses bilateral trade flows to estimate the distribution of global quotas among countries.[23] A further assumption for this analysis is that within-quota imports from small island developing economies are duty free. That is, the inquota tariff rate is not applied, implying that the initial rent accruing to small island developing economies is inflated.

The final key assumption relates to the quota fill rate (that is, the ratio of actual imports to the total tariff rate quota quantity of the product concerned). Ideally, the quota fill rate should determine the domestic price so that if the quota is unfilled, domestic prices should be determined by the inquota tariffs,

Figure 4.3   Quota rents with a binding out-of-quota tariff

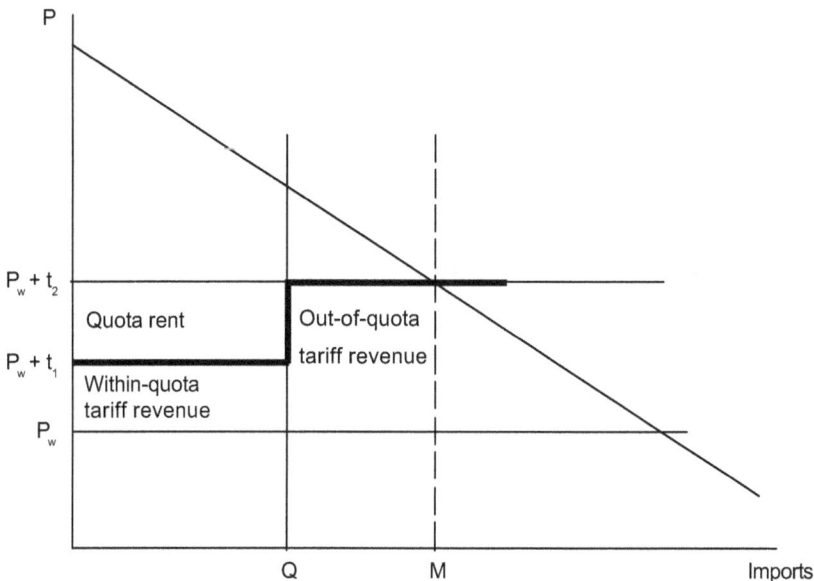

and prices should be high only if the quota is filled or overfilled. However, it is often observed that quotas are unfilled but domestic prices are nonetheless high. This may be because administrative constraints prevent the quotas being filled. More to the point, countries with high domestic prices are unlikely to be prepared to see them eroded by a shift in the supply of imports. As a result, the outquota tariffs (or possibly the applied tariffs) determine the domestic market price. This implies that global quotas should not exceed imports, and quotas are reduced to the level of imports where the data suggests this is the necessary. The calculation of tariff revenues and rents in the model is based on these assumptions.

The assumptions made above imply that changes in inquota tariffs and tariff rate quota quantities will not have price and production quantity effects, as these instruments are not binding. They do, however, change the distribution of rents.

Estimates of initial quota rents accruing to small island developing economies may be overstated because of the assumptions on inquota tariff rates and fill rates, but understated because of the method of allocating rent between countries. The calculation of initial rents affects the estimates of potential losses from liberalisation—the higher the rent, the greater the potential losses.

Data. Data on production quantity (2000) are compiled from the Food and Agriculture Organization (FAO) supply utilisation accounts (see FAOSTAT). Price data are from the FAO Yearbooks, using an average of the figures for 1996–98. Parameters on elasticities and feedshares are also provided by FAO. These are based on a trawling of the literature and are not econometrically estimated specifically for the model. Inquota tariffs, outquota tariffs and the size of the global quotas as notified to the WTO are obtained from the Agricultural Market Access Database 24 and aggregated to the Agricultural Trade Policy Simulation Model commodity level using a simple average wherever trade exists. Specific tariffs are converted to *ad valorem* equivalents based on unit values calculated for each country at the 'Harmonized System' six-digit level. Data on trade-distorting domestic support and export subsidies are derived from the notifications submitted to the WTO. Bilateral trade flow data for 1995, which were used to allocate global quotas to individual exporting countries, are provided by UNCTAD. The UNCTAD TRAINS database is a source of applied tariff information that determines whether cuts in bound rates are effective.

Current protection levels and rents

A good indicator of levels of border protection is global tariff revenues and rents, as these are the product of the level of protection and the trade flows. The base period data of these global indicators are shown in the first two columns in Table 4.6. Across commodities, temperate goods are subject to relatively higher level of border protection in developed economies than tropical products (with the notable exception of sugar and bananas). Developing economies, however, may levy substantial tariffs on tropical products.

Also shown in the table are the initial values of three variables important to small island developing economies: tariff revenues, export revenues and rent received. It is immediately apparent that sugar is the key commodity of small island developing economies, capturing more than 50 per cent of the total export revenues and 90 per cent of rents received. Sugar is followed in importance by vegetable oils (copra), coffee, cocoa and bananas. The bulk of the small island developing economies' export revenues and virtually all the quota rent received emanates from the EU and the US sugar policies. The major supplier of the EU sugar imports (1.3 million tonnes) is Mauritius with a quota of 487,000 tonnes. The United States also imports 1.1 million tonnes of sugar under a quota from developing economies plus Australia, the only developed economy exporter of cane sugar. China has imports of 0.6 million tonnes, the bulk of it from Cuba, Thailand, India and Australia.

Multilateral trade liberalisation will influence the level of the three variables. Tariff revenues and rent received are most likely to be reduced, while export revenues may improve. The next section examines the extent of such impacts and how they vary according to different trade liberalisation scenarios.

Four alternative scenarios

Taking into account the proposals and discussions made so far during the ongoing WTO negotiations on agriculture, the following four scenarios were selected for examination

- 'Ambitious': across-the-board reductions in outquota (MFN) bound tariffs using the Swiss formula with a coefficient of 25, and total elimination of export subsidies and production-distorting domestic support.
- 'Conservative—the Uruguay Round approach': a 36 per cent cut in outquota bound tariffs, 36 per cent reductions in export subsidy spending and 20 per cent cut in trade-distorting domestic support in developed economies.

Table 4.6   Global distortions: revenues and rents by commodity (US$m)

	World tariff revenue	Rent forgone	SIDS tariff revenue	Export revenue	Rent received
Apples	1,104	30	8	-	-
Bananas	537	492	1	91	28
Barley	411	613	0	0	-
Bovine meat	2,913	1,051	7	4	-
Butter	367	253	10	-	-
Cheese	886	530	16	6	1
Chocolate	1,283	139	9	7	-
Cigarettes	27	-	-	51	-
Cigars	3,684	-	14	41	-
Citrus fruits	508	43	1	23	-
Cocoa beans	61	-	-	118	-
Cocoa butter	48	-	-	10	-
Cocoa powder	44	-	-	4	-
Coffee extracts	18	-	-	0	-
Coffee green	576	3	1	183	-
Coffee roasted	19	2	-	11	-
Cotton linters	287	30	-	-	-
Maize	2,406	2,369	10	-	-
Milk, conc.	864	648	36	2	-
Milk, fresh	-	-	-	1	-
Oilseeds	2,496	326	8	34	-
Other mfr tobacco	666	-	1	-	-
Other tropical fruits	246	1	-	18	-
Pigmeat	482	199	6	-	-
Poultry	2089	259	37	3	-
Pulses	368	1	8	1	-
Rice	692	972	85	3	-
Roots and tubers	103	-	5	7	-
Sheep meat	236	594	24	-	-
Sorghum	67	25	-	-	-
Sugar	1,736	906	35	1,110	276
Tea	365	1	1	15	-
Tobacco leaves	2,112	81	1	75	-
Tomatoes	181	38	-	-	-
Vegetable oils	4,286	204	41	273	-
Wheat	1,515	2,687	27	14	1
Total	33,682	12,499	394	2,106	307

Source: The Agricultural Trade Policy Simulation Model (ATPSM) database <http://www.unctad.org>.

Two-thirds of these reductions in developing economies and no reductions in least developed economies.

- 'Tariff-50': 50 per cent cut in outquota bound tariffs in all countries.
- 'Compensatory': the previous scenario, plus removal of all tariffs on all small island developing economies' exports.

The 'ambitious' scenario—consisting of elements that have been proposed to the WTO negotiations on agriculture by major agricultural exporters such as the United States and the Cairns Group members—will lead to substantial agricultural liberalisation. A 'Swiss Formula' is designed in such a way that it eliminates tariff peaks and substantially reduces tariff escalation.[25] A maximum coefficient of 25 (as proposed by the United States and the Cairns Group) sets an effective tariff ceiling at 25 per cent, and achieves very deep cuts indeed— under this approach, tariff rates of 100 per cent, 200 per cent and 300 per cent are reduced to 20 per cent, 22 per cent and 23 per cent respectively.

The 'conservative' approach is almost a replica of the liberalisation approach employed during the Uruguay Round. The only difference is that, in this scenario, a linear cut of 36 per cent applies to the tariffs across all products, unlike the actual Uruguay Round approach, where tariffs on sensitive commodities were reduced by at least 15 per cent so long as an average cut of 36 per cent across products was achieved.

The 'tariff-50' scenario focuses purely on the impact of tariff cuts. Reductions in MFN bound tariffs—putting aside proposals to make reductions from the applied tariffs—are likely to have the greatest impact on small island developing economies, through the erosion of preferences causing reductions in quota rents. This scenario is also a reasonable middle ground between the 'ambitious' and 'conservative' scenarios, and will serve as a benchmark for assessment of the impact from the following scenario.

The 'compensatory' scenario examines the elimination of all outquota (MFN) rates applicable to small island developing economies, which is equivalent to an expansion of tariff rate quotas only to these economies. As the quota rents are determined by the outquota tariff rates and the quota quantities, changes in either of these variables (for example, global reductions of MFN tariffs) may possibly be offset by changes in the others (for example, small island developing economy-specific expansion of tariff rate quotas).

Results

In order to interpret the outcome of the simulations, we need to take into account the following elements. First, reductions in outquota tariff rates do not necessarily mean that the gap between domestic and world prices is reduced by the amount of the cut in the bound rate. In cases where applied tariffs are below the bound outquota rates, a 50 per cent cut in the outquota tariffs may result in a less than 50 per cent cut, or even no change at all, in the applied rates. Second, EU sugar and dairy production is assumed not to be responsive to changes in prices due to the existence of the production quotas for those products.

Prices. The impact on world prices for the first three scenarios is shown in Table 4.7. The price changes are correlated with the level of distortions removed. This is why the 'ambitious' scenario shows relatively greater price rises on products that are subject to high levels of tariffs, trade-distorting domestic support and/or export subsidies (including dairy products and wheat) than the other two approaches. The model estimates similar levels of price changes for the 'conservative' and 'tariff-50' scenarios. As anticipated, the results show that prices of tropical products (such as sugar, copra oils and bananas) increase less than temperate products, which implies a decline in the terms of trade facing the majority of small island developing states.

While price rises are indicative of the level of distortions, of greater interest to policymakers in small island developing economies is the impact of liberalisation on export revenues, tariff revenues, changes in quota rents and overall welfare. The welfare impact is calculated based on the changes in consumer surplus, producer surplus, and government revenues. These estimates are shown for small island developing economies and for the world in Table 4.8.

Export revenues. The comparison of estimated export revenues across different scenarios suggests that export revenues increase in proportion to the level of market access improvement. The increase in global export revenues under the 'ambitious' scenario (US$40.2 billion) is almost four times greater than the estimated increase under the 'conservative' scenario.

Under the 'tariff-50'—or benchmark—scenario, export revenues to small island developing economies rise from US$2.1 billion to US$2.4 billion, an

Table 4.7   Impact on world commodity prices of alternative scenarios

	Ambitious	Conservative	Tariff-50
	%	%	%
Bovine meat	8.4	2.9	3.0
Sheep meat	10.9	4.2	6.6
Pig meat	4.5	1.6	2.3
Poultry	7.2	1.8	3.7
Milk, fresh	−18.6	−4.2	2.9
Milk, conc.	11.4	1.5	2.1
Butter	19.7	6.0	5.4
Cheese	6.8	2.5	4.8
Wheat	13.3	4.5	2.3
Rice	3.1	1.0	1.6
Barley	2.5	0.6	1.4
Maize	4.0	1.3	2.3
Sorghum	0.8	0.3	0.4
Pulses	4.6	0.5	1.3
Tomatoes	3.1	1.6	2.3
Roots & tubers	3.5	1.0	2.6
Apples	3.9	1.9	3.2
Citrus fruits	1.5	0.7	1.2
Bananas	1.5	0.7	1.1
Other tropical fruits	3.8	1.1	2.2
Sugar	12.5	3.8	3.8
Coffee green	0.6	0.1	0.2
Coffee roasted	0.3	0.2	0.3
Coffee extracts	4.8	0.5	1.0
Cocoa beans	0.4	0.1	0.1
Cocoa powder	1.5	0.7	1.2
Cocoa butter	0.6	0.8	1.1
Chocolate	2.2	1.4	2.0
Tea	3.0	0.6	1.3
Tobacco leaves	3.9	1.4	2.6
Cigars	0.4	0.1	0.3
Cigarettes	0.1	0.0	0.1
Other mfr tobacco	0.2	0.1	0.1
Oilseeds	1.9	0.8	1.5
Cotton linters	1.3	0.3	0.5
Vegetable oils	8.0	1.2	1.6
Total*	5.5	1.7	2.1

Note: *Total is weighted by initial import values.
Source: Authors' model simulations based on the Agricultural Trade Policy Simulation Model <http://www.unctad.org>.

increase of US$190 million (or 9 per cent). Sugar (US$77 million), other tropical fruits (US$20 million), citrus (US$16 million) and bananas (US$16 million) are the major beneficiaries. This does not show changes in export revenues from the benchmark, due to the assumption that changes in quota rents alone do not affect the supply decisions of the producers of exported products concerned (hence the level of export quantity remains the same). This assumption is reasonable for small changes in quota rents.[26]

Tariff revenues. Tariff revenues are determined by the combination of the tariff rates, import quantities and import prices. The simulation results in Table 4.8 show a wide variation in the degree of changes in government revenue across different scenarios. Concerning government revenues at the global level, the 'ambitious' scenario will lead to smaller losses than the 'tariff-50' scenario because tariff revenues forgone are offset by reductions in domestic support and export subsidies. The continuation of spending on these government subsidies results in substantial losses in government revenues in the benchmark scenarios.

Looking at the 'compensatory' scenario, reducing tariffs on small island developing economies' out-of-quota exports involves losses in tariff revenues for importing countries equalling the gains in quota rents received by small island economy exporters. Importing government revenue losses are US$110 million over and above the US$5.22 billion in the benchmark scenario. The magnitude of a global loss in tariff revenues (or an increase in quota rents for small island developing economies, from US$181 million to US$72 million in Table 4.8) is determined by the degree of rent capture. These revenue losses effectively arise from transfers between taxpayers and producers and do not involve any efficiency gains or losses. Concerning small island developing economies, the benchmark scenario leads to a fall in tariff revenues from the estimated initial level of US$394 million to US$349 million, an 11 per cent reduction.

Quota rents. Global quota rents in the agricultural sector represented in the database are initially estimated to be around US$12.5 billion prior to any policy change. In total, small island developing economies receive US$307 million in the initial database, of which US$276 million is from sugar. The rents are reduced by US$181 million under the benchmark scenario, of which US$173 million can be attributed to sugar. Some US$29 million of this loss is

Table 4.8   Impact of alternative scenarios on key variables (US$m)

	Ambitious	Conservative	Tariff-50	Compensatory
Export revenue				
SIDS	466	161	190	190
World	44209	11218	23835	23835
Government revenue				
SIDS	−148	4.4	−44	−44
World	−3440	3241	−5216	−5326
Quota rents				
SIDS	−264	−145	−181	−72
World	−7297	−1504	−2763	−2654
Welfare				
SIDS	−217	−138	−151	−42
World	24051	8851	10833	10833

Source: Authors' model simulations based on the Agricultural Trade Policy Simulation Model <http://www.unctad.org>.

offset by allocative efficiency gains (due to tariff reductions in small island developing economies themselves) and increased export prices (due to tariff reductions in other countries).

The 'compensatory' scenario results in a US$72 million loss in the quota rents transferred from the initial level, and US$109 million improvement on the benchmark result. That is to say, removing tariffs to all small island developing economies' exports within and out of quota (which is equivalent to increasing the size of global quotas to accommodate all small island developing states' exports) is not sufficient to offset the US$181 million losses in quota rents resulting from a 50 per cent cut in MFN tariffs in importing countries.

Welfare. Putting together the various changes in production, exports, tariff revenues and quota rents, the greater the degree of liberalisation, the greater are the welfare gains to the world as a whole (the 'compensatory' scenario does not change global welfare from the benchmark). A greater global welfare increase under the 'tariff-50' (benchmark) scenario than the 'conservative' scenario arises from gains by developing economies as a whole, as more substantial tariff cuts by developing economies under the benchmark case increase largely due to consumer surplus increases in those economies. However, the impact of liberalisation on small island developing economies appears to be negative because of loss of quota rents and rising prices of imports.

Table 4.9 provides a breakdown of welfare impacts under each of the four scenarios across different groups of countries. Most groups gain more from deeper reform, but the picture is confused by the removal of export subsidies that raise the world price while providing allocative efficiency gains predominantly to the European Union. Least developed economies experience a welfare loss under the 'conservative' scenario due to a combination of higher import prices and the absence of efficiency gains from liberalisation (these economies are exempted from making reduction commitments), though they can make welfare gains in excess of US$900 million in other scenarios. Developing economy agricultural importers lose under the 'conservative' scenario for similar reasons. Providing compensation to small island developing economies does not make other developing economies worse, according to these estimates. However, this result is driven by the assumption that quotas are filled and therefore there is no trade diversion. The major cost of the compensation policy is borne by the developed economies that provide the compensation through extended preferential access, predominantly the European Union and the United States.

A breakdown of the welfare impact under the benchmark scenario for individual small island developing states by commodity is presented in Table 4.10. The largest welfare loss is anticipated to be by Mauritius, Jamaica and Fiji. The major losses by commodity occur in sugar (due to loss of quota rents) and wheat, dairy products and meat (due to increases in food import prices).

The importance of quota rents to the welfare figures highlights the assumption about their distribution. In an alternative simulation—where all rents are assumed to accrue to importers—the welfare of small island developing economies under the benchmark scenario rises by US$30 million rather than falling by US$181 million.

Some limitations

The limitation in this analysis is the lack of knowledge of the distribution of quota rents. Small island developing economies' rents received are underestimated because quotas are allocated according to historical data that are biased by overquota exports. However, quota rents are overestimated due to the assumption that quotas are effectively filled and that outquota or applied tariffs rather than inquota tariffs drive domestic prices. A final consideration is the assumption that producers don't respond to changes in rents, which further implies no trade diversion. These are reasonable for small policy changes but less so for elimination of tariffs. Preference erosion is expected to benefit low-cost producers through liberalisation of markets in which they had been excluded from preferential market access (Brazilian sugar in the EU market, for example). These limitations are unlikely to affect the overall results in this application because most of the quota rents accruing to small island developing economies derive from sugar exports, to which the concerns listed here are not so applicable.

CONCLUSIONS

In spite of the limitations listed above, several implications can be drawn from the results.

First, preferences provide significant benefits to some small island developing economies, and trade liberalisation will lead to some erosion of these preferences. This will have a significant impact in some cases, particularly for those small island developing economies currently enjoying quota rents. Sugar and banana producers are likely to be the sectors most affected. Yet, the magnitude of the overall impact depends on the chosen scenarios, the highest being in the 'Ambitious' scenario and the lowest in the 'Conservative' scenario.

Table 4.9   Impact on welfare of four scenarios

	Ambitious $m	Conservative $m	Tariff-50 $m	Compensatory $m
SIDS	−217	−138	−151	−42
European Union	9,027	4,471	2,838	2,745
United States	−564	599	506	494
Cairns Group	2,724	661	225	225
Developing importers[1]	4,249	−81	1,798	1,905
All developed	17,953	9,042	8,244	8,136
All developing[2]	5,180	−54	1,627	1,733
Least developed countries	917	−137	962	963
World	24,051	8,851	10,833	10,833

Notes: [1] Developing countries, excluding Cairns Group members. [2] Excludes least developed countries.
Source: Authors' model simulations based on the Agricultural Trade Policy Simulation Model, <http://www.unctad.org>.

Table 4.10   Welfare impacts by commodity group from 50 per cent tariff reduction (US$m)

	Beverages	Cereals	Dairy	Fruit	Meat	Oilseeds	Sugar	Tobacco & cotton	Vegetables	Total
Barbados	−0.02	−0.22	−0.51	−0.08	−0.67	−0.12	−8.54	0.01	−0.04	−10.20
Cuba	−0.03	−6.87	−2.37	0.28	−3.19	−1.00	19.31	0.79	−0.57	6.36
Dominica	0.02	−0.03	−0.05	−0.77	−0.21	0.00	−0.02	−0.01	0.00	−1.07
Dominican Rep.	0.16	−4.90	−1.19	−1.49	20.86	−1.52	−1.74	1.24	0.13	11.55
Fiji	−0.02	−0.24	−0.30	0.18	−0.91	0.30	−48.70	0.39	0.24	−49.05
Grenada	0.00	−0.10	−0.18	0.03	−0.37	−0.01	−0.08	−0.01	−0.01	−0.71
Haiti	0.01	2.08	−0.43	1.92	1.31	−0.45	−0.97	0.03	1.09	4.59
Jamaica	−0.04	−1.73	−1.55	−0.91	−2.91	−0.52	−27.23	−0.02	−0.01	−34.92
Maldives	−0.01	−0.15	−0.13	−0.06	−0.18	−0.01	−0.10	−0.02	−0.02	−0.69
Mauritius	−0.10	−1.23	−1.02	−0.31	1.45	−0.36	−65.86	−0.13	−0.09	−67.65
Papua New Guinea	0.49	−1.17	−0.20	0.51	−4.04	4.21	0.81	−0.01	0.63	1.24
Solomon Islands	0.00	−0.18	−0.02	0.00	0.12	0.41	−0.03	0.00	0.87	1.18
St. Lucia	−0.01	−0.08	−0.18	−2.01	−0.54	0.00	−0.06	−0.01	−0.01	−2.90
St. Vincent	0.00	−0.32	−0.07	−1.10	−0.33	0.00	−0.06	−0.01	0.02	−1.87
Trinidad & Tobago	−0.07	−0.84	−1.92	−0.13	−0.75	−0.54	−0.06	−0.04	−0.17	−4.52
Bahamas	−0.02	−0.07	−0.41	0.02	−1.01	0.00	−0.11	0.20	−0.02	−1.43
Cape Verde	−0.01	−0.27	−0.13	−0.06	−0.12	−0.07	−0.15	−0.01	−0.04	−0.87
Comoros	0.00	−0.14	−0.01	0.01	−0.17	0.00	−0.02	0.00	0.00	−0.34
Sao Tome	0.00	−0.04	−0.01	0.00	0.00	0.00	−0.02	0.00	0.00	−0.06
Seychelles	0.01	−0.05	−0.09	0.03	−0.06	−0.04	−0.03	0.06	0.00	−0.17
Vanuatu	0.00	−0.07	−0.04	0.00	0.06	0.14	−0.03	0.00	0.00	0.06
Total	0.36	−16.61	−10.81	−3.96	8.33	0.43	−133.68	2.46	2.01	−151.47

Source: Authors' model simulations based on the Agricultural Trade Policy Simulation Model, <http://www.unctad.org>.

Second, the results of the simulations suggest that there is scope for these countries to be compensated, if it is considered desirable. This involves expanding import duty-free quotas to cover all small island developing economies' exports. According to the model estimates, this would substantially but not entirely compensate for losses in rents. Given the high degree of specialisation by small island developing economies on a limited number of products, additional preferential quotas appear therefore to guard beneficiaries against the erosion of preferential tariff margins and quota rents. However, this assumes that beneficiary countries are capable of filling the additional quotas.

There might, however, be individual small island developing economies currently not capturing quota rents that may be inclined to favour liberalisation as estimates indicate that if quota rents are ignored there are positive net benefits from improved market access and efficiency gains from domestic reform. Similarly, low cost small island developing economy producers may find themselves shut out of markets by the import quota system and may be favoured by the erosion of preferences.

Finally, compensation, if any, might be sought both within the WTO framework and bilaterally. In fact, given the high geographical concentration of small island developing economy exports in few markets, there may yet be scope for improving the effectiveness of non-reciprocal preferential market access via expansion of product coverage, expansion of quantitative limits on preferential market access or lowering preferential tariff rates, with a view to offsetting the impacts of MFN tariff cuts.

ACKNOWLEDGMENTS

This paper is an updated and revised version of a chapter by the same authors in an UNCTAD report entitled 'Turning Losses into Gains: SIDS (Small Island Developing States) and Multilateral Trade Liberalisation in Agriculture' UNCTAD/DITC/TNCD/2003/1 July 2003.

NOTES

[1] UNCTAD considers 'small island developing states' as countries and territories with a population under 5 million people. While both the United Nations and the Commonwealth Secretariat make use of population as the benchmark for determining smallness, there is no officially agreed international definition of smallness. The Commonwealth Secretariat's *Vulnerability Report 1985* uses as a threshold a population of one million (subsequently increased to 1,5 million), but at the same time, regards as small states countries with a larger population such as Papua New Guinea and Jamaica. Others (Briguglio 1993; Downes 1988) use a composite index of population, land area and GNP.

[2] In 1994, a Global Conference on the Sustainable Development of Small Island Developing States (Barbados, April/May 1994) resulted in a Programme of Action for the Sustainable Development of Small Island Developing States. In September 2002, the World Summit on Sustainable Development (Johannesburg, RSA) in its Plan of Implementation (paragraph 55) requested the UN General Assembly at its 57th session to consider convening a new international meeting on the Sustainable Development of Small Island Developing States.

[3] See for example, Briguglio 1995; UNCTAD 1997; Commonwealth Secretariat, various years; Downes1988; Lockhart et al. 1993; Encontre 1999.

⁴   Pending the ratification process, the Agreement was put into provisional application on 2 August 2000, according to the modalities laid down in Decision No 1/2000 of the ACP–EC Council of Ministers of 27 July 2000 (2000/483/EC, Official Journal L 195 of 1.8.2000, p. 46).

⁵   Small island developing economies' new ACP members include Federal States of Micronesia, Marshall Islands, Palau, Nauru, Cook Islands and Niue.

⁶   Duty-free treatment is also granted to fish and fish products subject to specific rules of origin requirements.

⁷   On most such products, the pre-'Everything But Arms'–Generalised System of Preferences used to provide a percentage reduction of MFN rates rates, which would only apply to the *ad valorem* duties, thus leaving the specific duties still entirely applicable. This is no longer the case as all dutiable products that were previously granted only a limited margin of preference or were subject to quantitative limitations are now entirely liberalised for least developed economies.

⁸   For the basic US legislation on the Generalised System of Preferences program (Title V of the Trade Act of 1974 as amended) and for further details, please refer to the text and appendices of the Handbook on the Generalised System of Preferences Scheme of the United States, UNCTAD document ITCD/TSB/Misc.58, of June 2000, also available on the UNCTAD Generalised System of Preferences website. For detailed information about the African Growth and Opportunity Act, please refer to the Handbook on the Generalised System of Preferences Scheme of the United States, as published by UNCTAD, Document ITCD/TSB/Misc.58, of June 2000, also available on the UNCTAD Generalised System of Preferences website. All African Growth and Opportunity Act related documentation is available online at Internet: www.agoa.gov.

⁹   All designated African Growth and Opportunity Act (AGOA) beneficiaries, including non-least developed economies, have been granted duty-free treatment on all GSP-eligible products, including those on which only least developed beneficiary countries used to enjoy GSP treatment. This implies that former special Generalised System of Preferences least developed economies' preferences have been somewhat diluted since other sub-Saharan non-least developed economies in Africa can now benefit from them.

¹⁰ In addition, the 'African Growth and Opportunity Act-enhanced' Generalised System of Preferences benefits will be in place for a period of eight years, and this longer-than-usual period of time is expected to provide additional security to investors and traders in qualifying African countries.

¹¹ These countries are Antigua and Barbuda, Aruba, Bahamas, Barbados, Belize, Costa Rica, Dominica, Dominican Republic, El Salvador, Grenada, Guatemala, Guyana, Haiti, Honduras, Jamaica, Montserrat, Netherlands Antilles, Nicaragua, Panama, St. Kitts and Nevis, Saint Lucia, Saint Vincent and the Grenadines, Trinidad and Tobago, and British Virgin Islands

[12] For example, according to the Caribbean Textile and Apparel Institute, approximately 150 companies have closed their operations and relocated to Mexico since NAFTA came into force.

[13] However, the *ad valorem* equivalent of all rate components estimated by the US International Trade Commission is reported to be only 3.5 per cent (the US2002 Tariff Web-Database at http://dataweb.usitc.gov/scripts/tariff2002.asp contains further information).

[14] Anguilla, Antigua and Barbuda, Bahamas, Bermuda, Barbados, Belize, British Virgin Islands, Cayman Islands, Dominica, Grenada, Guyana, Jamaica, Montserrat, St. Kitts and Nevis, St. Lucia, St. Vincent and the Grenadines, Trinidad and Tobago, and the Turks and Caicos Islands.

[15] Under the scheme in force for fiscal year 2002–03, Japan granted preferential treatment to 164 developing economies. For detailed information on the current scheme, please refer to the Handbook on the Scheme of Japan 2002/2003 (document UNCTAD/ITCD/TSB/Misc.42), also available on the internet.

[16] With the recent addition of Zambia, Democratic Republic of Congo, Kiribati and Tuvalu to the list of Generalised System of Preferences beneficiaries, there are currently only two least developed economies (Comoros(*) and Djibouti) that, despite being eligible for duty/quota free treatment under the Japanese scheme, have yet to request so.

[17] The current initiative to dispute the EU sugar regime by Brazil and Australia at the WTO shows how critical the situation might become.

[18] See the 'Joint Declaration Concerning Agricultural Products Referred to in Article 1(2)(a)', containing the preferential treatment applicable to agricultural products and foodstuff originating in ACP states, Annex to Decision 1/2000 of the African, Carribean and Pacific–EC Committee of Ambassadors of 28 February 2000 on transitional measures valid from 1 March 2000, EU OJ L 217, 26.8.2000, p. 189 ff

[19] The entry price system trade regime has replaced the old reference price system as one of the results of the 'tariffication' process carried out in the Uruguay Round, whereby all no-tariffs measures had to be converted into bound tariffs. To explain briefly how the entry price system works, it is useful to think of it as a dual system where two separate sets of tariffs apply according to a core variable that is represented by the entry price. Applicable tariffs are either *ad valorem* or specific duties. In this system, as long as the c.i.f. import price of a particular product complies with the entry price (that is, is either equal or higher) a 'general' bound tariff applies. However, if the import price falls below the entry price, an additional duty is charged on top of the general one up to a maximum tariff level (also bound). In reality, the system is slightly more complex, since there are several entry prices for the same product, and for each of them a different additional duty applies. Indeed, and although set *a priori*, entry prices change according to seasons, being lower during the harvest season in the European Union so as to provide maximum protection to the EU local producers.

[20] Proposal for a COUNCIL REGULATION on The Arrangements Applicable to Agricultural Products and Goods Resulting from the Processing of Agricultural Products Originating in the African, Caribbean and Pacific States; Brussels, 21.06.2002 COM(2002) 335 final 2002/0129 (ACC).

[21] The Agricultural Trade Policy Simulation Model equation structure and other details can be found in Annex 2 or in UNCTAD (2002). The model can be downloaded for free from www.unctad.org/tab.

[22] The definition of small island developing economies is somewhat debatable. Possibly contentious in the Agricultural Trade Policy Simulation Model list are Cuba, a large sugar exporter, and Haiti. Other small island developing states countries included in the Agricultural Trade Policy Simulation Model are Bahamas, Barbados, Cape Verde, Comoros, Cuba, Dominica, Dominican Republic, Fiji, Grenada, Haiti, Jamaica, Kiribati, Maldives, Mauritius, Papua New Guinea, Sao Tomé and Principe, Solomon Islands, St. Lucia, St. Vincent and the Grenadines, the Seychelles, Trinidad and Tobago and Vanuatu.

[23] For this reason, estimated rents may differ from reality in cases where a country exports at the overquota level in addition to its quota share.

[24] AMAD is available to all users at http// www.amad.org.

[25] Swiss formula takes the following structure: $T1 = (T0*x)/(T0+x)$, where T1 is the new tariff rate, T0 is the initial tariff rate and x is the maximum coefficient.

[26] This assumption may no longer hold if suppliers depend on the receipt of rents to cover their costs. At some point declining rents will lead to a fall in production below the quota level.

[27] The Agricultural Trade Policy Simulation Model plus the documentation and data are available free from UNCTAD on request. Email atpsm@unctad.org to request a copy.

Annex 1	Preferential trading arrangements for small island developing economies in the quad

African SIDS

EU *ACP:* Cape Verde, Sao Tomé & Principe, Comoros, Seychelles, Mauritius *GSP:* as ACP + Maldives *GSP–EBA:* Cape Verde, Sao Tomé & Principe, Comoros + Maldives
United States *GSP:* Cape Verde, Sao Tomé & Principe, Comoros, Seychelles, Mauritius *GSP–LDC:* Cape Verde, Sao Tomé & Principe, Comoros *GSP–AGOA:* Cape Verde, Sao Tomé & Principe, Mauritius and Seychelles

Canada *GSP:* Cape Verde, Sao Tomé & Principe, Comoros, Seychelles, Mauritius + Maldives *GSP–LDC:* Cape Verde, Sao Tomé & Principe, Comoros + Maldives
Japan *GSP:* Cape Verde, Sao Tomé & Principe, Comoros (*), Seychelles, Mauritius + Maldives *GSP–LDC:* Cape Verde, Sao Tomé & Principe + Maldives

Caribbean SIDS

EU *ACP:* Bahamas, Dominican Republic, Antigua and Barbuda, Barbados, Dominica, Grenada, Haiti, Jamaica, St Kitts–Nevis, St Lucia, St Vincent and the Grenadines, Trinidad and Tobago *GSP:* as ACP + Cuba *GSP–EBA:* Haiti
United States *GSP:* Bahamas, Dominican Republic, Antigua and Barbuda, Barbados, Dominica, Grenada, Haiti, Jamaica, St Kitts–Nevis, St Lucia, St Vincent and the Grenadines, Trinidad and Tobago *GSP–LDC:* Haiti *CBI/CBTPA:* same as GSP

Canada *GSP:* Antigua and Barbuda, Bahamas, Barbados, Cuba, Dominica, Grenada, Haiti, Jamaica, St. Kitts and Nevis, St. Lucia, St. Vincent & the Grenadines, Trinidad and Tobago *GSP–LDC:* Haiti *CARIBCAN:* Antigua and Barbuda, Bahamas, Barbados, Dominica, Grenada, Jamaica, St Kitts–Nevis, St Lucia, St Vincent and the Grenadines, Trinidad and Tobago
Japan *GSP:* Antigua and Barbuda, Barbados, Dominica, Grenada, Haiti, Jamaica, St. Kitts and Nevis, St. Lucia, St. Vincent and the Grenadines, Trinidad and Tobago *GSP–LDC:* Haiti

Pacific SIDS

EU *ACP:* Fiji, Kiribati, Marshall Islands, Federated States of Micronesia, Nauru, Palau, Papua New Guinea, Solomon Islands, Tonga, Tuvalu, Vanuatu, Samoa *GSP:* as ACP *GSP–EBA:* Kiribati, Solomon Islands, Tuvalu, Vanuatu, Samoa
United States *GSP:* Fiji, Kiribati, Palau, Papua New Guinea, Solomon Islands, Tonga, Tuvalu, Vanuatu *GSP–LDC:* Kiribati, Solomon Islands, Tuvalu, Vanuatu, Samoa

Canada *GSP:* Fiji, Kiribati, Marshall Islands, Nauru, Papua New Guinea, Solomon Islands, Tonga, Tuvalu, Vanuatu, Samoa *GSP–LDC:* Kiribati, Solomon Islands, Tuvalu, Vanuatu, Samoa
Japan *GSP:* Fiji, Kiribati, Marshall Islands, Federated States of Micronesia, Nauru, Palau, Papua New Guinea, Solomon Islands, Tonga, Tuvalu, Vanuatu, Samoa *GSP–LDC:* Kiribati, Solomon Islands, Tuvalu, Vanuatu, Samoa

ANNEX 2

Some technical details concerning ATPSM

The Agricultural Trade Policy Simulation Model is a comparative static, deterministic, linear, partial equilibrium, global model with 36 commodities and 162 countries or regions. One principal characteristic of the model is that domestic prices are all a function of world market prices and the border protection or special domestic support measures. Thus, no data is provided about the domestic prices and no transaction costs (such as wholesale and retail margins) are taken into account. All protection measures are expressed in tariff equivalents.

A second characteristic is two-way trade. In the Agricultural Trade Policy Simulation Model database a country is often an importer and exporter of the one (aggregated) good. To accommodate this feature of trade data, composite tariffs for determining the domestic consumption and production price are estimated. The technique chosen to derive the composed tariffs is to divide the volumes into three groups, imports, exports and production supplied to the domestic market (Sd).

First, a domestic market tariff (td) is computed as the weighted average of two trade taxes, the export subsidy rate (tx) and import tariff (tm), where the weights are exports (X) and imports (M).

$$td = (X\ tx + M\ tm)/(M + X)$$

Then, a consumption (domestic market) tariff is computed as the weighted average of the import tariff (tm) and the domestic market tariff (td), where the weights are imports (M) and domestic supply (Sd):

$$tc = (M\ tm + Sd\ td)\ /\ D$$

Similarly, a supply (domestic market) tariff is computed as the weighted average of the import tariff (tm) and the domestic market tariff (td), where the weights are exports (X) and domestic supply (Sd) plus the domestic support tariff (tp):

$$ts = (X\ tx + Sd\ td)\ /\ S + tp$$

These calculations are applied both to the baseline and the final tariffs.

The system is essentially based on four equations, specifying domestic consumption, production, exports and imports.

The standard equation system for all countries has four equations.

$$\hat{D}_{i,r} = \eta_{i,i,r}\left[\hat{P}_{wi}\left(1+\hat{t}_{c_{i,r}}\right)\right] + \sum_{\substack{j=1 \\ i \neq j}}^{J} \eta_{i,j,r}\left[\hat{P}_{wj}\left(1+\hat{t}_{c\,j,r}\right)\right] \qquad (A4.1)$$

$$\hat{S}_{i,r} = \varepsilon_{i,i,r}\left[\hat{P}_{wi}\left(1+\hat{t}_{p_{i,r}}\right)\right] + \sum_{\substack{j=1 \\ i \neq j}}^{J} \varepsilon_{i,j,r}\left[\hat{P}_{wj}\left(1+\hat{t}_{p\,j,r}\right)\right] \qquad (A4.2)$$

$$\Delta X_{i,r} = \gamma_{i,r}\Delta S_{i,r} \qquad (A4.3)$$

$$\Delta M_{i,r} = D_{i,r}\hat{D}_{i,r} - S_{i,r}\hat{S}_{i,r} + \Delta X_{i,r} \qquad (A4.4)$$

where D, S, X, and M denote demand, supply, exports and imports, respectively;

$\wedge$ denotes relative changes and Δ absolute changes

P_w denotes world price

t_c denotes the domestic consumption tariff and t_p denotes the domestic production tariff

ε denotes supply elasticity, denotes demand elasticity, and denotes the ratio of exports to production

i and j are commodities indexes

r is a country index.

Equation A5.3 requires that the change in exports in each market is some proportion of the change in production. This proportion is determined by the ratio of exports to production. For example, if all the initial production is exported, all the change in production is exported. If half the initial production is exported, half of the change in production is exported. This implies that the proportion of exports to production is maintained. Equation A5.4 clears the market, so that production plus imports equals domestic consumption and exports. Further details on the model are available in UNCTAD (2002).[27]

COMMENT

Ray Trewin

On reading Monge-Roffarello et al., my first thoughts were that there was a third option to 'sinking' or 'swimming' and that was 'floating'. 'Floating'—just treading water and hoping external forces will do something positive—has been the approach of many small island developing states. I think the proactive 'swim' option has much more going for it in the long run, but it may require a different stroke to what has been used in the past—that is, introducing proactive policies that will facilitate structural adjustment towards more competitive industries and building on comparative advantage rather than relying on preferential access, aid or assistance. These thoughts are based on experiences I have had at the Australian Bureau of Agricultural and Resource Economics (ABARE), The Australian National University and now the Australian Centre for International Agricultural Research (ACIAR) over the last 30 years or so. I will draw on these experiences in my comments on the paper.

First, as I was invited to make these comments with my ACIAR hat on, I should mention that ACIAR has a number of relevant projects currently underway, such as the 'Impact of policy changes on the Fiji Islands' food sector'. This project will be looking at alternative policies to current approaches, including a sugar industry based around the type of preferential access outlined in the chapter, assistance to an uncompetitive Fiji dairy industry based on failed import replacement/self-sufficiency approaches, and bans on imported lamb flaps in the hope that locally produced foods will be taken up. One such alternative policy is higher levels of research and development in neglected local industries—such as taro—which have been crowded out by some current policies assisting other industries. Such alternative policies would not only have resource allocation benefits but also positive spillovers in terms of food health issues.

The ACIAR project previously mentioned has a structural adjustment aspect, but a more relevant story on this issue, concerns some work I was involved in on Tasmania—which could be considered a small island developing state— shortly after joining the Bureau of Agricultural Economics, now ABARE, some 30 years ago. At that time, the Huon Valley in Tasmania was highly dependent on apple exports (which had just lost preferential access to the UK market) and was also reliant on various other forms of assistance such as payments to equalise freight, payments if drinks contained apple juice as a sweetener, price support and compensation for exchange rate changes. A tree pull scheme was introduced with the loss of the UK export market, facilitating structural adjustment. Such a policy contrasts to some in Europe where payments might be made to avoid farmers having to adjust and to maintain the current rural environment. Industry and household surveys showed that adjustment took place in the Huon Valley, with some farmers replanting for new specialist markets (for example, high quality Fuji apples for export to Japan rather than poor quality juicing apples). New activities such as recreational and tourism services were also developed. This early experience was a strong lesson that policies which facilitate structural adjustment can work for the betterment of groups apparently disadvantaged by policy or market changes.

Returning to the paper, various problems are identified by Monge-Roffarello et al., but many of these could really be solutions (to quote John Lennon). For example, isolation can be an advantage for some growing 'castaway' tourism services and for specialist products, like Fiji water which is one of the country's fastest growing exports. Moreover, some of these 'problems' are diminishing. Smallness and remoteness, for example, are less of a problem now with new transport and communication technologies, and greater competitive forces from globalisation in these and other like sectors. Lastly, have Monge-Roffarello et al. identified the right problems? Often the lack of resources which is put forward as a problem is due to poor property rights such as in land-use rights.

One thing for certain is—as pointed out in the chapter—that preferential arrangements have distorted the economic structure of the relevant small island developing states away from comparative advantage, both in terms of the type of exports and their destinations. These distortions are likely to have had negative effects on the economic structure of all small island developing states, even those not directly involved in preferential arrangements.

Assessing the impact of future trade liberalisation options involves modelling. In the modelling described here by the authors, a number of key assumptions are made. First, it is assumed that partial equilibrium modelling will do the full job. However, structural adjustment is such an important issue in trade liberalisation that you would think some computable general equilibrium (CGE) modelling—with its ability to shift resources between sectors—would be needed at some point. Another key assumption made is that quota rents go to producers, which suggests the existence of some market power that is not evident in other aspects. Some sugar exported from Africa to the European Union (EU) under preferential arrangements has been shown to be originally EU sugar. This suggests that market power is elsewhere and rents are not all going to producers. The final key assumption made by Monge-Roffarello et al. is that changes in rents do not influence supply. Experiences in Australian industries such as eggs and dairy—where arrangements that produced rents have been changed—would suggest that large supply responses can occur. All these assumption are important in terms of the measured impacts of policy changes. Although the limitations of the analysis are acknowledged, they are ignored in the conclusions drawn by Monge-Roffarello et al. The paper puts forward more of the same special and differential (SAD) treatment approaches for small island developing states instead of a structural adjustment approach through investment in infrastructure, education and better policies. Some International Food Policy Research Institute (IFPRI) work in Asian developing countries has shown large returns can be achieved through such investments.

5

'POOLED REGIONAL GOVERNANCE' IN THE ISLAND PACIFIC: LESSONS FROM HISTORY

Greg Fry

Since mid 2003 the Australian government has been attempting to reshape and revitalise regional cooperation in the South Pacific around the concept of 'pooled regional governance'. As with its new hands-on engagement at the national level in the Pacific—in particular in Solomon Islands, Papua New Guinea and Nauru—this heightened commitment is ultimately motivated by security concerns. The Pacific island states are seen as 'fragile', or potentially fragile, and therefore prone to penetration by terrorist networks. As viewed by the Howard government, the tasks have therefore become those of getting serious about state strengthening, development, law and order, and 'good governance'. Whereas this has been previously promoted by aid conditionality, diplomacy and what was ultimately seen as weak regionalism, it is now seen as requiring more direct Australian management and, where necessary, the insertion of police and armed forces. It is also seen as requiring a more robust form of regional governance in which Australia would play a more forthright role.

Prime Minister Howard first promoted the notion of 'pooled regional governance' in July 2003 in the context of announcing his government's intention to lead a regional assistance mission to Solomon Islands.[1] Howard argued that the smaller Pacific states needed to share resources if they were to overcome the constraints imposed by their small size and lack of capacity. He illustrated the point by referring to the absurdity of each island country trying to run its own airline or train its police when these could be done through pooling resources.

By August 2003 'pooled regional governance' had become a major foreign policy objective for the Australian government. Prime Minister Howard vigorously promoted the concept at the Pacific Islands Forum in Auckland. After his discussions he claimed that other leaders had accepted the notion[2] although the New Zealand press interpreted these events slightly differently viewing the Australian push as too heavy-handed. The Forum agreed not only to take action on the particular cases the prime minister had raised in June— that of a regional police training unit and an Australian-sponsored study of civil aviation—but also to a major overhaul of regional arrangements under the auspices of the Forum. In some senses, the resulting Pacific Plan became the embodiment of a broader notion of 'pooled regional governance', not just the sharing of resources and saving of costs in particular sectors but also a commitment to ratcheting up the cooperative effort as implied in the term 'regional governance' as against 'regional cooperation' (MFAT 2004). Additionally, Howard lobbied hard and ultimately successfully to make sure that an Australian would be in charge of the development of the Pacific Plan.

'Pooled regional governance' could in theory take many forms in relation to the depth and breadth of regional integration, in the degree of obligation expected of sovereign states, in the form of institutional arrangements, and in the kind of political participation envisaged. Hypothetically we could imagine at one end of the spectrum a European-style union; and at the other, the existing form of regional cooperation in the Pacific with its limited functional cooperation, active collective diplomacy and its attempt at harmonisation of laws around issues of 'good governance', neo-liberal development and regional security. As the concept is currently being developed in the Pacific context certain things have become clear about the parameters within which the participating states envisage future developments. No Pacific leader is pressing for a Pacific union along the lines of the European Union or a regional currency (the Australian dollar) despite the publicity given to these ideas following the release of the recommendations of an Australian Senate Committee on *A Pacific Engaged* just prior to the Auckland Forum. Both the Australian government and leaders of Pacific island states rejected such ideas as premature. But all seem to agree on the need to go beyond what is currently in existence either to deal with globalisation, to promote regional security (Australia) or to halt the development of a 'ghetto of conflict and poverty' (New Zealand). There also seems to be agreement that this should be pursued under the auspices of the Pacific Islands Forum.

Within these broad parameters there is obviously ground for political contest over the depth, breadth, form and purpose of future regional governance and the shape of institutional arrangements. How far should regional governance go with integrating into 'one South Pacific regional economy'? Should it revisit the 'one regional airline' idea? What are the issues involved in significant integration of sectors in such ventures? If agreed on the need for regional governance to negotiate the impact of globalisation, how should that be pursued? There is also the perennial question of how the legitimacy of these reforms is affected by Australia's dominant role in promoting them? How institutionalised should regional governance become? How far beyond the representatives of independent states should political participation in regional governance go? In relation to institutional arrangements, do we move to one regional organisation rather than the existing set of functional agencies? Should the Secretary-General have a proactive role?

These are of course not new questions in a region where regional governance in various forms has been attempted for so long. As Fiji's Foreign Minister, Kaliopate Tavola, said when asked about the new notion of pooled regional governance in July 2003, 'Well the concept is not new, I mean, the name Prime Minister John Howard has given it is new…But the concept itself has been the basis of some of the regional initiatives' (ABC Online 2003). We can go as far back as British colonialism in the nineteenth century to see advocates of pooled regional governance in the Western Pacific High Commission or later in the 1930s in the creation of the Central Medical School in Suva to train Pacific islanders from British territories across the region. The South Pacific Commission established in 1947 was partly based on ideas of pooling resources for research information and training to promote development and eradicate disease. With decolonisation in the 1960s there was a move by Pacific island leaders to take control of regional organisation and cooperation most prominently through the establishment of the Pacific Islands Forum in 1971 and the South Pacific Bureau for Economic Cooperation in 1973.

Since its inception 34 years ago, the Forum has provided a focal point for several different models of regional governance. It is the starting point for this discussion that this experience provides some useful insights into the issues awaiting particular interpretations of the concept of 'pooled regional governance'. While one should recognise that there are new global conditions and Pacific states are at a very different stage of their political development, it seems to me that there are nevertheless lessons to be learnt from this history. It is at the very least important to remind some new commentators that there is such a history. The fact that Australian governments have made major attempts in the past to promote precisely this same agenda is important. In 1994, for example, Prime Minister Keating tried to create a new regional economic order with 'pooled regional governance' in all but name as the underlying concept and, as now, with airline rationalisation as a key policy objective (Fry 1994). This is not to mention the first decade of the Forum's history, when a narrow conception of 'pooled regional governance'—that concerned with regional integration of sectors of the economy including, most prominently, civil aviation—was unsuccessfully pursued as the main objective of regional cooperation.

At the risk of simplification, I divide this rich history of regional cooperation in the Pacific into five main forms of attempted regional governance with a rough correlation with different time periods in terms of their prominence: comprehensive economic integration (1971–74); sectoral integration (1971–78), collective diplomacy (1979–90); regional security community (1984–89), and harmonisation of national policies (1994–2003). We will then be in a position to distil from this experience some possible lessons for the new regionalism proposals promoted since 2003, sometimes characterised as 'pooled regional governance' or 'regional integration'.

COMPREHENSIVE REGIONAL INTEGRATION

The emphasis on regional economic integration in the early years of the Pacific Island Forum reflected the liberal economic and development thinking of the time. It proceeded on several simple premises that seemed to have common sense status and which bear a strong resemblance to the rationale for 'pooled regional governance' as promoted in the current context. These premises were that larger units do better than smaller ones (particularly very small ones); that rationalisation of industry across the region would maximise economies of scale or at least reduce the diseconomies of scale that would otherwise occur; that small countries could not each afford a shipping line, a university, an airline, and a development bank; and that a free trade area would be trade-creating for the region; and that cost-cutting could be achieved through bulk purchasing. These ideas were implicit in the early proposals of the Forum, in the tasks given by the first Forum to a committee on trade which met in 1971, and in the tasks given to the new South Pacific Bureau for Economic Cooperation in its founding agreement (South Pacific Forum 1971, 1972).

Proposals for comprehensive regional economic integration—economic union, free trade area and industrial rationalisation ideas—did not pass initial inspection by consultants and committees. They failed largely on the basis of the supporting arguments as examined by officials and consultants, rather than because of political positions of member countries in formal negotiations. Industrial rationalisation was thought to be premature when an industrial base did not exist in the island countries except in Fiji. Inter-island trade was minimal because their products were either the same (for example bananas) or, where different, were not the type of product that other island countries had the capacity to process (for example copper). While a regional free trade area was judged to benefit Fiji's economic development it would be damaging to the island economies. Incorporation in a wider free trade area with Australia and New Zealand was seen as having similar implications.

SECTORAL INTEGRATION

While comprehensive economic integration was effectively removed from the regional agenda in the early years of the Forum's activities, attention focused instead on sectoral integration, particularly in the areas singled out later by Prime Minister Howard as in particular need of pooled regional governance—education and training, and civil aviation. Some prominent regional institutions—the University of the South Pacific and the carrier Air Pacific—had already been created in these sectors in the last years of the colonial period. They became controversial in the 1970s as Pacific island leaders outside Fiji began to question whether these Fiji-based institutions were adequately serving their interests (Crocombe and Neemia 1983).

The idea of a regional airline, based on an extension of the existing Fiji Airways, was first developed in the late 1960s by the British, Australian, New Zealand and Fiji Governments. In 1968 the existing shareholders in the consortium—Qantas, Air New Zealand, British Overseas Airways Corporation (BOAC) and the Fiji Government—were joined by the Western Pacific High Commission on behalf the British Solomon Islands Protectorate, the Gilbert and Ellice Islands Colony, and the Kingdom of Tonga. In the following year Western Samoa and Nauru became shareholders and in 1971 Fiji Airways changed its name to Air Pacific.[3] By the early 1970s, however, it was evident that it was only Fiji, among the island states, that was keen to develop Air Pacific further as a regional consortium. Despite their shareholdings in Air

Pacific, the independent island countries were clearly interested in developing their own national airlines. Nauru had already established Air Nauru in 1969, and Polynesian Airlines, with the Western Samoa Government as major shareholder, was set up in the same year. In 1972, Nauru formally withdrew from the board of Air Pacific while retaining its shareholding. In the following year the King of Tonga announced his intention of establishing a national airline and Papua New Guinea established Air Niugini. The lack of commitment of the other island states to the development of Air Pacific was also demonstrated in their reluctance to increase their shareholdings as the metropolitan airlines withdrew. As a result, Fiji became majority shareholder and the airline became increasingly identified as a national carrier.

After the Rarotonga Forum in March 1974, Ratu Mara had warned that the 'Forum will stand or fall on civil aviation…Civil aviation will be the real test of Pacific regional cooperation' (Pacific Islands Monthly 1974). Two months later he was saying that 'civil aviation is a notable failure'.[4] The idea of a regional carrier was effectively at an end. While various proposals for cooperation among national airlines, such as rationalisation of air routes and cooperation on the purchasing of equipment would later be countenanced, full sectoral integration in the civil aviation field was effectively off the agenda until raised again by Prime Minister Keating (unsuccessfully) in 1994 and by Prime Minister Howard in 2003.

It is worth recalling the main reasons for the failure of this ambitious effort at 'pooled regional governance' of the kind recently advanced by the Australian government. The principal reason was the perception by island states that Air Pacific was dominated by Fiji. It was Suva-based; it had its origins in Fiji; Fiji was the main shareholder; Fijians gained most of the employment provided by the airline; and, it was claimed, Fiji subsidised internal airfares by setting fares on certain regional routes higher than they should be (Inder 1974). The bitterness that this issue engendered was not felt only on one side. It was clear that Fijian leaders, and particularly Mara, took offence at the rising complaints about Fijian dominance.

It is important to note that the failure of the 'one regional airline' concept had important spillover effects into other areas of regional cooperation. The neo-functionalist theory of regional integration underpinning European integration assumed spillover effects in a positive direction; this however was a spillover effect that threatened to take regional integration in the other direction.

This was the first major issue causing division among the Pacific island states. Although the negotiations were conducted largely outside the Forum meetings, the experience significantly affected the willingness of these states to cooperate on other substantive issues within the Forum in its early years.

By the end of the 1970s it was clear that Pacific island states were wary of economic integration schemes requiring high capital outlay, centralisation in one island state, or a sacrifice of national autonomy. The University of the South Pacific and the Pacific Forum Line were the only examples of a significant degree of sectoral integration. The University maintained its regional support by decentralising the campus. New campuses and units set up in Western Samoa, Kiribati and Tonga and promised at that time for Vanuatu, went some way to placate regional concerns about the uneven distribution of benefits (Crocombe and Meleisea 1988:359). The Pacific Forum Line succeeded because it did not involve high-level integration. The 'pooling' concept, involving an operating company that would charter ships from member countries, allowed an identifiable national component in this regional scheme and kept capital outlays to a minimum. In most areas of cooperation the emphasis shifted to the supplementation of national efforts through shared expertise, information and coordination rather than a more ambitious level of sectoral integration.

The South Pacific states were fortunate that they did not venture far down the path of comprehensive or sectoral integration common in other parts of the developing world at this time. Had they done so the experience would have likely poisoned any chance of moving to the more workable forms of cooperation later achieved. Their attempts at significant sectoral integration in tertiary education and civil aviation indicated the kinds of tensions that would have pulled more ambitious regional schemes apart. Regional management boards were not like corporation boards in the private sector. They were composed of representatives of national interest. The most desirable outcome for the region was not necessarily the most desirable outcome for individual states or the politicians running a state. Despite the assumption of shared smallness, isolation and product range which has informed the dominant approaches to regional development, there is in fact considerable variation among Pacific island states on each of these variables. These differences quickly revealed a serious rift between the centrally located, relatively large and well-off Fiji and the other participating states over the costs and benefits of sectoral integration (Neemia 1986).

There was not only the issue of equity; there was in addition the question of whether the individual state could have a more cost-effective result outside the regional scheme. There were also political costs. For politicians the visible national venture, however irrational in terms of economic theory, was far more likely to earn local support than the regional venture. The recent 'biscuit war' between Vanuatu and Fiji with Vanuatu banning Fiji biscuits because of their lower price in its market due to the operation of a free trade area, suggests that this tendency is still present.

COLLECTIVE DIPLOMACY

In the 1980s, Pacific regional cooperation found its strength in the shift in emphasis from regional integration, whether comprehensive or sectoral, to collective diplomacy. By collective diplomacy I simply mean joint regional action aimed at mediating, moderating or denying harmful global influences on the region and to maximise the benefits from positive international influences. Whereas regional integration looks inward, collective diplomacy looks outward. It is nevertheless a form of pooled regional governance in the broad sense in that it seeks to reach a compromise within the region in pursuit of a joint foreign policy and trades on the advantage of pooled diplomatic and negotiation resources.

Collective diplomacy was already evident right from the start of the Forum alongside sectoral and comprehensive integration as a major form of regional governance. The Forum employed this approach, for example, in relation to negotiations with the European Community (EC) over the Lomé Treaty. The Pacific Group, with coordination provided by the South Pacific Bureau for Economic Cooperation (SPEC), successfully represented the interests of Pacific island states. Also in relation to the Law of the Sea negotiations during the 1970s, they formed the Oceanic group which again successfully represented the views of the island states particularly in relation to the rights of archipelagic countries.

Pacific collective diplomacy came of age in the 1980s when regional integration as a form of cooperation was on the wane (in the Pacific and across the developing world). In particular it was the success of the anti-nuclear dumping campaign in turning around Japan's proposal to dump radioactive wastes in the Marianas Trench that first demonstrated the power of collective action. This was followed by a series of successful joint diplomatic campaigns altering the intended behaviour of larger states: Japan on drift-netting, Australia on its policy approach to regional security, and the United States on its position on Law of the Sea issues and on the incineration of chemical weapons on Johnston Island. While the Forum's campaign to support the decolonisation of New Caledonia did not influence France's explicit policy toward that territory, the success in gaining UN support on the re-inscription issue, despite French lobbying, demonstrated what concerted diplomatic action could achieve in international fora. It doubtless contributed to the increased confidence that was evident in later diplomatic campaigns, most notably on the drift-netting dispute and in the lobbying on environmental questions prior to the Rio Conference on Environment and Development in 1992.

Collective diplomacy was strengthened by the institutional developments of the late 1980s: the reorganisation and enlarging of the Forum Secretariat, the creation of a separate agency for dealing with environmental issues, and the acceptance of a compromise in the long-running battle over whether there should be one regional organisation or many organisations. The compromise was to create a cooperative network of organisations through the establishment of the South Pacific Organisations' Coordinating Committee. The decentralised, but coordinated, network of regional agencies in place by the end of the 1980s provided focus and commitment in particular issue areas—the environment and fisheries for example—and allowed several island capitals to enjoy the economic and status benefits of hosting a regional institution, a departure from the Suva and Noumea-centred regionalism of the 1970s.

A significant outcome of collective diplomacy has been the establishment of a series of regional legal regimes which seek to institutionalise the understandings reached between island states and the outside world. These include the *South Pacific Nuclear Free Zone Treaty* (1985), the *Convention for the Protection of the Natural Resources and Environment of the South Pacific Region* (1986), and the *Convention for the Prohibition of Fishing with Long Driftnets in the South Pacific* (1989).

REGIONAL SECURITY COMMUNITY

Alongside these collective diplomacy efforts of the 1980s concerned with the regulation of the impact of globalisation (broadly defined) on the Pacific was an attempt at another form of regional governance—the attempt by Australia and New Zealand to impose a regional security order. This was a push by Canberra and Wellington to promote a joint foreign policy orientation among Pacific island states around the notion of the 'strategic denial' of Soviet influence in the South Pacific. This was a form of collective diplomacy, of attempting a joint foreign policy stance across the region *vis-à-vis* matters related to the Cold War as interpreted in Canberra and Wellington. The regional governance in this case was, however, explicitly hierarchical. The joint foreign policy orientation expected of the island states was different from the foreign policy behaviour of Australia and New Zealand.

This is often represented as a successful Australian and New Zealand (on behalf of the West) strategy which somehow kept the Pacific states pro-West during the Cold War. However, this is not the case. Pacific states were anti-communist for their own reasons. This attempt at hegemonic regional governance ultimately failed. The hierarchy could not be sustained. The Pacific leaders did not like the second-class citizenship given to island states in the strategic denial formula. They could not understand why island states were denied diplomatic, economic and cultural contact with the Soviet Union when the Western powers, including Australia and New Zealand, enjoyed these links. In 1985, Kiribati entered a fisheries agreement with the Soviet Union. Vanuatu followed suit in 1986. By 1988, it had become clear to the Australian Foreign Minister, Gareth Evans, that Australia's past approaches to regional security were no longer workable. Recognising the effective challenge to existing Australian assumptions posed by the concerted actions of island leaders he announced a conceptual shift in policy to a doctrine of 'constructive commitment' emphasising partnership rather than agency for western interests, or Australian hegemonic aspirations, which he saw as dominating past approaches.[5]

HARMONISATION OF NATIONAL POLICIES

From 1994 there was a concerted effort by the Australian and New Zealand governments to re-establish leadership in regional governance around issues to do with economic reform, national governance, and small 's' security—drug-running, transnational crime, money laundering and tax havens. While this new push initially included attempts to promote a form of what is now termed 'pooled regional governance' (in the form of rationalised airlines and bulk purchasing) as well as new forms of collective diplomacy in relation to gaining better prices for tuna from distant water fishing nations, these were not taken up by the Pacific island states. The form of regional governance that began to dominate was what we might call regional harmonisation of national laws, regulations or policies, and was very different from collective diplomacy and from regional integration of a particular sector. Its focus was initially on creating the conditions for structural economic reform, and for neo-liberal development based on open markets. Like the regional security community this was explicitly hegemonic regional governance.

This form of regional governance had its origins in the Keating Government's attempt to create an Australian-led regional economic order in the Pacific. As the 1994 Pacific Islands Forum approached, the Australian Minister for Pacific Island Affairs, Gordon Bilney, stated that 'it is our hope that we shall be able to seize the moment to launch ourselves with fresh determination, on the crucial task of preparing our region for the challenges of a new century'.[6] Throughout the 1990s the structural reform agenda for Pacific states was managed regionally (Sutherland 2000). A donor-led agenda emphasised a regional harmonisation of national regulations and practices including privatisation, investment laws, lowering of tariffs, accountability, output-based budgeting. This harmonisation of national regulations and practices also began to cover security-related issues such as customs, drug-running, policing and money laundering, particularly after the incidents of 11 September 2001.

This form of regional governance was often contested or quietly resisted by Pacific island governments because it was seen as insensitive to local cultural practices, or involved political costs for local politicians, or economic costs for particular groups in society or because of the way it was imposed by Australia. For their part, Australia and New Zealand became increasingly frustrated with the slow pace of regional reform and the lack of obligation on the part of those who signed up to the regional standards to carry out what they had agreed to.

THE NEW REGIONALISM

The frustration felt in Canberra and Wellington with the failure of the attempted harmonisation of policies to bite sufficiently at the national level is partly responsible for the push for 'pooled regional governance' from 2003. In this context the use of the term 'pooled regional governance' suggests an attempt to move regional cooperation to a new level of commitment and obligation on the part of Forum members. For Helen Clarke, prime minister of New Zealand, this was necessary if the Pacific was not to descend into a 'ghetto of conflict and poverty' (*Sydney Morning Herald*, 17 March 2004:12). She was clearly intent on seeing existing regional commitments and agreements actually implemented. For the Australian government, this need to implement the regional agreements on national policies concerning border control, economic management and 'good governance' was made even more urgent by their concern to turn around state fragility in its patch in the War on Terror, something which Prime Minister Howard insisted was Australia's 'special responsibility' (Transcript of the Prime Minister's Press Conference, Canberra, 22 July 2003).

The new push for 'pooled regional governance' is not only about making the harmonisation of national policies around security, governance and economic reform more effective. Particularly as seen from Canberra, it is also about promoting sectoral integration in key sectors—purchasing, airlines, training—to save on the costs of government. This then is a return to a form of regional governance attempted in the early 1970s and again, briefly, in 1994–95.

This new regionalism is explicitly hegemonic. For the Australian government it necessarily involves Australian leadership both diplomatically and in the management of the Pacific Plan. The Australian prime minister lobbied hard to ensure that an Australian candidate would be Secretary-General of the Pacific Islands Forum at this crucial time. The push for a deeper form of regional governance with stronger obligation and pooled sovereignty at the heart of its institutional arrangements is clearly coming from Canberra and Wellington. Although the Pacific Vision of the Eminent Person's Group introduces other concerns, particularly around cultural identity, the draft Pacific Plan looks more like the security and economic agenda of the last eight years, but this time to be pursued in an institutional context in which they can be more effectively implemented.

The new notion of regional governance sits uneasily with recent moves by the Pacific states, since the late 1990s, to promote a regional free trade area and the proposal by the Senate Committee for a more radical economic union including Australia and New Zealand with one regional currency, the Australian dollar, and the possibilities of labour mobility. The Australian and New Zealand governments at this stage explicitly reject this more comprehensive notion of regional economic integration.

LESSONS FROM THE PAST

Certain general points can be distilled from the past experience with regional governance in the Pacific which may hold lessons for this current attempt to build 'pooled regional governance' and regional integration. The first is that in various ways the history of regionalism in the South Pacific has always been about negotiating Pacific engagement with globalisation, whether in the form of global trade, investment, colonial control, or the environmental impact or resource exploitation by larger powers. Regional governance has always had a double-edged role in this negotiation or mediation process. For outside powers such as Australia and New Zealand or for the international agencies it is seen as a vehicle to promote these globalising ideas and processes. For Pacific states it has often been seen as a shield against such processes or a way of moderating the impact as in the multilateral treaties regulating the rapacious activities of the larger powers.

Second, implicit in these various attempts at creating regional governance over the past 34 years is the creation of particular notions of regional community. The big lesson of this long history is that the political authority of regional governance is tied directly to the legitimacy, among Pacific islanders, of the particular notion of regional community that is being promoted. This legitimacy has depended on the answer to questions that a particular attempt at imposing regional governance raises: what does the community stand for as a set of ideas and purposes? Who can belong, and on what basis? Who can speak on its behalf? How is the regional community to be built?

As the main outside force attempting to shape regional governance since the mid 1970s, Australia has come up against this legitimacy issue a number of times. As Senator Evans found in his promotion of a two-tier security community in the 1980s and Prime Minister Keating and Minister Bilney found in the 1994–95 period in attempting to set up a new regional economic order, what looks like a successful new form of regional governance is not sustainable if it fails to gain legitimacy among Pacific states and peoples. The lesson from those past failures is that the problem lay partly in the hegemonic style of Australia's regional community building (exacerbated by its claim to shape a community of which it was not a member), and partly in what was being promoted as the way the community should live.

In these encounters two long histories are always potentially in tension. One is the history of the place of the South Pacific islands region in the Australian imagination. While individual Australians know very little about Pacific societies (it is completely absent from their school education), at the official level the idea that the Pacific is 'our patch' and that Australia has a special right to shape how people should live in this part of the world is a constant theme from the so-called Australasian Monroe doctrine of the nineteenth century to the formation of the South Pacific Commission, and throughout the post-colonial period. This self-appointed role on behalf of the Anglo-Saxons, the civilised world, the West, or on behalf of the United States in the War on Terror puts Australia at a disadvantage when approaching the Pacific in gaining legitimacy for its attempts to influence regional governance. The authority of Australian prescriptions is lessened further by the fact that Australia seldom sees itself as part of the South Pacific regional community for which it is prescribing a particular form of governance.

The long history with which this comes into tension is the history of Pacific island attempts to decolonise regional governance and defend regional sovereignty, particularly from 1965 to the 1980s. This is a story of a unified regional indigenous élite struggling step by step to gain control of what had been a colonially-controlled regional governance in the South Pacific Commission and to create their own institutions, most notably the South Pacific Forum. The Forum was founded on the ideal of self-determination. The right to have a Pacific islander in charge of the regional secretariat whether as head of the South Pacific Commission or the South Pacific Bureau for Economic Cooperation (later Pacific Islands Forum Secretariat) was seen as symbolic of the achievement of this ideal. Initially Australia supported this push for regional self-determination but increasingly from the 1980s they were in tension. It is evident that the current attempt by Australia to reshape the nature of regional community has pressed all these buttons, not least in insisting on overthrowing the symbolism of a Pacific islander being at the helm of the main regional institution set up by Pacific island leaders.

There is also a long and related history of Australia promoting particular concepts of regional development and regional security as the purposes of regional governance which take little account of Pacific viewpoints. Often driven by global or Australian security concerns or economic models, they have failed to gain legitimacy among Pacific islanders because they fail to take account of their security concerns, forms of governance, or ethics. Senator Evans was open about having learnt this lesson by the end of the 1980s after the authority of the Australian-led regional security order came into question. Minister Bilney also recognised—after some years of pressing land reform as part of regional economic reform—that he had learnt that this was much more complex than he originally thought (after listening to a special South Pacific Commission seminar on land by a number of Pacific island representatives). In both the security and economic prescriptions promoted by Australia as part of the new regionalism it appears that this lesson has not been learnt by everyone.

The lessons concerning the legitimacy issue in relation to past regional governance do not solely revolve around a tension between Australia and the Pacific islands. The other major trend in this regard is the tension between different groups of Pacific islanders over their respective rights and terms of participation in regional governance. The regional project has been seen as illegitimate because it has been too state-centric, too male-dominated, or dominated by larger countries such as Fiji. In general terms, there has been a tension between those who see the need for an opening-up of regional governance to include civil society, sovereignty movements and non-independent territories, and those who support a state-centric regional community.

Among participating Pacific island states, the authority of regional governance has partly depended on how they see their gains and costs relative to other member states. As we have seen, the lesson is that this becomes very obvious when regional integration in particular sectors is attempted. The early failure of the regional airline and the underlying tensions between Fiji and the other Pacific states was noted earlier. Even the regional success story, the integration of the university training sector in the regionally-governed University of the South Pacific, has some important lessons in this regard. The trend is to an increasingly decentralised university and to the creation of new national universities. Distance, relevance and local economic and political benefit are all factors in encouraging national rather than regional institutions in these areas of high sectoral integration.

The exact shape of regional governance under the Pacific Plan is still under negotiation. The lessons of the past suggest that serious regional integration of the kind attempted in civil aviation is probably not going to gain the legitimacy it requires for authoritative and sustainable governance. Harmonisation of domestic policies as a form of regional governance may also have the problems of legitimacy they experienced in the 1990s unless Australia and New Zealand engage more fundamentally with Pacific perspectives on the governance and security issues they seek to influence.

NOTES

[1]   Transcript of the Prime Minister, The Hon John Howard MP Press Conference, Canberra, 22 July 2003.

[2]   Transcript of the Prime Minister, The Hon John Howard MP, Doorstop Interview, Carlton Hotel, Auckland, 15 August 2003

[3]   Based on author's interview with Captain P. Howson, former Chairman of Air Pacific, Sydney, 19 July 1976.

[4]   Ratu Sir Kamisese Mara, Regional Cooperationion in the South Pacific, address delivered at the University of Papua New Guinea, Port Moresby, May 1974, p.13

[5]   See Gareth Evans, 'Australia in the South Pacific', address to the Foreign Correspondents' Association, Sydney, 23 September, 1988.

[6]   Gordon Bilney, Australia's Relations with the South Pacific—Challenge and change', address to the foreign Correspondents' Association, Sydney, 15 June 1999.

6

A COMMON CURRENCY FOR THE PACIFIC ISLAND ECONOMIES?

Ron Duncan

The question I examine here is whether the Pacific island countries—or at least a substantial number of them—should adopt a common currency (or currency union) as part of a process of regional integration. There are also related questions such as which currency they should adopt and when should they do so. The regional integration may only be between the Pacific states, or it may be with other countries. At present the only other countries under consideration for regional integration with the Pacific are Australia and New Zealand, but regional integration could potentially involve other countries in the Asia Pacific region. Choice of a common currency could involve the adoption of a 'Pacific dollar'—especially if the regional integration is only among the Pacific nations—or it could imply the adoption of one of the other non-Pacific currencies already being used by some of the Pacific countries—that is, the Australian, New Zealand, or US dollars.

Prior to the report by the Australian Senate Foreign Affairs and Trade Committee (Commonwealth of Australia 2003) recommending the consideration of a Pacific Economic and Political Community—including the adoption of a common currency—and the Forum Leaders' Pacific Plan for the investigation of further regional cooperation, there had been some discussion of the adoption of a common currency among the Pacific island countries and Australia and New Zealand (Duncan 1994, 2002; Duncan and Xu 2000; de Brouwer 2000; Hughes 2003 and Jayaraman 2003). Since the Senate Committee report, further discussion of the idea has ensued, mostly negative

(Chand 2003; Bowman 2004; Jayaraman 2005; Jayaraman et al. 2005 and Mawuli 2005). There has been little reaction from the Pacific to the proposal for a common currency, but what has emerged has also been mostly negative. As a long-time supporter of the idea of formal economic integration between those Pacific island countries that wish to do so and Australia and New Zealand (Duncan 1994)—including adoption of the Australian dollar as the common currency—I am happy to have this opportunity to re-examine the arguments for and against a common currency for the Pacific states. I believe that the case for adoption of the Australian dollar set out in de Brouwer (2000) and Duncan and Xu (2000) still holds, so I will mainly examine the subsequent arguments against the proposal.

The primary consideration for Pacific states in deciding whether to adopt a common currency and which currency to adopt is whether they form an 'optimal currency area'. However, there are also political economy and other considerations to take into account. Are the Pacific island nations themselves an optimal currency area, or do the Pacific nations and Australia and New Zealand—or the Pacific and any other possible regional partner(s)—satisfy the conditions necessary to form an optimal currency area? Or could changed conditions in the future mean that they would form an optimal currency area? These are questions that ultimately depend for answers on empirical analysis and much of the necessary analysis has not been carried out. Therefore, I will only offer arguments to support the claim that optimal currency area considerations are paramount and discuss some related issues, while examining the recent counter-arguments.

OPTIMAL CURRENCY AREA THEORY

In putting forward the theory of optimal currency areas, Mundell (1961) was concerned about the relationship within a country between the exchange rate and the economic conditions of different regions in that country. As he said,

> If labor and capital are insufficiently mobile within a country then flexibility of the external price of the national currency cannot be expected to perform the stabilisation function attributed to it, and one could expect varying rates of unemployment or inflation in the different regions (Mundell 1961:664).

To illustrate Mundell's point, consider the case of Tasmania. If there is an external shock—such as a commodity price decline—that adversely affects industries in Tasmania, labour and capital can freely move out of Tasmania and into the rest of Australia. But if labour and capital could not move in this way, there would have to be different prices for labour and capital in Tasmania than in the rest of Australia, or Tasmania would have different rates of unemployment or inflation. If Tasmania could not have different prices for capital and labour than the rest of Australia and if Tasmanian labour and capital could not move freely to other parts of Australia, then it would be desirable for Tasmania to have a different exchange rate from the rest of Australia. However, labour and capital can move freely between Tasmania and the rest of Australia and there can also be some differentiation in the prices of labour and capital. Tasmania can therefore have the same exchange rate as the rest of Australia.

To put it another way: in order for Tasmania to have the same exchange rate as the rest of Australia, it must experience the same external shocks as the rest of Australia; or if it experiences asymmetric shocks, it must either have freedom of movement for its labour and capital or have flexibility in differentiating the prices of its labour and capital. However, while the price of capital is flexible throughout Australia, we have to acknowledge that the price of labour is not flexible, especially in a downward direction, and regional differentiation of wages is limited. Therefore, there is greater importance on the freedom of movement of labour—which in this case is uninhibited, except for the costs of adjustment. The costs of adjustment of labour and limits on the scope for regional differentiation of wages—offset to some degree by inter-state transfers— could be seen as explaining any differences in rates of unemployment between regions within Australia.

The same logic applies to adoption of the Australian dollar by Pacific nations. For the Australian dollar to be an appropriate exchange rate regime, the Pacific must experience the same external shocks as Australia, or they must have independence in changing the prices of their labour and capital, or capital and labour must be able to migrate freely; or, alternatively, each of these three conditions must exist to a sufficient extent to provide the necessary basis for an optimal currency area. As well, there may be inter-state transfers to help compensate for any disequilibrium. De Brouwer (2000) has broadly discussed the extent to which each of these conditions applies and recognised that optimal currency area conditions may be satisfied by any one condition being fully satisfied or by two or more being satisfied to some extent. Here, I extend his arguments by exploring in more detail the extent to which the optimal currency area conditions are satisfied or need to be satisfied, or could be more satisfied in future.

First, it is important to distinguish between two sets of countries: the very small countries that already use the Australian or New Zealand dollar and those with their own currencies (I ignore the Pacific countries that use the US dollar, as the likelihood of their adopting the Australian dollar in the near term is not high). Kiribati, Nauru and Tuvalu are micro-states that use the Australian dollar, while Cook Islands, Niue and Tokelau are small countries that use the NZ dollar. Of most relevance to this discussion is that there is little in the way of private sector activity in these Pacific countries. Therefore, external shocks, the mobility of labour and capital, and the flexibility of their wages matter little as normal market adjustments to external shocks play a very minor role in their economies. Until circumstances change in these small countries with very limited private sectors, it appears that they have made the right choice by using the currency of a much larger country with sound monetary and fiscal policy and with which they have extensive trading relationships.

Hughes (2003) has argued that the similarly poor performances of the Pacific island nations using Australian or New Zealand currency and those with their own currency is an indication that it would not be advantageous for the other Pacific countries to give up their monetary independence. However, an argument about something so complex as economic growth on the basis of a single variable has limited use. The circumstances of the other larger Pacific states deserve more serious analysis with respect to their exchange rate regimes.

The countries of primary interest here are the countries that have their own currencies and central banks—namely Fiji, Papua New Guinea, Samoa, Solomon Islands, Tonga and Vanuatu. These are more substantial economies with larger private sectors—though unfortunately their private sectors are not as large as is desirable. In these cases, we have to consider not only whether a common currency would be a feasible alternative but also whether it would be desirable from the viewpoint of providing advantages in terms of fiscal and monetary management.

Empirical analysis of the extent to which these countries share common external shocks with each other or with Australia and/or New Zealand has not been carried out, except for the relationship between Papua New Guinea and Australia. Xu (1999) estimates the extent to which Papua New Guinea shares external shocks with its major trading partner, Australia. The results of Xu's econometric tests suggest that at least 75 per cent of the variation in industry output growth rates in the two countries can be attributed to industry-specific shocks common to both countries (such as international commodity prices), while 23 per cent is attributable to country-specific disturbances (such as domestic economic policy and natural disasters). Xu concludes that the results pointed to adoption of the Australian dollar or a currency board with the kina strongly fixed to the Australian dollar as the optimal exchange rate policy for Papua New Guinea.

It has been argued that the export baskets of the two countries are not the same and therefore movements in international commodity prices will not affect the two economies in the same way. However, as Duncan and Xu (2000) point out, there is substantial auto-correlation between international primary commodity prices (even though some of the markets appear to be unrelated), which can help to explain the high degree of commonality in the external shocks of the two countries. The Australian dollar is widely regarded as a primary commodity currency because of its co-movement with global primary commodity prices. The Papua New Guinea kina, which has been floating since 1994, can most likely be categorised similarly.

The economies of the other Pacific island countries with their own currencies—Fiji, Samoa, Solomon Islands, Tonga and Vanuatu—are also highly dependent upon primary commodities for exports. It is likely therefore that, similar to Papua New Guinea, their industry output has a high degree of commonality with Australia in terms of industry-specific shocks. This conclusion remains to be tested. However, if it is the case to a significant degree, the condition for an optimal currency area with Australia is satisfied and there is not so much need for the countries to have mobility of labour and capital or flexibility in prices of labour and capital. Asymmetry in industry-specific shocks and country-specific shocks may, however, still matter. Therefore, it is important to examine the extent of the flexibility in prices of labour and capital and the mobility of labour and capital.

Samoa and Tonga have had relatively easy emigration to New Zealand (and ultimately to Australia) for many years. In fact, despite still having quite high fertility rates, their emigration rate is so high that population growth in these two countries is close to zero. Investment in education in Samoa and Tonga is also relatively high, and can be interpreted as investment in the income risk diversification of households. Indeed, Tonga boasts more PhDs per head of population than any other country.

Apart from the Indo-Fijian population of Fiji, labour from the other four Melanesian countries has had limited emigration possibilities. There has been a steady stream of 5,000–6,000 Indo-Fijian emigrants since the 1987 coups, cumulatively totalling around 100,000. Of these, about 10,000 have been skilled to highly skilled professionals such as doctors, lawyers, accountants, computer specialists and teachers. In recent years, however, the aging of the populations of the high-income countries has opened up the possibilities for offshore employment of Melanesians, particularly in 3D (dirty, difficult and dangerous) semi-skilled jobs. For example, there are around 3,000 Fijians in the British armed forces, around one-half that number are employed as security guards in Iraq and Kuwait, and, if one believes newspaper reports, an estimated 10,000 Fijian 'care givers' are employed in the United States. Thus, with the continuing aging of the global population, the mobility of skilled and semi-skilled labour in these Melanesian countries—as well as in the other Pacific island countries—will only increase. This conclusion does not apply to the majority of the Melanesian population who are primarily poorly educated, rural dwellers. The recent interest in short-term work visas for Pacific peoples in Australia and New Zealand could lead to some employment opportunities for this category of workers, but it is hard to see such programs being large or growing very fast.

If labour mobility is poor for the large proportion of lower-skilled labour, how flexible are wages? As Forsyth (1998:86) notes

> The majority of the PDMCs [Pacific Developing Member Countries] either have not set a statutory minimum wage or have a rate so low as to be clearly 'non-binding', i.e., below the market-clearing rate, or have a potentially binding rate but do not police or enforce it. The only countries in which minimum wage rates clearly lie above the market-clearing rates are Fiji and Papua New Guinea.

Fiji and Papua New Guinea are the only Pacific nations with strong unions. But even in these countries, minimum wage laws only affect the small proportion of the labour force that is in formal employment. Most of the labour force earn livelihoods as smallholder farmers, through forms of semi-subsistence agricultural and fishing pursuits, and through urban informal activity. Therefore, for these parts of the labour force, real wages are not 'sticky'. In fact, as seen in Papua New Guinea with the large depreciation of the kina and the increased inflation in recent years, many have suffered large declines in real incomes. Thus, it would appear that for the semi-skilled and skilled workers in the

Pacific, labour mobility is quite high and increasing, while for low-skilled labour wages are flexible. While increased off-shore employment opportunities would be beneficial for the low-skilled labour force in these countries, they are not necessary for these countries to be an optimal currency area with Australia and New Zealand.

ARGUMENTS AGAINST ADOPTING THE AUSTRALIAN DOLLAR

Bowman (2004) criticises the idea of Pacific island countries adopting the Australian dollar on the basis of time series tests of the relationship between the independent currencies of Pacific states with the Australian dollar, the Japanese yen, the British pound and the US dollar, and a comparison of the trading relationships between Pacific nations and Australia and the Pacific nations and Asia. Bowman finds that, except for the Tongan pa'anga, the Pacific island countries' currencies are more highly correlated with the US dollar than with the Australian dollar. She also points out that the Pacific is beginning to trade less with Australia and more with Asian countries, and that these two findings argue against adopting the Australian dollar.

In this case, however, regression analysis of the relationship between the currencies is not an appropriate test for an optimal currency area. The exchange rates of the Fijian dollar, the Solomon Islands dollar, the Tongan pa'anga, and the Vanuatu vatu are fixed to individual baskets of currencies set by the central banks. The Papua New Guinea kina could best be described as a 'managed float'. Essentially, all that Bowman has done is estimate the weights of the currencies in the baskets of the adjustable currency pegs (which are not made public by the central banks). It is of interest to have these estimates, but they are not a test of the extent to which these Pacific countries and Australia share industry-specific shocks.

Moreover, with the Pacific island states and Australia being 'small countries' in trade terms, the extent to which they trade with each other is not as important as the extent to which they trade with other countries, and are therefore affected by changes in global conditions. That the Pacific may be moving away from trade with Australia to trade with Asian countries is not an argument against the Pacific being an optimal currency area with Australia. Australia's own trade has moved heavily towards Asia and this means that Pacific states and Australia will both experience the shocks coming from that trade link.

In his several publications arguing against the formation of a currency union between Pacific states and Australia and New Zealand, Jayaraman (2001, 2003, 2005, and Jayaraman et al. 2005) discusses various indicators that have been put forward in the optimal currency area literature as key deciding factors for a currency union—openness, intra-trade volume, degree of product diversification, similarity in industrial structures, correlation in economic activities, similarity in inflation rates, flexibility in wages and prices, and factor mobility. Further, Jayaraman (2001, 2003 and 2005) and Jayaraman et al. (2005) carry out tests on various indicators and find that the optimal currency area conditions are not satisfied. I find the tests undertaken and the arguments made unsatisfactory on several grounds.

Several of the conditions suggested as needing to be satisfied for the formation of an optimal currency are endogenous to regional integration that includes a common currency (as Jayaraman acknowledges). Others are of second-order importance to the primary conditions that I have discussed previously. Openness, intra-trade volume, output diversification, inflation rates, and factor mobility are all likely to change in Pacific states with closer economic integration with Australia and New Zealand. For example, forgoing monetary independence on adoption of the Australian dollar can be argued to be an important reason for Pacific nations to take this action, given the tendency of many towards high fiscal deficits with their adverse effects on inflation rates, interest rates, and exchange rates. Also, intra-trade volume can be expected to increase with use of a currency that reduces exchange rate risk and other transaction costs. Intra-trade volume, degree of product diversification, similarity in industrial structures, and high correlation in economic activities appear to be unimportant if the primary conditions for an optimal currency area are satisfied. The importance of country-specific risks could also be reduced with closer integration if, for example, it leads to reductions in political instability.

Jayaraman (2005) presents correlations of economic growth rates, inflation rates, interest rates, and exchange rates between Pacific countries and Australia and New Zealand as tests of an optimal currency area. Jayaraman et al. (2005) present time series regression results on convergence between the Pacific states and Australia and New Zealand in nominal exchange rates, real effective exchange rates, inflation rates, and real GDP growth rates. Tests of correlations or convergence in GDP growth rates appear to be beside the point in regards this issue. The nominal exchange rate is a mechanism for short-term, economy-wide adjustments to external shocks. What is of interest, therefore, is the coincidence of business cycles, not the rate of growth of the economies. As argued previously, the inflation rate should be a strongly endogenous variable to the formation of a currency union between these countries and therefore a comparison of inflation rates or measures of their convergence are not really of interest here. Also, as argued above, tests of correlations or convergence of nominal exchange rates are primarily reflecting the currency basket weights adopted by Pacific states. As de Brouwer (2000) points out, real effective exchange rates are endogenous within the country, reflecting the interaction of monetary and fiscal policies, and can therefore be expected to be endogenous to the formation of a currency union or adoption of a common currency.

Mawuli (2005:48) criticises Xu's (1999) conclusion that Australia and Papua New Guinea formed an optimal currency area on the grounds that his analysis ignored the

> ...dominant role that productivity plays in the determination of the foreign exchange rate of a currency and the dissimilarities of the two economies—the Australian economy is dominated by services, especially financial services, while the PNG economy is dominated by commodities together with a large base of subsistence production.

While the trends in exchange rates may be primarily influenced by productivity growth, it is the short-term reflection of external shocks that is of importance here. Also, dissimilarities in the structure of the economies, especially where these are largely in the form of non-tradables, is hardly relevant. As noted earlier, both the Australian and Papua New Guinean currencies are basically 'primary commodity' currencies because of the importance of primary commodities in their exports.

Mawuli (2005) also argues against adoption of the Australian dollar by Papua New Guinea by using the example that Liberia has used the US dollar for over a century and 'has experienced disastrous consequences—a persistent, broadly based depressed economy, which partly accounts for its political instability, civil war and social disintegration'. I fail to see how the use of the US dollar could be held responsible for these developments. Moreover, many examples could be found of countries using the US dollar that have been successful.

POLITICAL ECONOMY AND OTHER ISSUES

The political economy arguments over whether the Pacific should adopt a common currency have been well covered in the literature, so I will only discuss them briefly. Sovereignty is the first issue that comes to mind with many people. In the Pacific there is a perception that to move away from one's own currency means giving up part of one's sovereignty. As with any such issue, the decision should rest on the balance of the benefits and the costs. Countries in the European Union have been willing to adopt a common currency in the interests of closer political integration, with the ultimate aim of reducing the likelihood of future conflicts between them. In the case of the Pacific, the sense of a loss of sovereignty over giving up their own currency would seem to be far outweighed by the potential gains. These gains are largely in the form of encouragement of trade from reductions in transactions costs due to reducing the risks associated with their highly illiquid currencies: inflation rate risk, interest rate risk, and exchange rate risk.

Loss of monetary independence and thus the loss of a degree of freedom in economic management are also seen by some as negatives. But monetary independence has minuses as well as pluses. When I argued for Papua New Guinea and Solomon Islands to adopt the Australian dollar (Duncan and Xu 2000; Duncan 2002), my position was based on concern over the loss of central bank independence in these countries. While central bank independence has been bolstered in Papua New Guinea through legislation adopted since that time, and the international intervention in Solomon Islands has reduced the threats to central bank independence in that country, it would be taking an overly optimistic position to argue that central bank independence is now assured in these countries; or that it is assured in the other Pacific island countries with central banks. A point of major concern to me is that in small countries fiscal policy drives monetary policy. So, despite legislative protection, the threat of loss of monetary independence under future governments will continue. It should be remembered that legislative protection in Solomon Islands did not in the past prevent the government from central bank borrowing beyond its legislative limits.

An argument is also made that the central banks are one of the few institutions that have functioned relatively well in the Pacific. This is true. They have generally performed far better than most other government organisations. However, when fiscal policy dominates monetary policy, and when skilled people such as those employed in the central banks are in very short supply, it appears to be a misallocation of resources to have these people working in the central bank rather than in the treasuries or finance departments. The key question appears to be how to create conditions in treasuries, finance departments, and statistics offices that replicate the central banks' capacity to recruit and retain such skilled people.

An issue on which research is needed is the cost to small countries such as a Pacific country of running a central bank. It may be claimed that the profits from seigniorage (from printing currency) more than cover the cost of maintaining a central bank. However, if in the process of changing over to Australian currency there was an agreement for the Pacific state to hold a share of the Australian seigniorage (as I suspect would be possible), the seigniorage should not be included in the assessment of the benefits and costs of maintaining the existing central banks. My impression is that a central bank is a rather expensive luxury for small countries.

With respect to the debate over loss of monetary independence, I believe that some attention should be given to the issue of the 'trilemma' of macroeconomic policy. The policy 'trilemma' facing governments is that it is not possible simultaneously to peg the exchange rate, maintain an open capital market, and have monetary policy autonomy. Only two of these policy goals may be followed at the same time. For example, a government can follow the objectives of exchange rate stability and an open capital market by adopting a permanently fixed exchange rate, such as a common currency or a currency board arrangement, but in doing so it has to give up monetary independence. If it elects to have monetary independence and an open capital market, it can float the exchange rate but therefore cannot have exchange rate stability. Finally, if a government chooses the goals of exchange rate stability and monetary independence, it cannot have the goal of capital market integration.

Taylor and Obstfeld (2004) argue that what was known as the Bretton Woods system—currency pegs and capital controls as cornerstones—was derived from suspicion of open capital flows due to the crises of the 1930s and association of floating exchange rates with speculation and instability. Therefore, the architects of the Bretton Woods system (John Maynard Keynes and Harry Dexter White) espoused capital controls and fixed exchange rates in order to prevent the disruption of trade. Taylor and Obstfeld argue that this view of the global economy—that the world could be kept safe for trade by constraining flows of private capital—proved to be an illusion. The global gains from expanded trade in the 1960s and 1970s and the necessity for large payments transactions put pressure on the balance of payments and led to frequent adjustments in currency pegs. Eventually the system collapsed and trade and capital flows have flourished, to the benefit of both developed and developing countries.

However, as Keynes himself pointed out, people hold to ideas long after they have been shown to be false. The Pacific island policies can be seen to be influenced still by the ideas of the long-defunct Bretton Woods system, with its in-built bias against trade and capital flows. The decision as to which of the two policy goals to follow should be made in the light of what is most important for the economic development of the country. As small, isolated countries, the Pacific's greatest need is to be able to exploit the economies of scale available from trade with the rest of the world. To do this they need to be open economies in order to take advantage of whatever technologies become available to overcome their inherent disadvantages. Unfortunately, their reluctance to open up to trade and investment only magnifies the disadvantages due to their smallness and isolation.

Those Pacific island countries with adjustable pegged currency regimes have elected to forgo open capital markets and to have exchange rate stability and monetary independence (Papua New Guinea with its 'managed' floating rate could even be included here). Therefore, if the Pacific small island states were to move to open capital markets in order to promote trade and investment, they must forego either the objective of exchange rate stability or of monetary independence. That is, they must either have a floating exchange rate or give up monetary independence. I suggest that their choice should be to adopt open capital markets and exchange rate stability and give up monetary independence.

CONCLUSIONS

The arguments put forward and the conclusion reached by de Brouwer (2000) in favour of Pacific island countries adopting the Australian dollar in place of their local currencies still seem to me to be justified. As de Brouwer makes clear, the optimal currency area conditions for a group of countries may be satisfied by a combination of the sharing of common external shocks, factor mobility, and factor price flexibility. Much of the subsequent published testing and arguments against the proposition do not appear to be relevant to the debate.

In re-examining the literature, I have discussed the factor mobility and factor price flexibility issues in more detail. I have also argued that circumstances affecting labour mobility, such as the aging of the global population, are changing in a positive direction for use of the Australian dollar as a common currency. Regional integration arrangements implemented as an outcome of the Pacific Plan could also increase factor mobility and factor price flexibility. Many of the indicators that have been found wanting in examinations of the case for use of a common currency are endogenous factors that will change significantly upon closer economic integration between the Pacific island countries and Australia and New Zealand. In this respect, there could be a larger role for fiscal transfers between Australia and New Zealand and Pacific states. As McKinnon (1963) points out, the capacity for fiscal transfers within the common currency bloc can be another means of compensating for differences in unemployment between the countries.

In Duncan (1994), I argue the case for those Pacific nations willing to do so to form a closer economic relationship with Australia and New Zealand. This relationship would involve a freer flow of labour and a common currency, as well as openness to trade and investment. However, the arrangement would have to be a formal contract involving commitments on the part of both parties. The Pacific states would have to commit to the sound and stable economic policies needed to place them on a higher economic growth path. For their part, Australia and New Zealand would provide assistance to the Pacific in the design and implementation of sound policies. As well, they should be ready to provide financial and material assistance to the Pacific nations in the event of shocks such as declines in commodity prices or natural disasters. The only way in which I would change the advice that I offered in 1994 would be to put much more emphasis on the need for more effective institutions in the Pacific and assistance from Australia and New Zealand in achieving this goal (such as secure property rights and impartial enforcement of contracts, with their underlying implications for the absence of discriminatory behaviour on the part of politicians, bureaucrats, and the courts). It seems to me that the explicit conditionality on Pacific island countries to adopt sound institutions and policies as the result of signing such a treaty would be much more effective than the conditionality attached to Australia's aid commitments.

There are, of course, the important questions of sequencing or prioritising in adopting such an integrated relationship. In the first place, Australia and New Zealand would have to agree on the framework of the economic relationship with the Pacific. If it were to be a joint effort, it would have to involve a deepening of the economic relationship between the two countries, including with respect to labour mobility and currency arrangements. Should Australia and New Zealand agree to go ahead, should they negotiate with Pacific nations separately or as a bloc, or even instead of negotiation of the Pacific Agreement on Closer Economic Relations? Should there be a sequencing of the integration itself—of trade, investment, capital, labour, and currency arrangements? This is essentially the sequence followed by the European Union.

As far as sequencing is concerned, I would prefer to see improvements in property rights security and contract enforcement take place before going ahead with other reforms. Trade and investment liberalisation may have little pay-off in the absence of these basic institutions, although it is possible that trade and investment liberalisation could increase public demand for better institutions. As far as the other reforms are concerned, there seem to be good reasons for carrying out the integration simultaneously. In the case of the European Union, there were major gains to be realised from first opening up to trade, which created a favourable climate for the other reforms to follow. In the case of Pacific island countries, the transaction costs associated with using the illiquid local currencies may make the gains from trade liberalisation quite small. Therefore, the complementarity between simultaneously adopting a common currency such as the Australian dollar—with its associated openness to capital flows—and trade liberalisation could substantially increase the gains from trade.

7

GLOBALISATION AND GOVERNANCE: AN AFRICAN PERSPECTIVE AND A CASE STUDY OF MAURITIUS

Vinaye Ancharaz and Sanjeev K. Sobhee

Globalisation is not a new phenomenon. What is new, however, is the dramatic scale at which it has occurred in recent years. Trade and cross-border investment, readily identified as the key drivers of 'international economic integration'—a term widely used to distinguish economic globalisation from other forms of globalisation—have registered explosive growth over the past two decades, aided by the rapid spread of information and communication technologies. Foreign direct investment (FDI) flows, which totaled US$160 billion in 1991, rocketed to US$1.1 trillion in 2000. The volume of international trade has increased 16-fold over the past 50 years. In the 1990s, in particular, world trade expanded much faster than world output. A remarkable feature of this growth in trade is that it was propelled mainly by trade in components, rather than in finished goods as vertically-integrated multinationals increasingly outsourced the parts they previously produced at home (Sutherland 2002).

Only the volume of controversy that it has generated in recent years matches the pace of globalisation. On balance, the accumulated evidence suggests that globalisation has proved beneficial to those economies that embraced it. A World Bank (2002) study, for example, finds that the 'new globalisers'—a group that includes Brazil, China, India and Mexico—achieved per capita growth rates that were a significant four per cent higher than countries that liberalised more slowly. Srinivasan and Bhagwati (1999) and Lindert and Williamson (2001), among others, demonstrate conclusively that promoting openness and supporting it by sound domestic policies leads to faster growth.

Despite the positive growth effects of globalisation, there is a widespread feeling that the rising tide of trade and capital flows has increased economic vulnerability. While it is true that globalisation allows a more efficient allocation of resources based on comparative advantage—and therefore offers a fair chance to developing countries to integrate with the global trade arena—there are abundant examples of the adverse effects of (mismanaged) globalisation. Even as globalisation has promoted convergence of per capita incomes among countries, there is growing evidence that inequality within countries—both developed and developing—has increased (Masson 2001). This has raised questions about the effectiveness of globalisation strategies in alleviating poverty and raising living standards in a sustainable manner. Moreover, the kind of volatile capital flows that wreaked havoc in East Asia in 1997 remains a stark reminder of the dangers of pursuing unchecked financial globalisation.

The continuing process of globalisation has also raised a number of non-economic concerns that have fueled the anti-globalisation sentiment. There are fears that the multinational corporatisation of economic activity has increased the incidence of child labour, harmed women, and imperiled indigenous cultures and the environment. Bhagwati (2004), however, argues that globalisation is 'socially benign' and therefore asks how governance should be designed so as to enhance the positive outcomes of globalisation.

It is expected that greater openness will lead to a larger government as the latter is called upon to play a more important role as a provider of safety nets and support services to counteract the adverse effects of globalisation. Rodrik (1996) has formalised this idea through a model in which government spending increases to absorb the heightened volatility in domestic income and consumption arising from the greater external risk induced by globalisation. Rodrik measures external risk as the variability in a country's terms of trade and argues that, although in principle small economies can diversify away from this risk by participating in international capital markets, evidence suggests that in practice this is far from the case (Lewis 1995).

Hence, the task of mitigating external risks falls on the government, but the mechanisms in place to achieve this differ markedly between developed and developing economies. In countries with demonstrated administrative capability to implement social welfare programs, the government can effectively compensate losers from globalisation through transfer payments. In most developing economies, however, the government's risk-mitigating role is limited to providing secure public employment, retraining facilities and, to a lesser extent, safety nets to the vulnerable. Rodrik (1996) provides empirical evidence confirming these hypotheses.

Alesina and Wacziarg (1997) question Rodrik's (1996) findings on the ground that the latter omitted a critical control variable—country size—from his basic econometric specification. They argue, with supporting evidence, that

1 larger countries have smaller governments (because the per capita cost of providing a given level of public goods, characterised by fixed costs and economies of scale, falls with size)[1]

2 smaller countries tend to be more open (because they are compelled to embrace openness so as to expand their effective market size and benefit from economies of scale).

Taken together, these findings imply that more open economies have larger governments but that this relationship is mediated by country size. Alesina and Wacziarg (1997) show that, once country size is explicitly accounted for, the positive relationship between government size and openness uncovered by Rodrik (1996) no longer holds. Nevertheless, they do find evidence that the size of government transfers increases with openness, confirming Rodrik's hypothesis about the risk-mitigating role of government spending in open economies.

Against the above background, this chapter investigates the relationship between government size and openness in sub-Saharan African countries, with a special focus on Mauritius, which is often cited as a small, open economy with good governance.

GLOBALISATION AND GOVERNANCE: AN AFRICAN PERSPECTIVE

In the second half of the 1990s, sub-Saharan Africa recorded its highest rate of growth in two decades. Fischer et al. (1998) attribute this remarkable economic performance to better policies rather than to favourable external developments. Several positive changes have occurred in a number of sub-Saharan African economies during the 1990s. Many countries have implemented structural reforms and stabilisation measures, although with varying degrees of success. The region has also seen a movement toward democracy and greater political stability.

Africa's economic woes are far from over, however. The magnitude of the economic decline in most African countries was such that GNP per capita in sub-Saharan Africa was lower at the end of the last decade than in 1970. Moreover, a large body of evidence suggests that sub-Saharan African economies have made little progress with economic reforms.[2] The wave of democratisation also delivered less than it promised (Bratton and van de Walle 1997).

While most of sub-Saharan Africa was grappling with domestic problems, many developing countries elsewhere were taking fuller advantage of the opportunities offered by the globalisation of economic activity and the growth of world trade. The result has been the 'marginalisation' of Africa in the world economy (Collier 1995; Yeats et al. 1996). Sub-Saharan Africa's share of world exports declined from an already low 1.2 per cent in 1990 to 1.0 per cent in 2000 (Table 7.1), while its share of world foreign direct investment (FDI) flows has stagnated at 1 per cent over a comparable period (Table 7.2). Sub-Saharan Africa as a whole accounted for a little more than 1 per cent of world income in 2001.

In absolute terms, however, sub-Saharan Africa saw a significant increase in trade and FDI flows in the 1990s. The region has made a decent effort to catch the globalisation wave—a number of countries have successfully liberalised and achieved degrees of openness comparable to the 'new globalisers'.[3] In this section, we investigate the impact of globalisation on governance in sub-Saharan Africa using a simple reduced-form regression model. The primary hypothesis, motivated by the literature surveyed above, is that greater openness leads to a larger government that acts as a buffer against the disastrous consequences of globalisation.

The basic regression is

$$G/Y = g(PCY, DEP, URBAN, OPEN) \tag{7.1}$$

where G/Y is the share of government consumption spending in GDP at constant prices, PCY is real GDP per capita, DEP is the dependency ratio, $URBAN$ is the percentage of population living in urban areas, and $OPEN$ is the degree of trade openness. Several variants of this equation are estimated to verify the robustness of the findings and to test alternative hypotheses. Thus, population (POP) and terms-of-trade risk ($TOTR$) are introduced as explanatory variables subsequently.

Table 7.1   Sub-Saharan Africa in world trade, 1990–2000 (per cent)

	Exports				Imports			
			Change in market share	Average annual growth			Change in market share	Average annual growth
	1990	2000			1990	2000		
Developed economies	71.5	64.0	– 7.5	5.5	72.5	67.3	– 5.2	5.7
Developing economies	23.9	32.0	8.1	9.1	22.6	29.1	6.5	8.3
Asia and the Pacific	16.9	24.2	7.3	9.5	15.9	21.1	5.2	8.2
Latin America and the Caribbean	4.2	5.6	1.4	10.2	3.7	5.9	2.2	11.4
Sub-Saharan Africa	1.2	1.0	– 0.2	4.1	1.1	0.8	– 0.4	2.6
Transition economies	4.6	4.0	– 0.6	8.8	4.9	3.6	– 1.3	8.7

Note: South Africa is treated as a developed economy.
Source: UNCTAD, 2003. *Handbook of Statistics*, UNCTAD, New York..

Table 7.2   Foreign direct investment flows, 1991–2000

Host region	1991–96 (Annual average)		2002		Change in share
	US$m	Per cent	US$m	Per cent	(per cent)
World	254,326	100.0	651,188	100.0	-
Developed economies	155,091	61.0	461,088	70.8	9.8
Developing economies	91,052	35.8	161391	24.8	–11.0
Asia and the Pacific	59826	23.5	95129	14.6	–8.9
Latin America and the Caribbean	27069	10.6	56019	8.6	–2.0
Sub-Saharan Africa	2542	1.0	6698	1.0	-
Transition economies	8183	3.2	28709	4.4	1.2

Note: South Africa is treated as a developed economy.
Source: Author's calculations using data from UNCTAD, 2003. *Handbook of Statistics*, UNCTAD, New York..

The data are taken from the World Bank Africa Database 2002. All the variables, except terms-of-trade risk, are measured as averages over the period 1996–2000; *TOTR* is calculated as the standard deviation of terms of trade over the same period. The full sample comprises 42 sub-Saharan African countries for which reasonable data were available; the sample size falls to 38 countries when *TOTR* is accounted for.

The estimation results are reported in Table 7.3. In columns 1–3 of the table, the dependent variable is the share of government consumption in GDP.

Despite some notable departures, the results are broadly supportive of Rodrik's (1996) primary hypothesis. The coefficient of per capita income is positive and statistically significant at conventional levels (except in column 3), contrasting with both Rodrik (1996) and Alesina and Wacziarg's (1997) findings, but supporting Wagner's law. The dependency ratio is positive as expected but never significant. Conversely, urbanisation enters with a negative sign in all variants of the basic regression and is significant at the five per cent level or better.

Let us now turn to the estimated coefficients on openness, our key variable. Consider the results of column 1 to begin with. When openness is included

Table 7.3   Regression results

Independent variables	Dependent variable			
	log(G/Y)	log(G/Y)	log(G/Y)	log(PCG)
	(1)	(2)	(3)[§]	(4)
Constant	−7.241**	−7.337**	−7.338**	−7.277**
	(3.07)	(3.35)	(4.55)	(3.09)
log(PCY)	0.232**	0.234**	0.194	1.234***
	(0.100)	(0.104)	(0.139)	(0.101)
log(DEP)	0.657	0.658	0.579	0.662
	(0.591)	(0.599)	(0.682)	(0.593)
log(URBAN)	−0.349**	−0.350**	−0.326**	−0.352**
	(0.158)	(0.161)	(0.147)	(0.158)
log(OPEN)	0.470***	0.476***	0.539*	0.472***
	(0.168)	(0.187)	(0.317)	(0.169)
log(POP)		0.004	0.019	
		(0.051)	(0.080)	
TOTR			1.383	
			(6.446)	
log(OPEN)*TOTR			−0.254	
			(1.491)	
Adj. R-squared	0.258	0.237	0.125	0.896
F	4.57	3.56	1.76	89.1
No. of observations	42	42	38	42

Notes: Standard errors in brackets. *** significant at 1 per cent; ** significant at 5 per cent; * significant at 10 per cent. [§] Heteroscedasticity-consistent standard errors.

without controlling for country size (*POP*), the regression yields a positive and highly significant coefficient on the variable. The results imply that a one percentage-point increase in the trade-GDP ratio is, on average, associated with about a half percentage-point increase in the share of government consumption in GDP. This seems to be an important response by governments of sub-Saharan African countries to the challenges posed by globalisation.[4]

The results of column 2 are obtained when *POP* is explicitly introduced as an independent variable in the regression. Interestingly, this variable displays no statistical association with government size, contrary to Alesina and Wacziarg's (1997) claim that country size is a critical intervening variable in the relationship between government size and openness. Moreover, comparing the results of columns 1 and 2, we observe that the addition of *POP* does not affect the estimated coefficients of the baseline regression either in magnitude or in statistical significance. However, the sharp drop in the goodness of fit and in the F-statistic does suggest that country size is a redundant variable in the model specification.

In column 3, we have included two additional variables—terms-of-trade risk (*TOTR*) and the latter interacted with openness. The objective is to determine whether government size increases with globalisation because greater openness exposes a country to larger terms-of-trade shocks. The results suggest that this has not been the case in sub-Saharan Africa. The openness variable, however, remains statistically significant, albeit at the reduced 10 per cent level.

One interpretation of the above findings is that governments have grown in sub-Saharan Africa to protect their citizens against the many detrimental effects of globalisation, but that these effects have not included adverse changes in the countries' terms of trade.

Column 4 shows the results of estimating Equation 7.1 with government consumption per capita (*PCG*) substituted for *G/Y*. This variant of the regression is intended to serve as a robustness check. A notable finding is that income per capita, which had become insignificant in column 3, reasserts itself as an important determinant of government spending per capita, with an elasticity exceeding unity. Openness regains its former 1 per cent significance. On the whole, the results corroborate the findings reported earlier.[5]

INSTITUTIONAL REFORMS, GOVERNANCE AND GLOBALISATION IN MAURITIUS

In this section an exclusive investigation of the impact of globalisation on the size of the public sector in Mauritius over the post-independence period 1970–2000 is made. Mauritius has pursued a policy of outward-oriented industrialisation ever since its import-substituting strategy collapsed in the 1960s. In recent years, however, as the process of globalisation has gathered momentum, threatening to damage economic prosperity and livelihoods, the government of Mauritius has implemented a series of institutional reforms and set up compensation mechanisms in all the major sectors of economic activity to tackle the challenges posed by globalisation.

In the agricultural sector, the Voluntary Retirement Scheme has been introduced to encourage workers to opt for an earlier retirement, with attendant benefits. The scheme's objective is to enable the overstaffed sugar industry to downsize its workforce, cut back labour costs and achieve greater efficiency so that it can stand ready to face the cut-throat competition that would follow the eventual phasing out of the Sugar Protocol—of which Mauritius has long been a privileged beneficiary. Moreover, large-scale land reforms have allowed conversion of thousands of acres of agricultural land for commercial and residential purposes. A notable initiative in this area is the Integrated Resort Scheme, which seeks to attract foreign investors by offering them the possibility of acquiring immovable property in Mauritius. This scheme has led to the clearing of land under sugar cane cultivation to make room for the construction of luxury villas and hotel complexes.

In the manufacturing sector, the government has recently put in place a scheme to compensate workers who have lost, or would be losing, their jobs as a result of the dismantling of the Multifibre Agreement. Similarly, the Textile Support Emergency Team has been set up to advise struggling firms on the structural measures that they should take—again with assistance from the government—to survive the erosion of trade preferences. Moreover, a Clothing Technology Centre has been established to provide export processing zones using firms up-to-date knowledge on technology choices, with a view to upgrading technology in the textile and clothing industry.

The government of Mauritius has played an important role at the international level in trade negotiations on market access for both agricultural and manufactured products to safeguard the interests of the local business community but also to prevent further job losses and to delay unpalatable structural reforms. Indeed, Mauritius has been an ardent defender of the interests of small island developing economies, arguing that such economies deserve special and differential treatment in international trade to enable them to compete effectively with other countries. The government has also led a relentless battle for the preservation of the Sugar Protocol and, recently, for the extension of the third-country fabric derogation under the African Growth and Opportunity Act. The high-profile involvement of Mauritius in trade negotiations has called for massive government spending, both in terms of investment in training for negotiators and diplomats, and financing of missions abroad.

As regards the services sector, the government has taken steps to diversify the range of services that have traditionally been the bedrock of the Mauritian economy towards emerging services such as Freeport operations, offshore banking and financial services, and business process outsourcing. The government recognises that, in an economy with no natural resource endowments, with a small market and unfavourable geography, the services sector is the most promising avenue for future growth. Consequently, among a host of other measures, the government has made the firm commitment to transform the country into a 'cyber-island'. The completion of the first phase of the cyber tower at Ebene, the work-in-progress for the second phase, and the proposal to build another cybercity at Rose Belle all bear testimony to this commitment.

Empirical evidence confirms that good governance is a major driver of economic growth. Mauritius has ratified several international conventions pertaining to the rule of law, civil and labour rights, money laundering and corruption, and corporate governance, amongst others. This has led to wide-ranging institutional reforms and the creation of new organs of public administration, resulting in an increase in the size of government.

The above seems to indicate that the process of globalisation has imposed new commitments and responsibilities on the Mauritian government, which have caused an unprecedented increase in government spending. We now turn to a formal investigation of the relationship between government size and openness and, in the process, we expect to throw light on the dynamics of incorporating the challenges of globalisation in the domain of public policy-making.

Estimation issues and findings

Our basic specification is as follows

$$PCG = f (PCY, OPEN) \tag{7.2}$$

where the variables are defined as above. Since greater openness leads to deeper integration into the world economy rather slowly over time, it is useful to characterise the relationship between government size and openness as a dynamic one. We therefore study the short and long-run dynamics of this relationship using the co-integration technique.

As a routine exercise in time-series econometrics, Augmented Dickey Fuller (*ADF*) tests for unit root are performed on the three variables to ascertain their order of integration. The results are shown in Table 7.4.

The test results suggest that, while all the variables are non-stationary in level form, they become stationary in the first difference. This implies that the variables are all integrated of one and the same order, that is, they are all $I(1)$.

Next, we use the Johansen technique to determine whether *PCG* and *OPEN* are co-integrated. Based on the Trace matrix, we find a unique co-integrating vector which links up the dependent variable and the regressors. The Trace statistic of 18.85 is found to be significant at the 5 per cent level.[6]

Using a general-to-specific approach, the following error-correction model (ECM) is established, in which the optimal lag length turns out to be 1. The Banerjee et al. (1986, 1993) decomposition—which is particularly relevant

Table 7.4   ADF tests of unit roots

Variable	Computed ADF statistic	Optimal lag length
$\log (PCG_t)$	−2.9750	1
$\Delta\log(PCG_t)$	−4.5481*	3
$\log(PCY_t)$	−0.2912	3
$\Delta\log(PCY_t)$	−3.4635*	3
$\log(OPEN_t)$	−2.9730	2
$\Delta\log(OPEN_t)$	−3.3798*	-

Notes: * indicates significance at 5 per cent conditional on the critical value of −2.978 based on MacKinnon (1991). 'Δ' indicates the first order difference operator. Optimal lag length is determined on the basis of Akaike's Information Criterion (AIC).
Source: Computed

for small samples, is applied to compare the long and short-run elasticities of each of the explanatory variables. Such decomposition is not done by either the Engle-Granger method or by the Johansen technique. The latter two report only the short-run elasticity for each independent variable and the long-run disequilibrium parameter. The Banerjee et al. (1986, 1993) model is relevant in this context, more so because the sample size is small. Moreover, the short-run dynamics based on AIC allow the inclusion of lagged values of all variables, leading us to accept the ECM as reported below (t-ratios in brackets)

$$\Delta\log(PCG_t) = 7.28 + 0.804\Delta\log(PCY_t) - 0.0673\Delta\log(OPEN_t)$$
$$(4.28)^{**}\ (4.37)^* \qquad\qquad (-2.13)^{**}$$

$$-0.74\log(PCG_{t-1}) + 0.918\log(PCY_{t-1}) - 0.096\log(OPEN_{t-1})$$
$$(-4.08)^* \qquad\qquad (3.84)^* \qquad\qquad (-3.18)^*$$

$\overline{R}^2 = 0.56$, DW = 2.1, F = 8.3 (where * indicates significance at 1 per cent; ** indicates significance at 5 per cent).

This equation could now be parametrised to capture short and long-run dynamics as follows

$$\Delta\log(PCG_t) = 7.28 + 0.804\Delta\log(PCY_t) - 0.0673\Delta\log(OPEN_t)$$
$$(4.28)^{**}\ (4.37)^* \qquad\qquad (-2.13)^{**}$$

$$-0.74[\log(PCG_{t-1}) - 1.24\log(PCY_{t-1}) + 0.13\log(OPEN_{t-1})]$$
$$(-4.08)^* \qquad\quad (3.84)^* \qquad\qquad (-3.18)^*$$

$\overline{R} = 0.56$, DW = 2.1, F = 8.3 (where * indicates significance at 1 per cent; ** indicates significance at 5 per cent).

Table 7.5 shows the elasticity values derived from the estimates. These results show that while the size of the public sector increases with per capita income

Table 7.5   Short and long-run elasticities

Variable	Short-run elasticity	Long-run elasticity
GDP per capita (*PCY*)	0.8	−1.24
Openness (*OPEN*)	−0.067	0.13

Source: Computed

in the short run, this tendency is reversed in the long run, with a much larger effect. On the other hand, openness appears to cause a decrease in government spending per capita in the short run; over the long run, however, government size increases with openness. It is worth noting that both the magnitude and the sign of the openness elasticity change when the dynamics are accounted for. The coefficient of adjustment of −0.74 indicates that public spending adjusts rapidly to its long-run equilibrium level following any random deviation from the established long-run relationship.

To conclude, the evidence suggests that globalisation has caused an expansion of the public sector in Mauritius in the long run. This result is robust to the inclusion of a significant control variable—per capita income. Hence, it appears that the government of Mauritius is well set to address the challenges of globalisation through its policies and compensation schemes.

CONCLUSION

The relationship between openness and government size has recently generated significant interest and controversy in the literature. While it is reasonable to argue that the government, as a provider of social security and protection in socialist countries, should naturally grow bigger as it is called upon to play a more prominent role to cushion the adverse effects of globalisation on the domestic economy and its people, the accumulated evidence to date has been, at best, inconclusive.

This chapter set out to study the impact of globalisation on governance in sub-Saharan African countries, Mauritius in particular. The findings strongly suggest that greater openness has led to an expansion of the government both in sub-Saharan Africa and in Mauritius. For sub-Saharan Africa, this result is robust to the inclusion of a wide set of control variables. Further analysis indicates that the relationship between government size and openness is mediated neither by country size nor by terms-of-trade risk. Hence, sub-Saharan African countries, irrespective of their size (as measured by population) have witnessed significant growth of their governments as they have become more open. The finding that external risk is not a significant determinant of government size in sub-Saharan Africa suggests that globalisation has affected sub-Saharan African economies in ways other than through their terms of trade. This makes sense since sub-Saharan African countries are known to have comparative advantages in specific primary products, competition in which has scarcely been affected by the process of globalisation. On the other hand, greater openness has compelled African governments to adopt institutional reforms and policies that have resulted in a bigger bureaucracy and higher government spending. As the case study demonstrates, this is certainly true of Mauritius. The Mauritian government has initiated a series of sectoral reforms and other measures to circumvent the adverse effects of globalisation and the consequent withering away of preferential market access. Hence, it comes as little surprise that the size of the government in Mauritius has increased significantly over the long term.

NOTES

[1]   On the relationship between government size and country size, see also Alesina et al. (2000) and Spolaore (2000).

[2]   In a comprehensive review of trade policy reform in developing countries since 1985, Dean et al. (1995:187) conclude: 'Only in Africa do we find little progress towards a liberalised trade regime. Here there have been important cases of reversal of policy, no liberalisation, or increased import impediments during this period [1985–1993]'. In a recent survey of trade liberalisation in IMF-supported programs, Sharer (1998:33) reaches a similar conclusion: 'There were no clear-cut examples of sub-Saharan African countries that have implemented the same degree of trade liberalisation on a sustained basis as in the "good practice" cases'.

[3]   Examples include Ghana, Mauritius, Tanzania and Uganda.

[4]   Note that the coefficient on openness is much bigger than those reported in either Rodrik (1996) or Alesina and Wacziarg (1997).

[5]   Further robustness checks were performed by running the regressions in the levels, rather than in logs, of the variables. The results (available from the authors but not reported here) overwhelmingly confirm the relevance of openness as a determinant of government size, whether or not country size is controlled for.

[6]   The 5 per cent critical value is 11.41.

8

DEEPER INTEGRATION WITH AUSTRALIA AND NEW ZEALAND? POTENTIAL GAINS FOR PACIFIC ISLAND COUNTRIES

Robert Scollay

The seven million inhabitants of the Pacific island countries (5 million of whom are accounted for by Papua New Guinea alone) are scattered in more than a thousand islands over an area of ocean several times the size of Europe. Although the common label of 'small vulnerable states' suggests a degree of homogeneity, the Pacific island countries in fact exhibit great diversity in their economic characteristics. Dimensions of this diversity include population levels (from 5 million in Papua New Guinea to microstates with a few thousand inhabitants such as Niue, Nauru and Tuvalu); income levels (from over US$7500 per head in Palau to just over US$500 per head in Tuvalu according to Table 8.1); human development (from relatively high in Cook Islands and Palau to low Africa-like levels in Papua New Guinea and Solomon Islands—two of the most populous Pacific island countries), as also shown in Table 8.1; natural resource endowments (both land-based and marine); degree of industrialisation (from moderate development of light manufacturing in Fiji and to a lesser extent Papua New Guinea, to virtually zero in smaller Pacific island countries); and composition of exports and main areas of economic activity. Table 8.1 also shows that, while populations may be small, population density is very high in some Pacific Island countries, and that populations are also young and therefore likely to be fast growing.

Table 8.1   Selected economic indicators for Pacific island countries

	Per capita GDP (US$, 1999)[a]	Population density (per km², 2000)	% of population under 15[b]	Human Development Index
Cook Islands	4,727	81.0	35	0.822
FSM	1,810	168.1	43	0.569
Fiji	2,210	43.7	34	0.667
Kiribati	910	122.4	41	0.515
Nauru	7,292	521.4	42	0.663
Niue	4,375	6.9	37	0.774
Palau	7,613	40.0	28	0.861
Papua New Guinea	800	11.0	40	0.314
Rep. Marshall Islands	1,560	303.9	51	0.563
Samoa	1,060	59.5	41	0.590
Solomon Islands	750	14.6	47	0.371
Tonga	1,720	141.4	41	0.647
Tuvalu	571	380.8	43	0.583
Vanuatu	1,170	15.6	44	0.425

Note: [a] 1998 for Tonga, Tuvalu and Vanuatu; 1992 for Palau. [b] Various years 1989–99.
Source: Pacific Islands Forum Secretariat, 2002. *Regional Policy Support Document 2002*, Pacific Islands Forum Secretariat, Suva.

Table 8.2 shows that Pacific island states are heavily import dependent, with import to GDP ratios of over 40 per cent for all except the Marshall Islands. Export orientation on the other hand is much more variable. Exports are a significant factor in the economies of Fiji, Solomon Islands and the Marshall Islands, but much less significant in many other Pacific island countries. Tourism development is largely confined to Pacific island nations with direct air links to major tourism markets—especially Fiji and, to a lesser extent, also Cook Islands, Palau, Vanuatu, Tonga and Samoa.

It is important to keep these characteristics and dimensions of diversity in mind when considering the trade interests of the Pacific island countries.

The joining together of the fourteen Pacific island states with Australia and New Zealand reflects both the hegemonic role of Australia and New Zealand in the South Pacific, and also their special relationship with the Pacific island countries. The economic dimension of this relationship is now poised for further development, and this is the focus of this paper. The remainder of the paper is organised as follows. The next section reviews the traditional economic

Table 8.2   Trade ratios and visitor numbers

	Ratio of trade to GDP (%)		Visitor numbers (1995)
	Imports	Exports	
Cook Islands	42	3	47,899
FSM	60	5	
Fiji	48	37	318,495
Kiribati	67	14	2,653
Nauru	74	17	
Niue	50	n.a.	2,161
Palau	88	10	53,229
Papua New Guinea	57	10	
Rep. Marshall Islands	27	39	
Samoa	57	6	
Solomon Islands	54	59	2,072
Tonga	52	8	24,219
Tuvalu	82	9	922
Vanuatu	41	13	43,721

Source: Pacific Islands Forum Secretariat, 2002. *Regional Policy Support Document 2002*, Pacific Islands Forum Secretariat, Suva.

relationship between the Pacific island countries and Australia and New Zealand. The following section briefly summarises recent developments in the Pacific island countries' trade and economic relationships that have paved the way for new approaches to their economic integration with Australia and New Zealand. The final section explores the possible future nature of that economic integration and potential benefits for the Pacific island countries.

THE TRADITIONAL ECONOMIC RELATIONSHIP

Australia and New Zealand are the principal aid donors to the Pacific island countries, as Table 8.3 indicates—although Table 8.3 does not include the very substantial direct financial support provided to the US Trust Territories through their Compacts of Free Association (CFAs) with the United States. Table 8.4 shows that Australia and New Zealand are also major import sources for at least the Melanesian and Polynesian Pacific island countries—accounting for between 30 per cent and 55 per cent of the imports of each country shown. On the other hand, as Table 8.5 shows, these Pacific imports represent no more than a minor export market for Australia and New Zealand, accounting

Table 8.3   Average annual development assistance to the Pacific

	Per cent of total
Australia	42.6
New Zealand	16.1
European Union	12.7
UNDP	9.1
FAO	5.2
United Kingdom	4.8
Canada	3.1
Asian Development Bank	2.8
Japan	2.7
France	0.9
Total	100.0

Source: Pacific Islands Forum Secretariat, 2002. *Regional Policy Support Document 2002*, Pacific Islands Forum Secretariat, Suva.

Table 8.4   Share of Australia and New Zealand in trade of six Pacific island countries, 2002

	Australia	New Zealand	Combined
Imports			
Fiji	37.4	17.2	54.6
Papua New Guinea	49.3	4.4	53.7
Samoa	16.1	24.0	41.1
Solomon Islands	31.7	5.1	36.8
Tonga	13.2	30.7	43.9
Vanuatu	21.3	9.7	31.0
Exports			
Fiji	19.70	3.80	23.50
Papua New Guinea	24.20	1.35	25.55
Samoa	61.01	2.32	63.33
Solomon Islands	0.87	0.26	1.13
Tonga	1.37	3.40	4.77
Vanuatu	3.25	0.64	3.89

Source: International Monetary Fund, 2003. *IMF Direction of Trade Yearbook*, International Monetary Fund, Washington, DC

respectively for just under 1.5 per cent and just under 2 per cent of the two countries' total exports.

A second asymmetry in the trading relationship, is that Australia and New Zealand are much less significant to the Pacific island countries as export markets than as import sources. Figures in Tables 8.4 and 8.6 show that Australia and New Zealand are very minor export markets for Pacific island countries other than Fiji (with its significant garment exports to Australia), Papua New Guinea, and Samoa (with its special arrangement for assembly and export to Australia of wiring harnesses). The Pacific island countries account for only 1.2 per cent of Australia's imports and just under 0.5 per cent of New Zealand's imports (Table 8.5). On the other hand, Australia and New Zealand are important sources of tourists for those Pacific island countries with significant tourism industries.

The weak performance of Pacific island exports in Australia and New Zealand has occurred despite the existence of the South Pacific Regional Trade and Economic Cooperation Agreement (SPARTECA) since the early 1980s—and, in relation to Australia–PNG trade, also of the Papua New Guinea–Australia Trade and Commercial Relations Agreement—which provided duty-free access for almost all Pacific island exports to the two Forum partners. The development of Fiji garment exports and the Samoan wiring harness exports were two

Table 8.5   Share of Pacific island countries in trade of Australia and New Zzealand, 2002

	Exports	Imports
Australia		
Fiji	0.44	0.18
Papua New Guinea	0.82	0.93
Other Pacific islands	0.21	0.09
Total	1.47	1.20
New Zealand		
Fiji	0.93	0.17
Papua New Guinea	0.34	0.27
Other Pacific islands	0.59	0.03
Total	1.86	0.47

Source: International Monetary Fund, 2003. *IMF Direction of Trade Yearbook*, International Monetary Fund, Washington, DC

significant developments under the South Pacific Regional Trade and Economic Cooperation Agreement. Access under the agreement—along with the availability of quota access to the US market—was a major factor facilitating the emergence of the Fiji garment industry in the late 1980s. Such successes, however, have been few and far between.

This lack of success can most likely be attributed to the SPARTECA rules of origin, which are based on the 50 per cent area content rule in the Australia–New Zealand Closer Economic Relations Agreement with some provision for relatively minor derogation. Arguably, this rule took little account of the realities of manufacturing in small island economies, where the lack of a significant manufacturing base made it inevitable that manufacturers would be more than usually dependent on imported inputs. Pacific island exporters also perceive quarantine regulations, and their implementation in Australia and New Zealand, as a very significant non-tariff barrier to their exports.

There is a strong mercantilist streak running through Australian and NZ trade policy toward the Pacific island countries. Market access has been vigorously pursued, for example, through the WTO accession negotiations of Vanuatu, Samoa and Tonga, and also since the late 1990s, through pressure for a new preferential trading relationship. Australia and New Zealand strongly resisted Pacific island pressure for liberal rules of origin in the early years of SPARTECA, and subsequent derogations were only grudgingly granted in the

Table 8.6   Main markets for Pacific island countries' exports, 1999 (per cent)

	Australia and New Zealand	Japan	United States	Other Asia Pacific developing countries	Other
Fiji	37.5	4.5	14.8	10.9	32.3
Kiribati	2.3	40.0	15.0	13.4	29.3
Papua New Guinea	26.5	11.7	4.6	15.0	42.2
Samoa	69.4	0.9	12.0	2.2	15.5
Solomon Islands	2.0	35.4	0.8	43.4	18.4
Tonga	11.5	59.0	19.0	2.0	8.5
Tuvalu	2.0	n.a.	n.a.	5.9	92.1
Vanuatu	1.6	11.2	25.3	5.5	56.8

Source: Pacific Islands Forum Secretariat, 2002. *Regional Policy Support Document 2002*, Pacific Islands Forum Secretariat, Suva.

face of repeated requests from the Pacific island countries. Facilitation of Fiji garment exports through introduction of the 'extended rules of origin' (allowing Australian and NZ content to count towards satisfaction of the area content rule) and Australia's Import Credit Scheme was motivated at least as much by support for the Australian cloth industry as by any desire for the development of Fijian industry, which could accurately be described as an accidental by-product of Australian policy towards its own industry. When the Credit Scheme had to be terminated following Australia's defeat in a related WTO dispute, the 'SPARTECA TCF' scheme, introduced to compensate Fiji partially for the impact of the disappearance of the Import Credit Scheme, continued the tradition of seeking to provide support for Australian cloth manufacturers while at the same time responding to calls from Fijian garment manufacturers for greater flexibility. It did so by introducing a system of Excess Local Area Content (ELAC) points, whereby over-fulfilment of the SPARTECA area content rules by using Australian cloth generates credits that Fijian garment makers can use in exporting garments made from cloth from other sources that would not meet the agreement's normal area content requirement. The increased ability to use cloth from other sources is thus effectively presented as a 'reward' for using Australian cloth.

CHANGING PACIFIC ISLAND COUNTRY APPROACHES TO PREFERENTIAL TRADE

Pacific countries' traditional approach to trade policy has been based around tariffs on imports and non-reciprocal preferential access for their exports to the markets of developed country partners. Tariffs were, and in a number of cases still are, an important source of revenue, and have also served a significant protective function in some Pacific island countries, notably Fiji and Papua New Guinea, where light manufacturing has developed behind the protective barriers. In addition to SPARTECA, non-reciprocal preferential market access agreements have included the Lomé Convention and its successor the Cotonou Agreement between the EU and the African, Caribbean and Pacific (ACP) states[1], and the Compact of Free Association (CFA) between the United States and its former trust territories.

As in the case of SPARTECA, the effect of the preferential arrangements with the European Union in encouraging Pacific island country exports has been limited to a very small number of products, mainly sugar from Fiji (via the Sugar Protocol) and canned tuna exports from Fiji, Papua New Guinea and the Solomon Islands, while very little increased export to the United States by its former trust territories has been developed through the CFA preferences. Quota-based access to the United States under the Multi-fibre Agreement did, however, facilitate the development of significant garment exports to the United States from Fiji, and intermittently also from the former trust territories. In some cases a side-effect of preferential access was a lack of pressure to achieve and maintain international competitiveness, for example in the Fiji sugar industry, where competitiveness has deteriorated alarmingly. At the same time, high tariffs imposed for revenue-generating purposes in some Pacific island countries have raised cost structures and undermined international competitiveness.

This model of trade policy has been under steadily increasing threat since the late 1980s. Preferences began to be eroded with the implementation of unilateral tariff reduction programmes by Australia and New Zealand, and the implementation of Uruguay Round commitments by WTO members. At the WTO's Doha Ministerial meeting in 2001, further erosion occurred when the European Union had to accept a demand from Thailand and the Philippines for a reduction in tariffs on canned tuna as the price for securing a further waiver for the non-reciprocal preferences granted to the African, Caribbean and Pacific states under the Cotonou Agreement. Since then, challenges have continued to mount. The European Union's 'Everything But Arms' initiative and similar initiatives by other developed countries have provided non-African, Caribbean and Pacific least-developed countries access with market access equal to, or in some cases better than, that enjoyed by non-least developed African, Caribbean and Pacific countries, while the US African Growth and Opportunities Act has motivated some international clothing firms to relocate from Fiji to Africa. The WTO panel and appellate body decisions on EU sugar subsidies will inevitably force a major revision of the European Union's sugar regime, leading at the very least to a substantial fall in the EU sugar price and a corresponding fall in the value of the preferential access of African, Caribbean and Pacific sugar exporters such as Fiji. Fiji's garment exports to the United States are also threatened by the ending of textile quotas under the terms of the WTO Agreement on Textiles and Clothing and by China's entry into the WTO. A successful outcome to the Doha Development Agenda will inevitably bring with it further preference erosion.

The effect of these challenges to preferential access is ironically now being compounded by the accelerating worldwide trend to proliferation of preferential trading arrangements. When these arrangements are formed between trading partners with whom the Pacific island countries have no preferential trading arrangements (or preferences of a relatively limited nature such as Generalised System of Preferences), the Pacific island countries find themselves in the position of being victims of trade discrimination, due to their exclusion from these arrangements. The threat of this discrimination is particularly acute in East Asia, and, for Pacific island countries other than the 'freely associated states', in the United States. Both East Asian countries and the United States are beginning to develop important networks of preferential trading arrangements, and so far participation in these networks has not been offered to the Pacific island countries.

One other very disturbing historical trend has been the decline in the Pacific island countries' apparent ability to attract foreign direct investment (foreign direct investment). A recent study by Forsyth (2003) concluded that foreign direct investment inflows are now failing to keep pace with the depreciation of the existing capital stock. This trend poses a major threat to future economic growth in the Pacific African, Caribbean and Pacific states. Two sets of factors can be cited to explain this trend

- intensifying competition among developing countries to attract foreign direct investment and to be included in international production networks, and the inherent handicaps faced by the Pacific island countries (along with many other developing countries) in competing with more attractive investment destinations.
- lack of certainty offered to foreign investors, due to lack of an enabling policy environment, perceptions of policy instability and political threats to economic policy, and land tenure issues.

A further obstacle to the Pacific island countries' trade and economic development is the severe political impediments to the liberalisation of the key 'infrastructure' sectors of telecommunications, transport (sea and air), and financial services, and the inefficiencies that result from insulating these sectors from competition. Of these key sectors, significant progress toward liberalisation has been possible only in the case of air services, with the conclusion of the Pacific Islands Air Services Agreement (PIASA). The value of the agreement has been compromised, however, by Fiji's reluctance to join it.

Faced with these mounting challenges and the broader challenge of globalisation, the Pacific island countries had decided by the late 1990s that their traditional trade policy model was unsustainable, and the decision was made in principle to move to a more outward-looking policy approach. At the same time, there was great nervousness at the prospect of any immediate removal of barriers, due to concern in some cases over the impact on local industries and in other cases over the impact on government finances of the resulting loss of tariff revenue. Accordingly it was decided to investigate a Forum free trade area as an initial step, and studies on this concept were undertaken in 1998 (see Scollay 1998; also Stoeckel and Davis 1998).

An interesting debate followed on whether the proposed free trade agreement should be a Pacific island country-only arrangement or whether it should include Australia and New Zealand. Australia and New Zealand initially insisted that their status as Forum members entitled them to foundation membership of any such free trade agreement. The Pacific island countries, on the other hand, were fearful of the consequences of opening their economies up to free trade with Australia and New Zealand on a reciprocal basis. Although the studies showed that a Pacific island country-only agreement offered them only very limited potential benefits, the Pacific island countries considered that the correspondingly more limited adjustment that would be required of them made such an arrangement a more suitable first step into the world of reciprocal free trade, that could be followed later by negotiation of a free trade agreement with Australia and New Zealand. They therefore resisted Australian and NZ pressure for inclusion in the proposed free trade agreement, and in the process gained some very valuable experience in the practice of trade negotiations.

The atmosphere changed when it became evident that, under the terms of the Cotonou Agreement, the Pacific island countries would shortly be called upon to enter negotiations for a 'WTO-compatible' (and therefore reciprocal) free trade agreement with the European Union as the replacement for their existing non-reciprocal trade arrangement. Instead of insisting on entitlement as Forum members to immediate participation in a Forum free trade agreement, Australia and New Zealand began to insist on the principle that they could not accept being placed in a disadvantaged position relative to the European Union in Pacific island country markets, and this principle was also readily accepted by the Pacific island countries.

The result was the conclusion of two agreements, a Pacific Island Countries Trade Agreement (PICTA) providing for free trade among the Pacific island countries, and a Pacific Agreement on Closer Economic Relations (PACER), providing a framework for future trade relations between the Pacific island countries and Australia and New Zealand, including a future free trade agreement.

The Pacific Island Countries Trade Agreement is a conventional free trade agreement providing for elimination of trade barriers over a lengthy transitional period, with the exception of products placed by each Pacific island country on a 'negative list'. One discovery made by many Pacific island countries when they came to formulate their 'negative list' was that the number of sensitive industries requiring permanent protection from other Pacific island country exporters is relatively small. Fiji, which has a larger range of protected industries, decided that only a tiny fraction of these needed to be excluded from a Pacific island country-only trade agreement. Bucking this particular trend was Papua New Guinea, which insisted on an unnecessarily lengthy negative list, including even products not made in Papua New Guinea and not likely to be made there in future.

Two significant extensions of the Pacific Island Countries Trade Agreement have been envisaged, and some preliminary work has been done on both proposed developments. The first is the extension of the agreement to cover trade in services. As well as the potential benefits of liberalising trade in services, this could have the further merit of precipitating a review of service sector regulation in Pacific island country economies. The second is the expansion of the agreement to include some or all of the French and US Pacific territories. This would provide Pacific island countries with preferential access to markets that are very affluent by Pacific island country standards and that, at least in the case of the French territories, are highly protected against imports from other non-European sources. Cautious steps are being taken at present towards the possible opening of negotiations between the Pacific island countries and New Caledonia.

The Pacific Agreement on Closer Economic Relations responds to Australian and New Zealand concerns by providing that any Pacific island country or group of Pacific island countries that enters into negotiations with a developed country partner for a free trade agreement[2] must undertake consultations with Australia and New Zealand as soon as practicable thereafter, 'with a view to the commencement of negotiations for free trade arrangements'. The agreement further provides that eight years after it is entered into force—in the absence of any triggering of this provision in the meantime—the Pacific island countries will enter into negotiations with Australia and New Zealand for a reciprocal free trade agreement. The 'price' received by the Pacific island countries for agreeing to this was the commitment by Australia and New Zealand to provide financial assistance for mutually agreed trade facilitation programs. After some initial skirmishing, this has resulted in the established of a substantial Regional Trade Facilitation Programme, funded by Australia and New Zealand.

In the meantime negotiations have commenced between the Pacific island countries and the European Union for an Economic Partnership Agreement (EPA) to replace the trade provisions of the Cotonou Agreement, as provided for under the latter. These negotiations are scheduled to conclude by 31 December 2007, to coincide with the expiry of the waiver that the European Union has obtained from WTO members for the trade provisions of the Cotonou Agreement. It remains to be seen whether this will lead to negotiations for a free trade agreement within the meaning of GATT Article XXIV:8, as specified in the Pacific Agreement on Closer Economic Relations, and if so how many of the fourteen Pacific island countries will eventually decide to participate in the negotiations.

In the meantime, however, the Cotonou Agreement has provided in conceptual terms a very useful example of an attempt to establish comprehensive linkages between trade arrangements, development assistance and development policies, all with the purpose of promoting sustainable development, and combined with an acceptance that the arrangements eventually agreed must address the specificities of the situation of the developing country parties to the agreement. This in turn has provided the Pacific island countries with the motivation and justification to develop and propose their own ideas on the kind of agreement best suited to achieving the avowed objectives of the Cotonou Agreement, given their particular circumstances.

The Economic Partnership Agreement negotiations are very demanding for the Pacific island countries, tying up a large proportion of the trade policy expertise. At the same time, the impact on the Pacific island countries of granting reciprocal preferential access to the European Union is not expected to be dramatic. A much more significant impact will result from a consequential agreement to concede reciprocal market access to Australia and New Zealand.

In this sense, the Economic Partnership Agreement negotiations can be usefully viewed as a 'trial run' for the eventual negotiations with Australia and New Zealand. The final section of this chapter considers some of the lessons that might usefully be transferred to those later negotiations.

NEXT STEPS WITH AUSTRALIA AND NEW ZEALAND

Hitherto the Pacific island countries' stance toward Australia and New Zealand on the issue of a free trade agreement has been entirely defensive, aimed at giving themselves 'breathing space' to prepare for the very substantial adjustments likely to be imposed by reciprocal free trade with Australia and New Zealand. Some Pacific island countries need this space to plan and begin to implement the restructuring of their fiscal systems that will be needed to cope with the loss of significant amounts of tariff revenue. Others need to build the capacity to engage more effectively in two-way trade, and to prepare for the structural changes in their economies that will follow from free trade with Australia and New Zealand.

The provisions of the Pacific Agreement on Closer Economic Relations make it inevitable that negotiations will have to begin with Australia and New Zealand at some point, the only questions being the timing, and, in the case that the negotiations are triggered by Article 6 of the agreement (rather than Article 5), how many Pacific island countries will be obliged to participate, or will choose to participate, in those negotiations. The agreement does not require that the negotiations reach a successful conclusion, so it remains open to the Pacific island countries to reject proposals from Australia and New Zealand they deem unacceptable. The Pacific island countries thus still have a number of cards that they can play if they continue to be defensively-minded in their stance toward Australia and New Zealand.

There is, however, a potential positive agenda that could be developed for negotiations with Australia and New Zealand, and it is here that the experience of the Economic Partnership Agreement negotiations with the European Union can prove instructive. As noted in the previous section, those negotiations require the Pacific island countries to consider how a 'development-oriented' agreement suited to their own specific situation and purposes should be designed. If the negotiations with the European Union go well, the resulting agreement can provide a precedent upon which the Pacific island countries may rely in their negotiations with Australia and New Zealand. In any event, there is nothing to prevent the Pacific island countries from adapting the positions they develop for negotiations with the European Union to form the basis also of their position in negotiations with Australia and New Zealand. A further argument in favour of adopting a positive agenda is that prolonged pursuit of a defensive strategy in the face of the rapid changes in the international economy, including the proliferation of preferential trading arrangements, can only result in the increasing marginalisation of the Pacific island countries. If this outcome is to be avoided, the Pacific island countries have to judge the correct moment to move proactively toward constructive engagement with major economic partners. The conclusion of negotiations with the European Union may provide that moment in the case of Australia and New Zealand.

While the Pacific island countries' position toward the European Union has yet to be fully articulated, the main outlines that it should take are clear enough, and could easily provide a 'model' for a position to be taken toward Australia and New Zealand. It should include strong proposals on market access for goods, trade facilitation and promotion, trade in services, investment, and the development of key tradeable sectors in the Pacific island country economies.

On market access, given the almost complete duty-free access currently enjoyed by the Pacific island countries, the main area to be explored is rules of origin. It is worth investing effort into investigating whether the Pacific island countries can design and propose rules of origin for at least some products that might make feasible the development of new lines of exportable manufactures that are not possible under the current rules. There are grounds for hope that the European Union may be receptive to such proposals, which could in turn establish a useful precedent for negotiation with Australia and New Zealand.

On investment and trade facilitation and promotion, the message will be that market access by itself is unlikely to be effective, especially from a development perspective unless backed by strong provisions in each of these areas. The Regional Trade Facilitation Programme provides a solid basis on which to build further trade facilitation measures, and trade promotion is also an area that readily lends itself to capacity-building assistance. Investment is a problematic area, in that it involves inherent handicaps faced by the Pacific island countries that are not easily overcome, including small market size and isolation, as well as the intractable problems related to land tenure. Innovative strategies will be needed to overcome these difficulties, and it is not clear at this stage what those strategies will be. In the case of the European Union, the

Pacific island countries are sure to insist also that EU agencies such as the European Investment Bank and Centre for Development of Enterprise modify their programs and procedures to make them more accessible to the scale of businesses typically found in the Pacific island countries. Australia and New Zealand will have lot of ground to make up before they can match these facilities.

On services trade, the key demand will be for increased mode 4 (mobility of persons) access, since this is the mode for which the Pacific island countries have the biggest supply potential, and arguably the mode in which expanded access could make the biggest contribution to development. Mode 4 access involves temporary movement rather than permanent migration, so that the skills developed from expanding this form of services access will not be permanently lost to the Pacific island countries. This is not to say that the Pacific island countries could not also benefit from provisions for longer-term mobility as well, but mode 4 is undoubtedly the place to start, given the sensitivities associated with migration issues.

Increased mobility of persons between the Pacific island countries and Australia and New Zealand is likely to be one of the measures with greatest potential to contribute to development of the Pacific island countries, with impacts that extend well beyond the initial exchange of services. In cases where some two-way mobility already exists it is clear the sending Pacific island country derives considerable benefit from the resultant return of both capital and business and entrepreneurial skills. This will not be an easy issue for Australia and New Zealand to address, and there will be many complexities also to be considered from the Pacific side, but it must be confronted if the parties are serious about making maximum use of the potential of trade arrangements to promote development.

The Pacific island countries are also likely to insist that an integration agreement that purports to promote and support their economic development must also pay attention to the key tradeable sectors in their economies, such as tourism and fisheries. The approach to tourism, for example, would not necessarily involve a separate tourism agreement, but rather a drawing together of all existing commitments of the parties relating to tourism, to emphasise that these commitments should be viewed and treated as an integrated package. These would include commitments under trade in services and investment provisions of the new arrangements, commitments of the developed country partners to development assistance, and commitments of the Pacific island countries to implementation of enabling policies.

The proposed strategy thus represents a holistic approach to economic integration between the Pacific island countries and Australia and New Zealand, based around the development needs and priorities of the Pacific island countries, and moving away from the approach heavily emphasising market access that Australia and New Zealand have tended to follow in the past. This holistic approach is already foreshadowed in Article 2 of the Pacific Agreement on Closer Economic Relations, in which the parties agree that their objectives include the provision of a 'framework for economic cooperation leading over time to the development of a single regional market'. The 'single market' concept as conventionally understood by trade economists includes free movement of labour and capital as well as free trade in goods and services. This provision was proposed by the Pacific island countries instead of the reference to eventual inclusion of services and investment suggested by Australia and New Zealand, to make it clear that future developments must include all aspects of economic integration of interest to the Pacific island countries, and not simply those aspects of particular interest to Australia and New Zealand.

The proposed approach, however, involves not only a holistic approach to economic integration, it also involves bringing together economic integration and development policy under a common purpose, as envisaged by the Cotonou Agreement. This could be something of a challenge for Australia and New Zealand, given the separation between trade policy and development policy recently adopted in the policy framework at least in New Zealand's case. Re-asserting the link between trade and development would, however, arguably represent a logical extension of the proposed Pacific Plan.

NOTES

[1]   Under the Lomé Convention eight Pacific island countries were included in the ACP group (Fiji, Kiribati, Papua New Guinea, Samoa, Solomon Islands, Tonga, Tuvalu and Vanuatu), but with the signing of the Cotonou Agreement the remaining six Pacific island countries were included also, so that now all fourteen are African, Caribbean and Pacific states (known for Cotonou Agreement purposes as the Pacific African, Caribbean and Pacific states or PACPs).

[2]   Defined as an agreement within the meaning of GATT Article XXIV:8

9

FISHING FOR A FUTURE

Hannah Parris and R. Quentin Grafton

The development challenges facing the countries of the southern central and western Pacific Ocean (collectively Melanesia, Polynesia and Micronesia—or Pacific island countries) are daunting despite substantial in flows of development assistance.[1] The difficulties facing these countries include the unsustainable use of key resources, such as fisheries, high rates of unemployment and underemployment, low levels of economic growth and, in some countries, social unrest and political instability (World Bank 2000b; Asian Development Bank 2004). To help address these concerns, Pacific island countries have embraced the sustainable development agenda and are active participants in a variety of fora, including the Barbados Plan of Action for Small Island Developing States. In the forefront of the development agenda of many Pacific island countries is how to utilise the region's natural resources—such as, fisheries, forests and tourist potential—to promote both social and economic goals.

In this chapter, we focus on the western and central Pacific region's highly prized fish stocks, found in the exclusive economic zones of Pacific island countries, and in the high seas in between, and how they might be used to sustain development. In section two, we briefly review broad measures of well-being and economic performance of Pacific island countries, and describe the importance of the tuna fisheries and the challenges faced by the region's countries. Section three highlights the major challenges to cooperatively managing tuna resources to maximise the benefits to the island states. In particular, we examine whether the recent 'Convention on the Conservation and Management of Highly Migratory Fish Stocks in the Western and Central Pacific Ocean' (hereafter the 'Tuna Convention') can deliver the potential benefits of cooperation. Later, we examine other constraints—in particular the quality and capacity of public institutions—that prevent Pacific island countries from making the best use of the resource rents from their tuna fisheries. We conclude by proposing two approaches that Pacific island countries, with assistance from donor countries, may wish to consider to sustain the region's development.

TUNA-LED SUSTAINABLE DEVELOPMENT IN PACIFIC ISLAND COUNTRIES

Income levels in the Pacific region are low by world standards, but there is substantial variability among countries. Table 9.1 indicates that only one country, Palau, has an upper middle level of income, and all others fall in the lower half of the world's countries in terms of their 'Human Development Ranking'.[2] Some countries have also experienced negative economic growth in the recent past, and many Pacific island countries have the challenge of ensuring rising living standards in the face of rapid increases in population.

Although the 14 independent countries and the eight dependent territories that constitute the region have very small populations (only Papua New Guinea has a population greater than one million), their exclusive economic zones extend 200 nautical miles from land and represent a huge area of the Pacific Ocean. Not surprisingly, marine resources are critically important to the well-being of some Pacific island countries, especially those with a large exclusive economic zone, a small population and a tiny land mass. In the case of the Federated States of Micronesia and Kiribati, the value of fish caught in their exclusive economic zones exceeds their gross national income, while in the Marshall Islands and Solomon Islands it almost equals their national income. Pacific island countries, however, receive only a tiny fraction of the benefits from the fisheries found in their territories because about 90 per cent of the fish caught in their exclusive economic zones are harvested by 'distant water fishing nations', and these nations only pay approximately 3–4 per cent of the landed value in access fees (Petersen 2005).

The failure to realise fully the potential benefits from their fishery resources is of major concern for Pacific island countries. Many thought that the Pacific islands countries would experience an economic 'bonanza' on being granted exclusive economic zones under the third United Nations Convention on the Law of the Sea.[3] It was hoped that fisheries would address two major challenges: reduce the risks of overexploitation of a common-pool resource and provide the Pacific island countries with a reliable source of income with which to finance economic development (Chand et al. 2003). Whatever exclusive economic zones may have delivered to Pacific island countries, they have coincided with a substantial increase in fishing effort and harvests. For instance, Figure 9.1 shows that the total harvest of tuna has more than doubled since the 1980s, and the region now supplies about 40 per cent of the world's global catch of tuna. The latest data suggest that catches of some tuna in the region may have peaked, such as yellowfin tuna, and that some stocks, such as bigeye tuna, may even be overexploited (Langley et al. 2005). Another worrying trend has been a 70 per cent decline in the catch per unit of effort of yellowfin tuna in the western Pacific over the past 50 years, although exactly what this implies about overall tuna populations is disputed (Hampton et al. 2005; Myers and Worm 2005).

Table 9.1   Development and fishery statistics of selected Pacific island countries

	Population ('000)[a]	Annual population growth 1990–98	GNI per capita (US$)[a]	Mean gross fisheries revenues 1993–98 (% of GNI)[a]	Adult literacy	Life expectancy at birth	Global HDI rank
FSM	120	2.1	2,150	215	71.3	65.7	120
Fiji	824	0.9	2,130	-	92.9	66.6	101
Kiribati	93	2.1	830	503	92.2	61.6	129
Marshall Islands	53	3.6	2,190	85	74.4	65.0	121
Palau	20	2.4	6,730	5	91.4	69.0	46
Tonga	101	0.3	1.530	-	99.0	68.0	107
Samoa	171	1.2	1,520	6	95.7	66.6	117
Solomon Islands	432	3.3	580	87	30.3	64.7	147
Vanuatu	203	2.7	1,050	-	33.5	65.8	140

Notes: [a] 2001 figures. FSM = Federated States of Micronesia. GNI = gross national income.
Source: World Bank, 2000a. *Small States: meeting challenges in the global economy*, Commonwealth Secretariat/World Bank Joint Task Force report, London; World Bank, 2003. *Sustainable Development in a Dynamic World: transforming institutions, growth, and quality of life*, Oxford University Press, New York; Petersen, E.H., 2005. *Institutional Economics and Fishery Management*, Edward Elgar, Cheltenham (in press); and authors' calculations.

Most tuna in the region are caught by large purse-seiner vessels worth up to millions of dollars and almost exclusively owned and operated by 'distant water fishing nations'. Of the total landed value of fish in the Western and Central Pacific—approximately US$2 billion—only about US$60 million is paid in access fees to Pacific island countries (Gillett et al. 2001). These access fees are low compared to those paid in other parts of the world (Chand et al. 2003; Inhedru 1995). This is explained, in part, by

- Pacific island countries' lack of bargaining power relative to 'distant water fishing nations'
- provisions imposed on 'distant water fishing nations'—such as transhipment of fish (Duncan and Temu 1997)—that reduce returns to fishing
- the linking of development aid and assistance with access fees
- current fishing effort seemingly exceeding the economic surplus maximising level (Bertignac et al. 2000).

Figure 9.1   The volume of tuna resources harvested in the Western and Central Pacific, 1950–2003

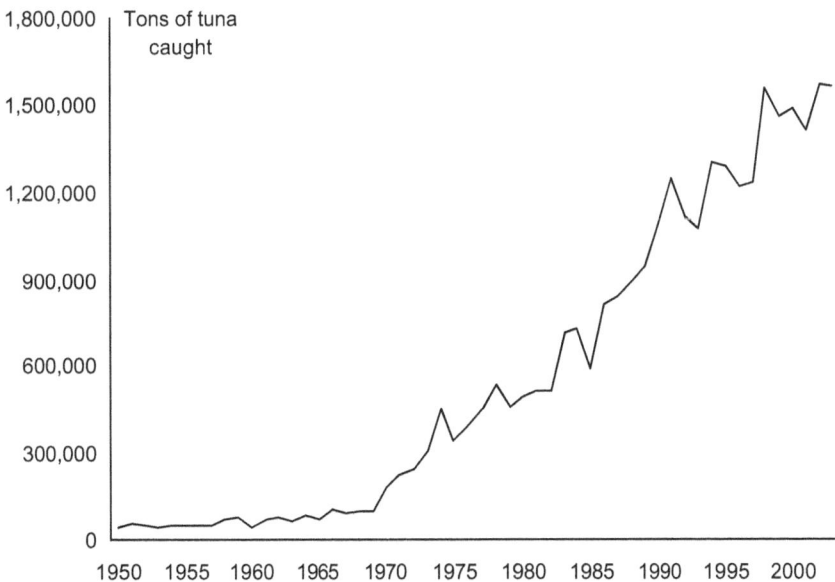

Source: Food and Agriculture Organization, 2005. *Total Production 1950–2003*, Fishstat Dataset, FAO, Rome.

Bargaining power

Pacific island countries' initial attempts to gain reasonable access to resource rents accruing from their fisheries were hampered by their negotiation experiences with the Japanese, who in the early 1980s harvested about three-quarters of the tuna stocks. Moreover, relatively unsuccessful experiments with multilateralism in other areas, such as air transport, in the 1970s (Fry 2005) left some Pacific island countries reluctant to collaborate and bargain as a group. This made it easier for the Japanese to manipulate negotiations through a 'divide and conquer' strategy. By refusing to negotiate with Pacific island countries collectively, and ensuring that at least one access arrangement to an exclusive economic zone was always in operation, the Japanese were able to keep Pacific island countries in competitive positions with respect to one another (Schurman 1998). This strategy was enhanced by the fact that the benefits and costs to Pacific island countries of implementing collective bargaining are likely to be unevenly distributed, thus lowering the incentive for these countries to form cooperative arrangements.

It appears that Pacific island countries have become more adept in bargaining with 'distant water fishing nations' over time and have realised the benefits of cooperating in discussions of access. For example, the formation of the Nauru, Palau and Federated States of Micronesia agreements represent successful efforts at coordination, although these agreements only explicitly cover licensing conditions. In addition, the Nauru Group appears to have improved access agreements and payoffs to Pacific states (Munro et al. 2004), and Japan seems increasingly receptive to discussing a multilateral agreement with Pacific island countries. Over time, Japan's relative importance has also diminished (see Table 9.2) in the face of increased access and competition by the Taiwanese, Korean, Chinese and US fleets, forcing the Japanese to concede to more reasonable access fees (Schurman 1998; Petersen 2005). Unfortunately, increased harvests from the new entrants appear also to have reduced overall returns and the ability of 'distant water fishing nations' to pay increased access fees.

Bundling of aid and fisheries access

It is common practice in the Pacific for donors to bundle in-kind or financial development assistance in the expectation that they will be favourably considered in negotiations over access to resources and fees. Schurman (1998) cites the example of the National Fisheries Corporation of the Federated States of Micronesia receiving 'gifts' of training boats, while the Asian Development Bank observes that almost half of the 'access fees' paid by US boats actually takes the form of development aid (Duncan et al. 1999). Given the secrecy surrounding the bilateral access arrangements it is difficult to determine the extent of this practice, but it does appear to have reduced the access fees paid to Pacific island countries.

Fostering a domestic and commercially competitive fishing industry

Many Pacific island countries have pursued 'domestication'—developing and/ or then integrating domestically located harvesting and processing sectors to serve export markets—to extract more of the economic benefits from their tuna fisheries. This they have encouraged, first, by publicly financing national industrial enterprises to kick-start a domestic tuna industry, and, second, by attaching industry development conditions to the licensing arrangements for 'distant water fishing nations'. Typically, this second approach has seen Pacific island countries requiring foreign vessels to use domestic infrastructure and/or use nationals to crew boats, as well as maintaining and completing compliance procedures such as those set out in the FSM Agreement.[4] Unfortunately, these strategies have largely failed (Petersen 2002, 2005; Schurman 1998; Chand et al. 2003; van Santen and Muller 2000; Duncan et al. 1999), but some benefits have been generated through direct and indirect employment in the tuna

Table 9.2   Average annual tuna catches in the Western and Central Pacific region for selected countries

Country	Estimated catch (average 2000–03)
Japan	225,567
Taiwan	282,458
Korea	190,761
United States	97,422
Solomon Islands	19,063
Vanuatu	9,593
Papua New Guinea	112,098
Federated States of Micronesia	22,747
Australia	1,892
Total	961,599

Source: FAO, 2005. *Total Production 1950–2003*, Fishstat Dataset, FAO, Rome; and authors' calculations.

industry and also through foreign currency earnings (Barclay and Yoshikazu 2000; Gillett et al. 2001).

In general, Pacific island countries have chosen to focus on the harvesting sector in terms of their public sector investment. Unfortunately, the harvesting of tuna generates highly variable revenues, requires large upfront sunk costs and substantial high technical requirements. The high investment costs and the fickle nature of fishing has meant that mistakes have been made that are financially burdensome for some Pacific island countries (Duncan et al. 1999).[5] The lack of appropriate technical skills domestically has also meant that Pacific island countries have often had to rely on foreign investment partners to implement projects, or enter into partnerships with foreign firms, reducing the potential financial gains from projects. Van Santen and Muller (2000) summarise some of the investments made by three Pacific island countries (Federated States of Micronesia, Fiji and Marshall Islands) in tuna harvesting, which total over US$70 million a sum in excess of the region's annual access fees. In general, these investments have been made by the public sector and many have failed to yield a positive financial return (Petersen 2005).

Equally important is whether Pacific island countries could receive a greater amount from access fees alone rather than a mix of access fees and an export-orientated domestic industry (assuming the investment by Pacific island countries generates a positive rate of return). The answer depends on the relative cost efficiency of 'distant water fishing nations' (Munro 1979). If 'distant water fishing nations' have lower harvesting costs, as seems likely given their ability to harvest tuna resources profitably and pay access fees, the potential economic surplus is *greater* than if Pacific island countries were to do the harvesting.

Another consideration for Pacific island countries, in terms of the domestication of their fishing industry, is the very substantial cost associated with fisheries management. In a number of countries outside the region, the costs of fisheries management exceed the potential benefits from the fisheries (Schrank et al. 2003). This suggests that a 'go-it-alone' strategy in terms of harvesting and managing tuna may be a costly exercise generating few, if any, net benefits for Pacific island nations. The question for advocates of 'domestication' is, therefore, what should be the nature of the partnerships between Pacific island countries and 'distant water fishing nations' that will maximise the payoffs to the Pacific states?

CHALLENGES TO COOPERATION IN THE WESTERN AND CENTRAL PACIFIC

There are a number of potential payoffs to Pacific island countries from cooperating over the use of their fishery resources. These include better bargaining power in terms of access fees with 'distant water fishing nations' from the current mean level of about 40 per cent of the total rent;[6] increased resource rent and greater population resilience from moving to lower rates of exploitation that could more than double the resource rent from the fisheries (Bertignac et al. 2000); higher returns from harvesting older age classes of fish and mitigating the 'race to fish' and, finally, better management from economies of scale and scope associated with shared monitoring, enforcement and stock assessments. Pacific island countries and 'distant water fishing nations' could be made better off with cooperation that reduces current harvesting and directs it to older age classes to raise the overall resource rent. Obtaining such an agreement would require that every country be at least as well off with cooperation. Moreover, there would be significant transitional losses in moving to a lower harvest, but the benefits from higher fish stocks would be unevenly distributed among 'distant water fishing nations' and Pacific island countries. Thus, to achieve an agreement, some form of 'side-payments' in terms of harvest rights or monetary compensation would be required from the winners to the losers as well as incentives for all countries to comply with a cooperative agreement. It would also require barriers to entry for new participants or countries that might also wish to benefit from increased returns from cooperation.

Chand et al. (2003) propose a possible way to achieve a cooperative agreement by the creation of a commission, composed of both Pacific island countries and 'distant water fishing nations', that would allocate harvesting rights as a percentage of a total allowable catch denominated by species and area based on exclusive economic zones and historical fishing patterns. These harvesting rights would be transferable and divisible between vessels flagged by the countries that are signatories to the agreement. Other countries could enter the agreement, but would be required to buy or lease harvesting rights to catch tuna legally in the region. Population assessments and monitoring and enforcement would be paid for out of rentals based on the allocated rights, and, because of economies of scope, could significantly reduce overall management costs. To give greater transparency to the size of the resource rents in the fisheries, Chand et al. (2003) recommend that a small percentage of the total rights held by all countries would have to be tendered for sale every year and the prices for the rights made available to all parties.

Unfortunately, the Tuna Convention does not incorporate the features recommended by Chand et al. (2003). Nevertheless, the Western and Central Pacific Fisheries Commission (hereafter 'Fisheries Commission'), the secretariat of the Tuna Convention, offers significant changes in terms of how Pacific island countries and 'distant water fishing nations' cooperate. Table 9.3 summarises key features of the Tuna Convention and its ability to deliver on the aspirations of Pacific island countries. Although the Tuna Convention will not, by itself, allow Pacific island countries to achieve the full economic potential offered by their fishery resources, it is a genuine multilateral regime that includes all Pacific island countries and allows for, and encourages full membership for 'distant water fishing nations'.[7] It also explicitly recognises the importance of sustainability, ecosystem management and interdependencies of tuna management. As with many international treaties, the key to its success is in how its various articles are applied and enforced, and whether resources are sufficient to achieve the treaty's objectives.

The Tuna Convention allows Pacific island countries to maintain full decision-making power with respect to their national exclusive economic zones. While this may be understandable from a political point of view, the retention of access fee arrangements by Pacific island countries means that the potential for 'distant water fishing nations' to 'game' the fee negotiations remains, along with the potential to limit the extent to which Pacific island countries can gain financially from the fishery. To this end, the Tuna Convention does little to help Pacific island countries work cooperatively to maximise resource rents at a sustainable level. Thus the Tuna Convention is not an economic treaty as such (it is a treaty about the amount of fish to be caught) and, therefore, does not address the economic/financial issues inherent in resource management. Moreover, the Tuna Convention does not prevent the Pacific island countries from attaching conditions to access and licensing similar to those set out in the Nauru, Palau and Federated States of Micronesia arrangements.

As with all new institutions, the future of the Tuna Convention depends on the strength of its implementation processes. The Fisheries Commission is charged with determining the total allowable catch or total level of fishing

Table 9.3   Selected features of the Western and Central Pacific Ocean Tuna Convention, with comments

Desirable features of a convention	Features of the WCPO Tuna Convention
Well-defined objective based on commonly agreed goals derived from sustainability principles	Yes, but multiple criteria make it difficult to understand the processes to arrive at sustainable harvest levels.
Management framework based on an ecosystems approach to fisheries management	In theory, yes, but the Fisheries Commission lacks the financial resources to implement the approach.
Well-defined property rights and system of and agreeing to and distributing 'entitlements' over common-pool resources	Rights exist at national level, but are not well defined at the fisher level.
Direct link between resource ownership/control and economic return	No
Incorporation of 'expert' advice based on scientific and socioeconomic research	Yes. Articles 11–14 establish scientific and technical subsidiary bodies to advise the Commission.
Clear mechanisms for dispute resolution between Convention members and between members and non-members/other convention areas.	No. some procedures are set out covering potential disputes with non-parties to the Convention, but these are weak and rely on diplomatic pressure.
Mechanisms to ensure adaptability in the future	Partial. The Tuna Convention claims to make use of the 'precautionary principle'
Mechanisms to prevent further entry into the fisheries	No
Mechanisms to prevent economic overfishing	Not a management objective or criterium for setting TACs.
Mechanisms to address social and environmental externalities	In theory, yes, as environmental and social externalities form part of the list of issues 'taken into account' in managing and conserving fish stocks. However, exact mechanisms to account for these issues are not defined.
Clear decision-making procedures established. Decision-making processes are transparent and open to scrutiny by third parties	Yes, decisions made in the first place by consensus. If not achieved, then decisions made by voting. Voting parties divided into two 157 chambers— those who are members of the FFA and those who are not. Article 21 allows for participation of third parties where appropriate, as a mechanism to promote transparency.
Mechanisms to ensure compliance with Convention goals and targets	Enforcement of provisions of convention on fishing vessels lies with flag state. Sanctions may be used to enforce compliance by flag states in the event of vessel non-compliance. Convention also establishes a regional observer program to promote compliance. No provisions to force member states to translate provisions in Convention into national laws.
Convention supports and develops the capacity of member countries to implement Convention goals	In theory, yes. Article 30 recognises the 'special needs' of developing country members and provides for financial, technical and other assistance as appropriate. Current budget, however, precludes such capacity development.
Secretariat is adequately resourced	No. The Fisheries Commission is under-resourced by several orders of magnitude (less than US$1 million in 2005).

effort within the region. To assist, the Fisheries Commission is to be served by a subsidiary scientific committee and a technical compliance committee. Crucially, however, the setting of total allowable catches to maximise the economic yield or surplus from fishing is not a criterium of the Tuna Convention. The allocation of effort or fish after setting of the total allowable catch is to be made by consensus by signatories to the Tuna Convention.

The effectiveness of the Fisheries Commission is limited by the political will of the member countries and the economic resources that they make available to carry out its mandate. It will be another organisation—along with the Secretariat of the South Pacific Community, located in New Caledonia, and the Forum Fisheries Agency, based in the Solomon Islands—that will provide support for fisheries management. It is not clear how responsibilities will be divided among the organisations, or what coordination there will be between the three organisations, and to what extent, if any, resources will be shared in terms of fisheries management. Thus, although the Forum Fisheries Agency was recently awarded US$11 million over five years from the Global Environment Facility to support fisheries management in the Pacific (FFA 2005), the budget of less than US$1 million allocated for the Fisheries Commision's 2005 operations is a matter of concern (Fisheries Commission 2004).

CAPACITY AND GOVERNANCE OF PACIFIC ISLAND COUNTRIES

The ADB identifies four key principles to good governance: accountability, participation, predictability and transparency (Abbott and Pollard 2004). The inability of Pacific island countries to promote and implement these principles is generally recognised as one of the key factors underscoring poor socioeconomic performance across the Pacific (Abbott and Pollard 2004). Many observers, AusAID included, argue that poor governance and poor institutional quality are major barriers to future development of Pacific island countries (AusAID 2005).

Causes of poor governance lie in a complex mixture of sociocultural and historical factors. Poor institutional performance is also linked to lack of suitably qualified people able (and willing) to address governance issues (Abbott and Pollard 2004). It is most strongly expressed in the low quality of the national public institutions, political instability, weak parliamentary systems, corruption, a politicised public service, and a failure to establish strong institutions of governance (such as auditors or ombudsman).

Figures 9.2 and 9.3 provide estimates of Pacific island countries' ability to control corruption and a measure of their governments' effectiveness in 2004. For comparison purposes, the estimated levels for Australia and New Zealand are also shown. Both figures place most Pacific island countries in the lower half of world rankings, with some countries, such as the Solomon Islands and Papua New Guinea, listed in the lowest decile of countries. While poor institutions and governance structures are critical factors in explaining the historically poor economic performance of tuna fisheries (Chand et al. 2003; Petersen 2002, 2005; Duncan et al. 1999; Schurman 1998; Hinds 2003), it is difficult to pinpoint any direct causal relationship, other than one of influence. Poor institutions and governance practices are pervasive rather than being specific to tuna management itself, and thus poor management in the fisheries is a symptom rather than a cause of poor economic performance. Moreover, the evidence relating to poor governance, as it directly affects tuna management, tends to be anecdotal although it is possible to make some general observations.

First, the historical approach of setting access conditions and fees is both non-transparent and non-participatory. A secret agreement between national governments makes it extremely difficult for analysts, or the Pacific communities themselves, to identify whether these common-pool tuna resources are being used in the most efficient manner. This is reinforced by the (explicit or implicit) bundling of donor assistance with access—although the provision of aid is of benefit to the Pacific island country in question, it is impossible to determine whether the combination of fees and aid represents the best economic outcome that could be derived from scarce tuna resources (Petersen 2005). This tendency towards 'bundling' is reinforced by the traditional and governance cultures pervasive in the Pacific—that is, the traditional familial links between politicians and their communities and the expectations that these connections will deliver financial benefits.

Governing for sustainability in tuna fisheries adds further layers of complexity. Sustainable governance arrangements for fisheries should, at a minimum, include harvest allocation mechanisms that provide incentives for sustainable fishing practices (Grafton et al. 2005). Chand et al. (2003) also argue that, in addition, fisheries management should include co-management of fisheries between public institutions and fishers, exploitation rates set to ensure long-term sustainability, a coincidence of public and private benefits and incentives in exploiting the tuna resources, and cooperation of all parties who have some financial or other interest in the resource (Chand et al. 2003). Clearly, the bilateral arrangements that have served as the main allocative institutions have incorporated few, if any, of these features.

Petersen (2002) also highlights the importance of governance in stimulating private sector participation in the tuna fisheries. Here again, poor governance and inappropriate economic policy settings appear to have failed to stimulate extensive private sector participation in the fisheries. Evidence of this is anecdotal for specific tuna fisheries across the region because the failure to develop a viable private sector is a general, rather than a tuna specific, issue. For example, Gillett et al. (2001) discuss the Papua New Guinea National Fisheries Authority, which, it is claimed, has insufficient internal and external controls, obscure licensing processes subject to manipulation, poor record keeping, mismanagement of trust accounts, and extensive use of influence rather than merit to determine management decisions.

Potential for a resource curse

Over the longer term, even with the successful implementation of the Tuna Convention, tuna-led development presents more governance challenges to the Pacific island countries. If Pacific island states are able to increase their access fees, this has the potential, in the absence of strong institutions, to generate a 'resource curse' (Auty 2001; Sachs and Warner 2000) for some countries. Pacific island countries require capital to promote their economic development, but in the absence of good governance these funds could contribute to political, economic and social problems that have arisen elsewhere with resource-rich developing countries.

The potential for a resource boom to initiate a 'resource curse' pattern in Pacific states is real. Both Papua New Guinea and Nauru have experienced the resource boom–bust cycle to various degrees, but the potential for a fisheries-induced resource curse in the Pacific region, and its potential consequences, have been largely ignored.

Resource booms may have both positive and negative consequences on the socioeconomic conditions of resource rich countries. These are often referred to as 'transmission' mechanisms, and usually include phenomena such as declines in the non-resource export sector, crowding out effects, poor decision-making at the government level, and a decline in the quality of institutions. Unfortunately, it is possible to discern many of the typical 'transmission'

Figure 9.2   Measure of the control of corruption for selected Pacific island countries

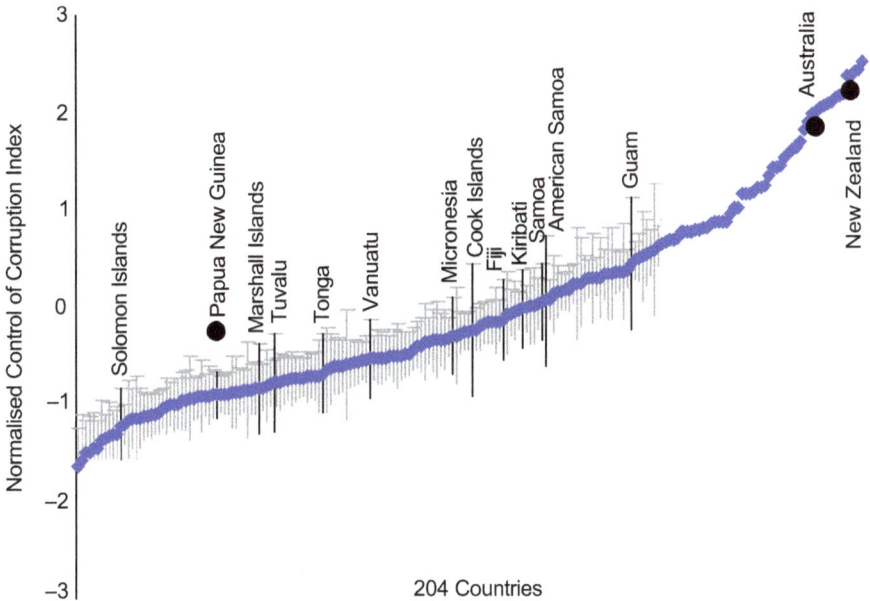

Key: Control of corruption measures perceptions of corruption in terms of using public power for private gain. Chosen comparator is the year 2000. All scores are normalised to be between –3 and 3 where a higher score indicates greater control of corruption. Confidence intervals are denoted by the upper and lower bars for each country.
Source: Authors' calculations and Kaufmann, D., Kraay, A. and Mastruzzi, M., 2005. 'Governance matters IV: governance indicators for 1996–2005', *World Bank Economic Review*, 18(2):253–87.

dynamics in existence in the Pacific. For example, corruption is key in spreading the impacts of the resource curse, and is also an unfortunate feature of some public institutions in the region.

Avoiding the curse

A major development focus should be to improve the quality of institutions and governance in the western and central Pacific. In other words, simply ensuring sustainable and economically profitable tuna fisheries is unlikely to be sufficient to bring about sustained development. A successful example of managing fisheries and their revenues is provided by the Falkland Islands

Figure 9.3   Government effectiveness, 2004
              (chosen comparator also shown for selected countries)

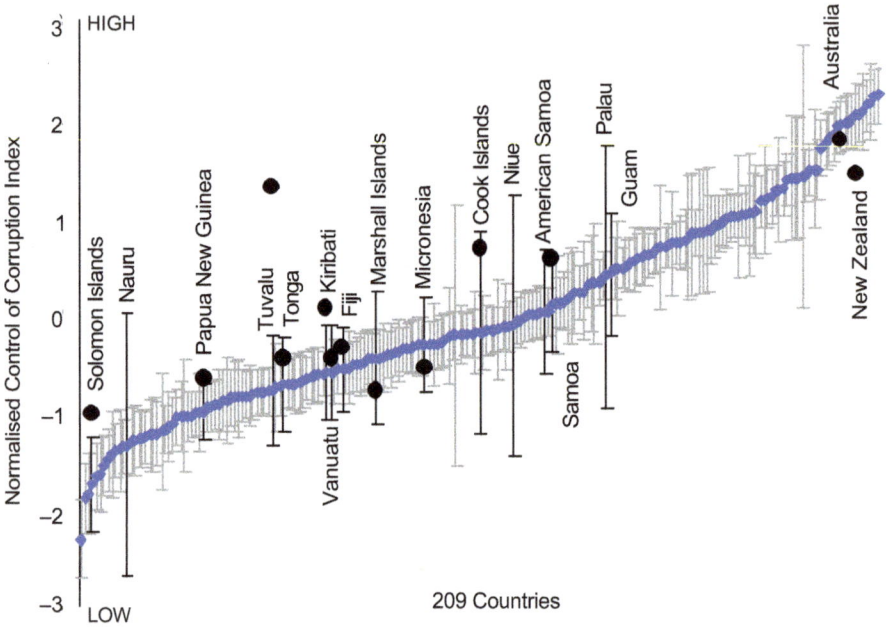

Key: Control of corruption measures perceptions of corruption in terms of using public power for private gain. Chosen comparator is the year 2000. All scores are normalised to be between –3 and 3 where a higher score indicates greater control of corruption. Confidence intervals are denoted by the upper and lower bars for each country.
Source: Kaufmann, D., Kraay, A. and Mastruzzi, M., 2005. *Governance Matters IV: governance indicators for 1996–2005*, World Bank, Washington, DC.

government, which suggests that very large fisheries revenues, if used wisely, can provide substantial social and economic benefits (Thomas 2002). For instance, the Falkland Islands government has been able to extract substantial access fees while also ensuring monitoring, data collection, surveys and analysis of catch and abundance data to manage the resources sustainably (Falkland Islands Government 2005).

In addition to supporting capacity and institutional development, Pacific island countries and donors could develop 'trust funds' which would be managed separately from other government revenues. The money in the trust funds could be independently managed and audited and any expenditure from the fund—beyond a pre-determined level—would be prohibited without an act of parliament or legislation. It would also be possible to specify the sort of expenditures (such as physical infrastructure) that would be permitted from the fund. Trust funds cannot substitute for good quality institutions, but can provide greater transparency in terms of both fishing revenues and expenditures. A trust fund could also provide a sustainable revenue stream for both present and future generations. The successful use of a trust fund by Kiribati for its phosphate royalties—which has generated returns long after mining ceased (Petersen 2005)—suggests that similar funds should be seriously considered by Pacific island countries to deal with fishery access fee revenues.

CONCLUSIONS

The countries and the territories of the western and central Pacific face formidable challenges to promote their sustainable development. Their shared fisheries resources—and in particular tuna—provide the possibility for 'tuna-led' economic development for some states. This opportunity is, however, constrained by economic overfishing, the inability to deter new entrants and fishing effort, and failed strategies to develop a profitable domestic, but export-orientated, industry. The countries of the region also face problems with corruption and government effectiveness, posing a real risk that fishing revenues will not generate a sustainable flow of income to sustain the region's long-term development.

To address these problems, Pacific island countries and donor nations should consider a twin strategy to maximise the development potential of the region's fishery resources. First, given the potential for cooperation to make every stakeholder better off (including 'distant water fishing nations'), greater effort should be directed to supporting multinational institutions that reduce harvests, increase the transparency of access fee arrangements, and allow for transferability of harvesting rights across countries and vessels. Second, to ensure the most effective use of funds generated from fishing resources, greater attention should be given to increasing capacity in the public sector and improving government effectiveness. This could include, but should not be limited to, developing innovative ways to reduce corruption and prevent the misuse of public revenues by the creation of trust funds for fishing access fees. Both strategies, if successful, increase the possibility of sustained development in the western and central Pacific.

ACKNOWLEDGMENTS

We are grateful to the Australian Research Council and the Bureau of Rural Sciences for partial funding of this research. We thank Tom Kompas, Kate Barclay and participants at the International Workshop on Pacific Integration and Regional Governance, Canberra, 8–9 June 2005, for helpful comments and suggestions.

NOTES

[1] Not including aid from France to New Caledonia and French Polynesia, total development assistance is a little less than US$100 per capita, although some countries receive substantially more than this amount.

[2] 'Human Development Ranking' is an index of life expectancy at birth, educational achievement (adult literacy and combined gross primary, secondary and tertiary enrolment) and real per capita GDP.

[3] The United Nations Law of the Sea Convention is a universal legal framework designed to manage and conserve marine resources at the international level. It incorporates many different areas of marine and ocean governance, of which the granting of exclusive economic zones to coastal states and the management of fisheries is just one part. It was finalised in 1982 and came into force in 1994.

[4] One compliance mechanism is the requirement to participate in a vessel monitoring system (VMS) run by the Forum Fisheries Agency. The vessel monitoring system allows Forum Fishing Agency members to track the location, speed and direction of licensed boats operating in the exclusive economic zones of member countries (van Santen and Muller 2000).

[5] The Asian Development Bank cites the following reasons why port development has not been a successful strategy: fleet operators prefer to service vessels in the same ports where they service fish, the later usually lying outside the WCPO Region; volatility in Pacific islands governments' access arrangements; the variable and seasonal nature of resources, which makes use of single ports impractical; poor port and other services; and concerns about law and order in some ports (Duncan et al. 1999).

[6] A 'back of the envelope' calculation of the proportion of the resource rent accruing to Pacific island countries is to take the estimated total access fees paid of around US$60 million in 1999 (Gillett et al. 2001) and divide by the estimated resource rent in 1996 of some US$160 million (Bertignac et al. 2000). Given the high risks associated with tuna harvesting it would be surprising if Pacific island countries were able to obtain, on a long-term basis, more than half the available resource rent in the form of access fees.

[7] As of March 2005, the republic of Korea and Chinese Taipei are the only members that are distant water fishing nations.

COMMENT

Tom Kompas

With the decline in fish stocks throughout the world, fisheries management has drawn severe and generally justifiable criticism (Grafton et al. 2005). In this regard it is easy to be critical of fisheries policy in Pacific island states, especially with respect to the management of tuna stocks, since little effective management infrastructure exists and overfishing is widespread. However, Australia, with its own considerable resources, has not performed much better in fisheries management. In the past 10 years the Australian government has committed over US$80 million per year to fisheries research and ecologically sustainable development, undertaken substantial buybacks of fishing vessels, implemented detailed scientific fishery management plans that incorporate strong stakeholder involvement, and expanded its system of marine reserves (Grafton et al. 2005; McLoughlin and Findlay 2005). Despite such management strategies, considerable effort creep and total allowable catches that are either too large, or not binding at all, have contributed to a three-fold increase in the number of Australian Commonwealth fisheries classified as overfished in the past 10 years (Caton and McLoughlin 2004). The Eastern Tuna and Billfish Fishery itself is under extreme financial pressure with dramatically falling profits and stocks of tuna and swordfish in particular that are under threat. If Australia is struggling, what hope is there for Pacific island countries?

The paper by Parris and Grafton (2005) highlights the failure of fisheries management and the impending crisis in Pacific island fisheries, especially with regard to tuna. It is packed with insight, but the story is not a happy one. It is clear that the potential gains from Pacific island cooperation on the management of shared tuna stocks are huge, and especially so now that recent, dramatic increases in catch and declines in catch per unit of effort imply that resource rents are falling, perhaps considerably. A cooperative decrease in fishing effort and a rebuilding of fish stocks will thus result in substantial gains, with the potential for more than double the resource rent from these fisheries (Bertignac et al. 2000). This is the good news. The bad—that Parris and Grafton identify and explain—is that cooperation to this end is highly unlikely, and the failure of the recently formed *Convention on the Conservation and Management of Highly Migratory Fish Stocks in the Western and Central Pacific Ocean* (Tuna Commission) will do nothing to improve the situation. By Parris and Grafton's account, the Tuna Commission is under-resourced, to say the least, with a budget of US$1 million in 2005 and no real power or ability to enforce a stock recovery plan in any event. It has also, sadly, failed to incorporate any of the recommendations contained in Chand et al. (2003).

The difficulty is compounded since the measures needed for effective cooperation will also almost always imply relative gains and losses among Pacific island states and, more to the point, stock recovery generates a 'transitional losses' problem that is difficult to overcome in any industry or country. The rebuilding of tuna stocks requires severe cuts in catch now, and for some period of time. In addition, although the larger future resource rents that would accrue from this action would more than compensate for transitional losses—this is the nature of a move to an optimal position where resource rents are maximised—it is difficult to convince those that fish, or those that currently benefit from the fishery, that the process is worth it. Planning horizons in Pacific island nations are undoubtedly as low as they are among fishers in Australia, and no capital market or government agency is likely to fund a stock recovery program with such inherent risk of failure. If transitional losses dominate, cooperation to reduce stocks is all but impossible.

The question then arises is there a benefit to each Pacific island state from going alone in fisheries management? The answer from Parris and Grafton is no. Shared tuna stocks across Pacific island countries imply that cooperation is necessary, at least for tuna, and when it comes to other stocks of fish, local governance and management infrastructure is not up to the task, at least for the moment.

Out of exasperation, it is tempting at this point to toss one's hands in the air, and give up. Perhaps 'tuna-mining' is the best approach in this sort of world? But even here, Parris and Grafton are sceptical. They point to the low bargaining power in the Pacific with 'distant water fishing nations'—with consequent low returns in the neighbourhood of 3–4 per cent of the value of total landings by some estimates—and that rents are dissipating in any case. Indeed, even if there are sufficient rents still to be gained Parris and Grafton argue effectively for the presence of a 'resource curse' in these countries, with rents squandered in unproductive uses. If a lack of bargaining power is a problem, what about Pacific nations developing their own tuna fishing industry instead? Parris and Grafton show that under current practice, rates of return for domestic fishers are low if not negative. A domestic industry, as it currently stands, thus cannot hope to extract resource rents with a positive return, much less compete with the gains achieved by 'distant water fishing nations'.

What is the solution? Parris and Grafton argue for greater efforts at reducing harvest through multinational institutions and the transferability of harvesting rights across nations, on the one hand, and the creation of trust funds for fishing access fees to limit the squandering of rents through corruption and misappropriation on the other. All this is good, but what do Pacific states do before this can be accomplished? And can it be accomplished? In the short term, a fish cartel is one possibility, something that collectively extracts more rentals from 'distant water fishing nations', but if Pacific nations can cooperate to this extent surely they can also probably cooperate on protecting tuna stocks as well. Both are unlikely. For now, tuna-mining seems to be the only practical option for any one Pacific island state, extracting the most rents possible before the tuna fishery collapses.

What is needed from Parris and Grafton is a practical plan, something that avoids the tuna-mining trap, a plan that forms a set of policies and incentives that foster and implement the establishment of cooperation among Pacific countries to protect stocks and increase resource rents; one that also overcomes the problem with transitional losses. If properly managed, the Pacific region's tuna stocks can remain highly prized. Indeed, if properly managed, these tuna stocks can all but fully finance the economic development of many Pacific states. The challenge is to find a way to make this happen.

10

DEVELOPMENTS IN PACIFIC ISLANDS' AIR TRANSPORT

Christopher Findlay, Peter Forsyth and John King

South Pacific regional aviation has faced a range of problems for many decades. These have been documented and analysed, for example by the World Bank (1993), Forsyth and King (1996) and most recently by the Pacific Regional Transport Study (Pacific Islands Forum Secretariat 2004).

The core problem facing the Pacific region is one of low density and remoteness—the region has long thin, aviation routes, and these are inherently costly to serve. This problem of low density reflects geography, low population and the size of tourism markets. However, new developments on both the supply and demand sides of the market may offer options for challenging some of these constraints. Furthermore, there is evidence of greater interest in removing some of the policy impediments to change.

OLD PROBLEMS

In aviation, there are substantial economies of density. Larger aircraft are, per passenger, cheaper to operate. In addition, there are economies on the indirect cost side as well. Routes that serve few passengers either have to be operated by aircraft that are small and have high per passenger costs, or they can be operated with larger aircraft but only at low frequencies. Importantly, traffic is sensitive to frequency, especially business travel. At the same time, good schedules, which enable low connection times and fit in with infrastructure (such as hotel) availability, are important for tourist travel.

The overall small scale of operations means that the range of aircraft types is limited. Thus airlines tend to operate aircraft types which are suitable for some routes but not for others, for example, a mid-sized Boeing 737 may be optimal for Nadi to Wellington but when operated Nadi to Apia, it can only operate infrequently as the route lacks density.

Low density is more of a problem on routes within the region than to and from it. Inevitably, fares within the region are high relative to fares in more dense markets. In addition, several of the routes within the region are quite long, also adding to the cost. Low frequencies mean that connections are poor, making travelling around the region difficult and multiple country visits unattractive to tourists.

Low density also affects travel to the region from the Pacific Rim countries. The smaller island countries have medium-sized aircraft providing the linkage and whilst fares are reasonable for tourism markets, the airlines sustain very small fleets (Air Vanuatu and Polynesian each having only 1 jet aircraft) and thus typically provide sub-optimal schedules. Fiji has some moderately dense routes and is comparatively well served, with services in larger aircraft such as Boeing 747 or 767 aircraft, which are able to reap the economies of large-scale aircraft.

So far, there has not been much development of hub and spoke networks, especially for traffic from outside the region. Hub and spoke networks enable higher density routes, but they require good connections, high frequencies and well coordinated service, which are difficult to achieve. In addition, the length of some routes in the region lessens the advantage of hub and spoke operations over point to point services.

It can be seen there are inherent difficulties in aviation in the Pacific region: geography, population and aviation technology all make it inevitable that services are relatively high cost and inconvenient (this is true not just for aviation, but also for other aspects of transport and communications, such as shipping and telecommunications). In addition, the region is beset with a range of other obstacles. Some, though not all of these, can be addressed and include the following.

Diseconomies of small fleets

Many of the airlines in the region are very small, and operate small fleets. They are not able to gain the economies of fleet size. To serve very diverse markets they may have several aircraft types, which in turn prevents them from gaining the economies of having only one or two aircraft types. The small fleets mean that they have no back-up aircraft, contributing to unreliability of services should any aircraft be out of service.

Restricted traffic rights

International air services in the Pacific region are governed by bilateral agreements, which considerably restricts the ability of an airline based in one country to operate and market its services between other countries. Thus it may make good sense for an airline from country A to fly to C via B, but, if it cannot carry traffic from B to C, the flight may not be viable. Bilateral restrictions make it very difficult for an airline to operate a hub outside its own country. This encourages point to point services, which are less frequent and more costly.

Limited competition

The low densities on most routes make the development of strong competition unlikely. However, policy also restricts competition. As a result, airlines are less open to the threat of competition than they need be, and thus are under less pressure to perform.

Poor financial performance of airlines

Pacific airlines have long sufered financial instability. Some airlines have performed poorly for decades, leading to the cancelling of services, difficulties in funding new investment, and protectionist pressures. Most of the airlines of the region are publicly owned, but the institutional framework within which they operate is usually ill defined. Although airlines obtain financial support from their government owners, it is not on any systematic or conditional basis, often resulting in chronic underperformance, periodic crises, and occasional collapses. Crises and collapses are not unique to the South Pacific, but they are particularly costly in this region where the alternative transport options are scarce. The risk of these crises is increased by an institutional structure that does not set clear incentives to meet policy objectives, and frequently does not even have objectives.

Many of these problems have been recognised for a long time, and attempts have been make to limit them. In practice, the region's airlines have established many strategic alliances to overcome the problems of remoteness, small scale and low density (see Forsyth and King 1996). Over time, technical cooperation between airlines has developed. The airlines were early in their use of code shares and joint services to enable individual airlines to build up viable networks and schedules. As with all strategic alliances, there is a trade off between gains from greater cooperation and lessened opportunities for competition. However, cooperation between airlines has lessened the problems of their operating environment. It is possible that better institutional and ownership arrangements will encourage further cooperation and shared problem-solving.

Airport and related infrastructure is another issue confronting the Pacific island countries. As elsewhere, the problem is getting the level of investment right. Too little investment will mean inadequate infrastructure. This will impose costs on users. For example, inadequate runways will force airlines to use less suitable, higher-cost aircraft to serve a destination, or they may require airlines to operate flights less than fully loaded, leading to higher costs. Poor terminal facilities will impose costs of discomfort on passengers, and they will make it difficult to make the most of retail opportunities. On the other hand, if infrastructure is excessive, costs will be too high. Governments will have to provide subsidies to fund losses, or charges to users will be unnecessarily high. In the first instance, airlines will pay, but they will pass the higher costs on to passengers. The ultimate result is reduced opportunities for the community in which the airport is located. The issue of getting investment right has been highlighted by the growth of low-cost carriers which usually wish to make use of fairly simple but cheap terminal facilities. Some airports such as Singapore Changi, for example, are building simple, low-cost terminals to satisfy the requirements of low-cost carriers.

RECENT DEVELOPMENTS

There are important forces for change in aviation policy in the region. Conditions now are significantly different compared to those as little as two years ago, even though many of the usual problems remain.

Attitudes to financial problems are changing. In 2003, four airlines reported a combined loss of A$19.94 million and three airlines made a combined profit of A$35.34 million. Several airlines have not been profitable for some time. In 2002, five airlines made a combined loss of A$30.11 million and three airlines made a combined profit of A$6.11 million. In the past, governments absorbed these financial burdens, but their capacity to continue doing so has declined. The recent shutdown of Royal Tongan and the restructuring of Polynesian Airlines are illustrations of the tightening budget constraints.

Donors also now say they are reluctant to continue to provide support to economies of the region if government budgets are run down by airline losses— a situation that contributed to support by Australia for the recent Regional Transport Study (Pacific Islands Forum Secretariat 2004).

The shift in political attitude to the airline positions was reinforced in August 2004 when Forum Leaders adopted a set of regional transport principles, a theme of which is a commitment to commercial orientation and good governance in airline operations and related infrastructure. These principles are listed in an appendix to this chapter.

Another development is the design of a new region-wide air services agreement (Pacific Islands Air Services Agreement), currently being adopted but yet to be ratified and implemented (a minimum of 6 ratifications is required, and this target is expected to be achieved, although debate on the policy will continue between the signature and ratification points in the participating economies).

Further drivers of policy change come from the markets themselves. The level of competition on routes to the region has increased as a consequence of the entry of so-called 'low-cost carriers', such as Pacific Blue and Freedom Air. Implementation of the bilateral agreements on market access in the region has been flexible, as illustrated by introduction of these new opportunities, as well as a long history of various forms of inter-airline cooperation in the region. However, higher levels of competition on routes to the region make it more difficult to sustain profits, which offset losses on other services within the region. This also adds to the budget pressure on governments who want to sustain their own airline.

Expectations imposed on the airlines often extend beyond flying operations. They are expected to provide services which support other sectors of their economies (tourism for instance), maintain connectivity within economies by offering services to remote areas, and to maintain connectivity within the group of economies as a whole. In some cases, they also serve to support the nation status of their home economy. Many of these concerns are acute for smaller economies. But, as noted, the capacity to reach this mix of policy targets is challenged by developments in the market place.

Another change, on the supply side, is the development of new aircraft technology that offers options for jet services of 30–90 seats. Smaller jet (rather than turbo-propelled) aircraft operate at higher frequency (to which travel demand responds significantly in other markets) than offered by the mid-sized jets currently employed, offering new opportunities for developing routes within the region. Industry observers are cautiously optimistic about the prospects for the introduction of these aircraft in the region.

Expectations are now widely held for growth of tourist traffic from Asia—China and India in particular—to the Pacific region. While some economies in the region welcome the prospect of rapidly rising tourist numbers, others are concerned about the impacts on local economies. The very small economies, who offer highly differentiated and distinct holiday experiences, often based on environmental features, are concerned about their ability to sustain their position in the market at the same time as establishing links with these increasingly important origin countries.

There may be returns from working together on developing strategies for the new Asian markets. This could include sharing information on forecasts, identifying the services likely to be sought, analysing options for meeting the demand, reviewing programs in training institutions, and noting the role of foreign investment, including the hotel sector and perhaps from the home countries of the visitors.

Cooperative work in this area should add to policy advisors' capacity to make assessments of the implications of tourism industry measures, including a variety of both taxes and subsidies, as well as other regulatory measures. This includes a deeper understanding of the role of, costs of support for, and protection of, airline operators for tourism industry development.

In this chapter we offer an extensive discussion of four policy related aspects of this set of issues, namely, the impact of the Pacific Islands Air Services Agreement, the entry of low-cost carriers, the moves to privatisation and the questions of infrastructure development. We conclude with some remarks on what we regard as the key elements of the policy agenda in this sector for Forum island countries.

PACIFIC ISLANDS AIR SERVICES AGREEMENT (PIASA)

The Pacific Islands Air Services Agreement was developed at the request of Pacific islands forum Ministers in 1998 and was finally endorsed for signature at the 2003 Pacific Forum Leaders meeting. Its objectives were to establish a framework for a transition to a 'single market'. Six parties must ratify the agreement before it comes into force. Five nations (Samoa, Tonga, Nauru, Vanuatu and Cook Islands) have so far signed the agreement and one more economy is expected to join that group shortly. The critical issue is the non-adherence to the agreement by Fiji.

The Pacific Islands Air Services Agreement is more liberal than many other plurilateral agreements, especially in its treatment of designation (the equivalent in this setting of trade in services as a rule of origin for trade in goods). A better specified accession clause would add to the agreement's degree of openness.

The Forum island countries agreed that it was desirable to open their own markets before integration with other countries, although the parties may agree to extend the agreement to others subject to further negotiation and to the consent of all members. The terms of accession are therefore in the hands of the current membership, rather than being specified at the foundation of the agreement and there is the risk that the current membership, at some point, will decide to close the membership in order to limit the competitive effects of further entry.

Rather than being subject to the consent of all existing parties, a more liberal form of this clause would be to say that the members are obliged to accept new members as long as they meet the same conditions as existing members.

The Air Services Agreement is to be implemented in three phases. The first phase commences six months after the agreement comes into force and liberalises the third, fourth and sixth 'freedoms' (that is, services between the parties—see Table 10.1). In the second phase, starting at 12 months, the fifth 'freedoms' amongst the parties are liberalised. Thirty months after the agreement comes into force, the fifth freedoms on routes to non-members of the agreement are open to all member airlines (subject to the bilateral agreements with the non-member states). Australia and New Zealand may accede to the agreement only at the beginning of the third phase. Wet leasing (of aircraft and crew) is permitted and there is no price regulation. However, domestic services (rights of cabotage) are excluded.

The terms of designation (of airlines with access to the terms of the agreement) vary between the stages of implementation. In the first stage, designated airlines must be 'substantially owned and effectively controlled by one or more of the Parties to the Agreement and/or their nationals'. This clause is relatively liberal since, even though it imposes the usual ownership and control clause, it also permits accumulation of ownership shares among the members.

The first stage also allows for the case where the ownership of the airline shifts outside the parties: an airline can be designated as long as it is then 'effectively controlled' by the parties and has its principal place of business in the territory of the designating party. Further, if the party does not own/control an airline when the agreement comes into force, it can designate another which has its principal place of business in the territory of the party.

These clauses are especially relevant as countries within the Pacific region effectively designate foreign-owned carriers to operate on their routes. For example, the restructuring of Polynesian Airlines has led to the establishment of a new airline—Polynesian Blue—a joint venture with Virgin Blue but majority owned by Polynesian interests (49 per cent by the government, 2 per cent by a local investor). The new airline (to be operated by Pacific Blue out of New Zealand) will take over the international routes of the previous Polynesian Airlines while the latter will retain its turbo-prop regional operations.

From stage 3, designation is even more liberal. A designated airline can meet either the ownership and control clause of the principal place of business test. These terms of designation not only reduce barriers to entry, they also make it easier for airlines in the region to be consolidated without losing their rights of market access. In the third stage, equity funding can also be raised from outside the region and the rights of market access maintained, as long as the airline is based in a designating party.

The agreement refers to various 'business' and competition policy matters. It is important to treat these matters explicitly in the absence of other institutions to respond to complaints by an airline located in one party about actions of another party.

The rights of designated airlines to set up offices, bring in staff, do their own ground-handling, sell tickets, remit currency and pay for local expenses in local currency are identified. User charges for airport services, air navigation and security 'may reflect, but shall not exceed, the full cost' and should not be discriminatory.

An article on pricing allows governments—on behalf of their designated airlines—to complain about discriminatory practices, abuse of a dominant

Table 10.1   Freedoms of the air

First freedom
The grant by country A to country B, for country B's airlines to fly over country A's territory without landing.

Second freedom
The grant by country A to country B, for country B's airlines to land in A's territory for non-traffic purposes (eg refuelling, aircraft maintenance).

Third freedom
The grant by country A to country B, for country B's airlines to carry traffic from B to A.

Fourth freedom
The grant by country A to country B, for country B's airlines to carry traffic from A to B.

Fifth freedom
The grant by country A to country B, for country B's airlines to carry traffic between country A and any other country, provided that the flight is part of a service that originate or terminates in country B's territory.

Sixth freedom
The grant by country A to country B, for country B's airlines to carry traffic between A and any other country via a point in B's territory.

Note: The sixth freedom is a combination of a third and fourth right (for example, see below)

A   X   B

Passengers from A to B via X on a carrier designated by X is travelling on a fourth freedom service from A to X and a third freedom from X to B. Sixth freedom traffic is assumed and not specifically negotiated.

position, as well as direct or indirect subsidies. Other items for complaint are fares below cost or the addition of 'excessive capacity or frequency', as long as these practices are sustained rather than temporary, cause 'significant economic damage' and have the 'apparent intent or probable effect' of driving another airline from the market.

Disputes are resolved by setting up a panel, drawing on a list of experts maintained by the International Civil Aviation Organisation (but according to rules and principles that the parties agree when they set up the panel, for example, on the question of whether the panel's decision is binding or whether they seek a resolution of facts).

The Air Services Agreement has been the subject of much discussion in the Pacific region. The most recent assessment was reported in the Pacific Regional

Transport Study (PRTS) in which the study team argued that an important reason for supporting a regional agreement was that it would add to the pool of potential entrants to routes within the region (a very high proportion of which are currently served by only one carrier). The transport study also noted some points to be clarified in the Pacific Islands Air Services Agreement text but concluded that

> ...considerable effort has been made recently in negotiating a Pacific Islands Air Services Agreement (PIASA). Whilst it has support from most FICs there are some reservations notably from Fiji. There are also certain points that may require clarification. Given the resources that have gone into PIASA the study team recommended the following:
>
> *Recommendation R2:* Pacific Forum Members should renew efforts to obtain a workable and strengthened Pacific Islands Air Services Agreement (PIASA) that is supported by all countries in the region. Negotiations to achieve a workable agreement should be conducted through the PIF.

The study team further recommends that Forum island countries examine the option of negotiating an agreement that would expand cabotage to a regional concept.

A significant group of Forum countries is interested in joining the agreement. Their participation may provide them with some important 'first mover' advantages in more open markets in the region. It is possible that new hubs will emerge, perhaps at Apia in Samoa to the West or Port Vila in Vanuata to the East, whose role would be supported by an arrangement which included those points.

Fiji is currently the central node of the regional network. This gives its carrier substantial advantage. The agreement opens the scope for restructuring the networks and therefore challenges Fiji's position.

Figures 10.1 and 10.2 show the route structure into the Pacific island region and within the region respectively. The figures show the key role now played by Fiji, supported by its location. Figure 10.3 shows the traffic volumes to selected destinations from Australia: Fiji data are plotted against the left-hand scale and all others against the right.

These data suggest that Fiji is in a strong bargaining position. Competition from other destinations may eventually draw Fiji into the agreement, and the most likely competitor is now Samoa (discussed further below). In the shorter term, however, negotiation to encourage Fiji's entry is likely to be more effective than competition for that purpose. Options for designation of the Fiji based

Figure 10.1   Routes to the Pacific region

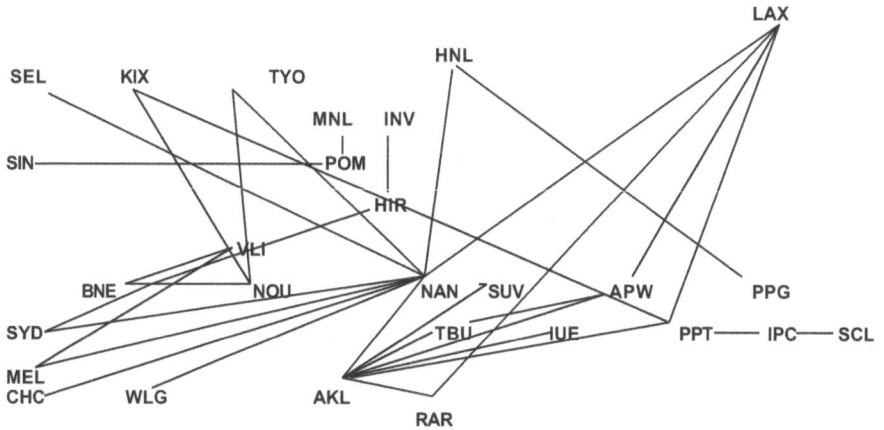

Figure 10.2   Routes within the Pacific region

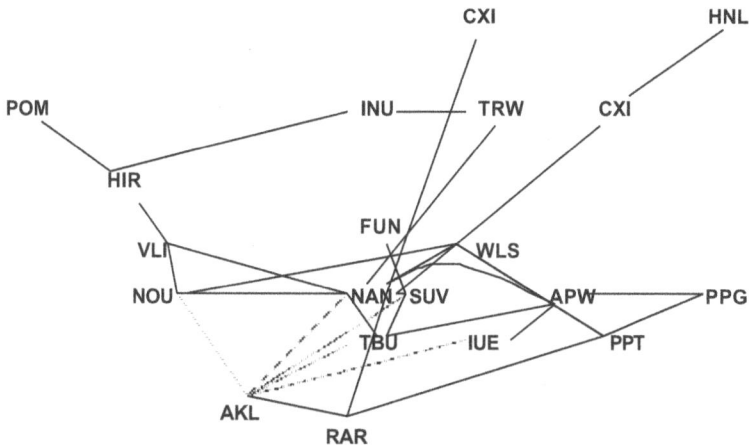

airline, Air Pacific, by other countries in the region which is possible under the terms of a strengthened Pacific Islands Air Services Agreement are some of the talking points that may draw Fiji into the agreement. 'Outer' countries, like the Cook Islands or Vanuatu may be candidates for such discussions. Also of interest is that the Solomon Islands (not yet a signatory to the agreement) has

Figure 10.3   Outbound monthly passengers from Australia

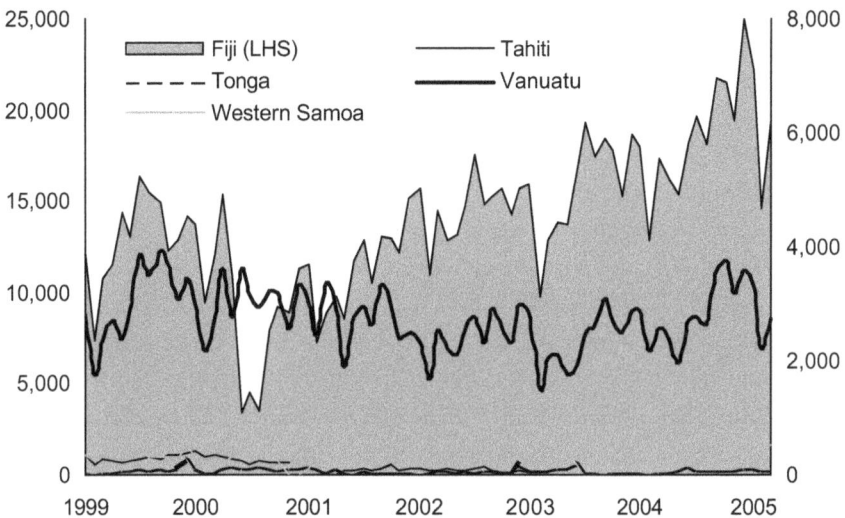

Source: Bureau of Transport and Regional Economics, 2003. *International City Pairs Time Series 1999–Current*, Department of Transport and Regional Services, Canberra. Available from http://www.btre.gov.au/statistics/aviation/international_time_series_downloads.aspx.

already designated Air Vanuatu on limited routes and has wet-chartered aircraft on the Australia route from both Air Vanuatu and Air Nauru.

No significant empirical study of the costs and benefits of the Pacific Islands Air Services Agreement, based on its text, has yet been made. Work of that type in the context of various scenarios for industry development (such as tourism growth outlooks, the impact of new technology, the effects of operations by low-cost carriers, for example) would assist the policy debate in the region, and help develop the arguments for Fijian participation. AusAID is now funding such a study.

The sorts of effects which might be examined in this study have been identified in early work by the Productivity Commission (Gregan and Johnson 1999) on the effects on competition of this type of plurilateral agreement. The effects could be significant, and not just within the networks affected. There are gains, first, from the effects on competition within the network covered by the club, contributing both to lower margins over costs and also to a movement of actual costs closer to the 'frontier' levels. Second, cost savings are available within the membership from new options for network design, including new hub points. These advantages also spill over into higher levels of competitiveness on routes not covered by the club agreement.

Regulatory reform within a route (even though barriers to entry by third parties remain) can have significant effects on performance. Micco and Serebrisky (2004) examine the determinants of air freight rates on routes to and from the United States. As they explain, during the 1990s, the United States implemented a series of Open Skies agreements (which liberalise entry and capacity of carriers eligible for designation). They examined air freight rates on routes with and without such agreements and found that the agreements reduced costs by 8 per cent. However, they also found that other policy-related variables were more significant influences on performance, such as infrastructure capacity and quality of regulation. In their sample 'an improvement in airport infrastructure from the 25th to 75th percentiles reduce(d) air transport costs by 15 percent. A similar improvement in the quality of regulation reduce(d) air transport costs by 14 percent.'

There is value in documenting how implementation of the Pacific Islands Air Services Agreement affects participants and non-menbers in the region. Similar agreements in the rest of the world have been difficult to implement, and a dialogue on that experience would be valuable, perhaps begining with a review of experience in Africa and South America. The ASEAN economies are also considering a similar approach to reform of aviation arrangements.

In a related development, a couple of the Pacific Islands Air Services Agreement members have also joined the Multilateral Agreement on the Liberalization of International Air Transportation (MALIAT), current membership of which is Singapore, New Zealand, United States, Chile, Brunei, Samoa and Tonga (see http://www.maliat.govt.nz). Parties to the agreement have the rights to unlimited capacity for their designated airlines on routes among the members. This creates, for example, the opportunity for an airline designated by Samoa under the agreement to fly across the Pacific to the United States or to Chile, also with links in the other direction to Singapore (the latter potentially being an important gateway for Asian tourism growth into the region). This option, plus the recent restructuring of Polynesian Airlines by Virgin Blue bolsters the options for Samoa to emerge as a competitor hub for Fiji in the region, though its easterly geographic position limits the network options.

LOW-COST CARRIERS

Low-cost carriers are now operating on routes to Fiji, Cook Islands and Vanuatu. Recent developments are summarised in Table 10.2.

Ergas and Findlay (2004a) suggest some key differences in the business model implemented by low-cost carriers (or 'value-based airlines' as they call them):

> Firstly, value based airlines usually have lower costs than full service carriers. Their business model is based on features such as the use of online reservation systems, the development of star-structured networks (that is, point to point, short haul operations) with a simple fleet composition, no interlining, and single class cabins. They start from a low 'greenfields' cost base and the structure of their operations is such that the turnaround times of their aircraft are typically shorter than those of full service carriers.

> Secondly, the relative simplicity of their business model also extends into the realm of pricing. While value based airlines use 'yield management' to maximise their profits, the range of fares they offer tends to be narrower than that offered by full service carriers.

> Thirdly, value based airlines also differ in the extent to which they seek to attract high yielding business travellers. Value based airlines typically adopt different business and marketing strategies (including frequencies and lounge facilities) relative to rival full service carriers, for whom attracting business travellers is particularly crucial. This is not to imply that value based airlines do not target business travellers—they must do so to be viable. But the approach they use can, and usually does, differ from that employed by full service airlines.

Ergas and Findlay (2004) argue that the competitive threat from low-cost carriers is likely to be significant. Their flat fare range means that they can discount heavily with less fear of cannibalisation of higher fare tickets. That is,

> ...the relatively flat fare ranges (of the LCCs) are equivalent to a commitment to having low opportunity costs from replacing the sale of an uncertain but potentially higher priced fare later by the sale of a certain but lower priced fare now.

On the other hand, full-service carriers as a result of their application of yield management strategies have a wider range of fares and have less incentive to engage in vigorous price competition. To some extent, they must meet the competition, but these effects limit their response and also the extent to which they can recoup contributions to common costs by charging higher fares to higher-yielding passengers.

Ergas and Findlay (2004) also explain how the value-based airlines can 'cherry pick' and earn a contribution to common costs from customers who can be

Table 10.2   Low-cost carriers' Pacific entry and capacity

Carrier			Initial weekly frequency	Initial weekly capacity	Subsequent weekly frequency	Subsequent weekly capacity	Effective date of change
	Route (all return)	Entry					
Virgin Blue/Pacific Blue							
ex Australia	MEL–VLI	Aug-04	1	180	-	-	May-05
	BNE–VLI	Aug-04	1	180	2	360	May-05
	BNE–NAD	Sep-04	3	540	4	720	May-05
	SYD–NAD	Jun-05	4	720	4	720	n.a.
	MEL–NAD	Sep-04	3	540	3	540	n.a.
ex New Zealand	CHC–RAR	Nov-04	1	180	1	180	n.a.
Freedom Air	HLZ–NAD	Apr-03	1	142	2	284	Apr-05
	PMR–NAD	Apr-03	1	142	2	284	Apr-05
	CHC–NAD	Apr-03	1	142	2*	284	Apr-05
	WLG–NAD	Feb-04	2	284	4	284	Apr-05

Note: *Supplemental services CHC–NAD return 10–24 July.

attracted by lower fares without the package of services that the full service carriers provide.

Air Pacific (on routes to Fiji) responded to low-cost carrier competition by changing its fare structure before the entry of Pacific Blue. Table 10.3 shows the fares from Australia to Fiji (similar changes occurred in fares for travel in the reverse direction). Fares were reduced prior to entry, and by a larger proportional amount for 'initiative fares'. The more open fares received different degrees of discount. 'Top' level fares, on the other hand, increased (a negative sign in the percentage change column indicates an increase).

The experience on routes to Vanuatu was different to that on routes to Fiji. The Air Vanuatu fare structure (other than business class and the little used full economy fare) were 'inclusive tour' fares requiring a bundling of air and ground content. When Pacific Blue commenced operations with its point-to-point unbundled fares, Air Vanuatu responded by introducing unbundled excursion fares for the general public and by establishing volume discounts for tour operators. The fences around 'inclusive tour' fares mean that it is very difficult to compare the fares in the two periods (pre and post Virgin Blue), other than to say that the cost to travellers has fallen, as have yields to Air Vanuatu.

Table 10.3   Air Pacific fares from Australia to Fiji (return economy, A$)

	Pre June–04 (A)	Air Pacific initiated— June 2004 (pre-Pacific Blue)	% decrease vs (A)	NOW (post-Pacific Blue)	% Decrease vs (A)
BNE–NAN					
Initiative*	499	368	26	338	32
Bottom#	836	368	56	368	56
Middle#	887	788	11	788	11
Top#	989	1028	–4	1028	–4
MEL–NAN					
Initiative*	599	498	17	458	24
Bottom#	887	498	44	498	44
Middle#	938	888	5	888	5
Top#	1040	1208	–16	1208	–16

Traffic volumes to Fiji and Vanuatu are shown in Figures 10.4 and 10.5 respectively (these are extracted from Figure 10.3). A vertical line marks the starting date of the low-cost carrier services. Both series show higher peak traffic volumes following low-cost carrier entry (based on the previous two peak values: values in trough months appear to lie on the same trend as previous values). Also of interest is that the usual mid-year peaks in traffic to Fiji appear to have been delayed by expectations of low-cost carrier entry. The significance of the impact of low-cost carrier entry on total traffic volumes is less clear and a more powerful test depends on access to a longer timeseries.

As suggested by the fare data in Table 10.3, there were different patterns of response by incumbent carriers. The capacity of Air Pacific remained the same following low-cost carrier entry and the airline also managed to maintain its traffic (based on comparisons of data in each month in the 2004–05 period compared to the same month in the 2003–04 period). The low-cost carrier, once established, carried 15–18 per cent of traffic each month (about the same as its capacity share).

On routes to Vanuatu from Australia, the incumbent appears to have increased capacity following entry but then returned to the original level of capacity after five months. After increasing capacity, it carried about the same

Figure 10.4   Traffic volume to Fiji from Australia

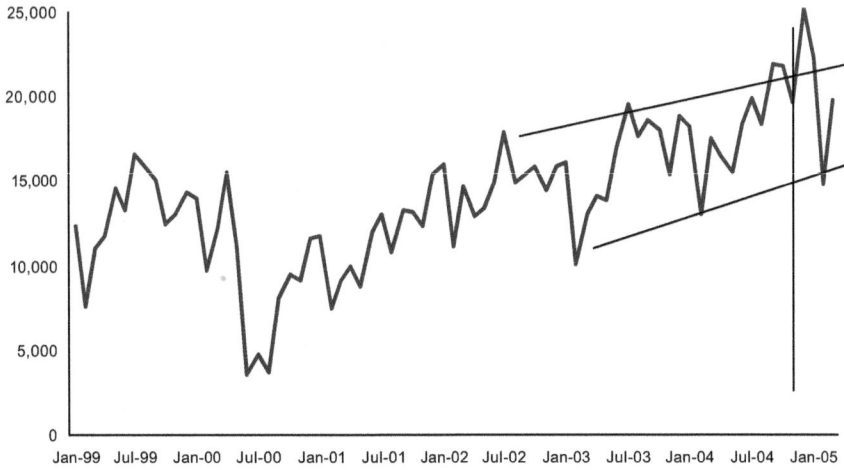

Figure 10.5   Traffic volume to Vanuatu from Australia

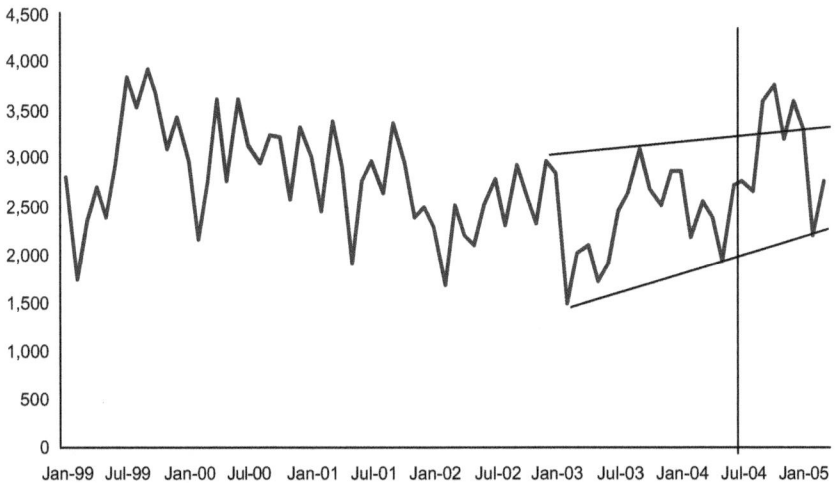

Source: Bureau of Transport and Regional Economics, 2003. *International city pairs time series 1999–current.* Department of Transport and Regional Services, Canberra. Available from http://www.btre.gov.au/statistics/aviation/international_time_series_downloads.aspx.

number of passengers as in the same period a year earlier but then its traffic numbers increased in February and March 2005. It has, however, maintained its market share at 73–75 per cent throughout this period.

The discussion of the low-cost carriers' impact, so far, has concentrated on the impact on routes to and from the region. Questions remain about the scope for low-cost carriers to operate within the region. Some of the uncertainties include the following.

- The same problems that have inhibited development within the region also constrain the low-cost carrier operators, such as geography and density, although higher traffic volumes based on Asian tourism may relax some of these constraints.
- The Pacific Islands Air Services Agreement offers options for building new networks, but the absence of Fiji, with its traffic volumes, weakens the business case for low-cost carriers' entry.
- New aircraft options, such as regional jets, may relax some of the constraints, but those aircraft are reported to have relatively high costs per seat/km (on the other hand, lower-cost turbo-prop aircraft favoured by some regional airlines have other disadvantages on the relatively long haul routes in this region).

If the low-cost carriers aggressively seek market share, they will put considerable pressure on fare levels, and could lead to a boom in travel. It is not clear, however, whether this strategy is sustainable in the long run. Alternatively, they may seek to gain a small but stable share of a profitable market. To do so, they will need to schedule a small amount of extra capacity, and cut fares to a limited extent.

The experience of Virgin Blue may provide some guidance. At different stages in its past, Virgin Blue was an aggressive competitor, increasing its scheduled capacity quite rapidly. In the past year, however, it has retreated from this strategy, and become much more cautious. It is likely that Pacific Blue will also exhibit this caution. Thus vigorous price wars, such as those that occur in the United States and Europe, are not likely be present in the South Pacific. The growth of low-cost carrier traffic is likely to be more measured (which would be in keeping with the tourism infrastructure constraints in most countries of the region).

Thus, overall, the introduction of low-cost carriers does contribute a little to resolving the old problems facing the region. For those countries that have a route density sufficient to attract low-cost carriers, lower fares and greater traffic flows will lessen their degree of remoteness. Smaller tourism destinations, which are not able to attract low-cost carrier services, are not likely to be much helped. Furthermore, the introduction of low-cost carriers is not likely to make much difference to routes within the region. Low-cost models for low density, long routes have not yet been developed, and it has yet to be seen if they are feasible. As is now the case in other regions such as Southeast Asia, the presence of low-cost carriers actively seeking access to routes will put pressure on the regulation of international aviation. Current regulations limit their development, and the success of low-cost carriers on the routes they are allowed to fly on raises questions about the wisdom of restricting their access to other routes.

PRIVATE EQUITY

Airlines in the region are unlikely to be able to survive the competitive pressures that now apply without further injections of equity. Governments will not be able to provide the funding required (or may do so only at high opportunity cost), so their operation depends on private equity. Sources of equity within the region are not likely to be sufficient, and foreign investment will most likely be sought. These considerations are already evident in the process of sale of Polynesian Airlines, discussed above.

The opportunities for foreign investors to enter the markets are limited by current rules on ownership and control in the bilateral agreements. Exploring new rules on ownership that will work within the region and that will be accepted by partners outside the region is a priority. Some options are available from the International Civil Aviation Organization and from the consideration of similar issues in other sectors by the World Trade Organization (in the context of the GATS negotiations). The Pacific Islands Air Services Agreement too has options for relaxing rules on ownership and control some time after implementation, as already noted.

Higher levels of private ownership have the advantage prompting efficiency gains in airline operations and establishing a commercial focus in decision-making. This has implications for market performance and the nature of competition in regional markets. It has implications for incentives for cooperation among airlines. It was observed that airline cooperation driven by markets was more likely to be successful than that established by committees of governments. The experience of mixtures of competition and cooperation among airlines in other markets is of interest in the transition to higher levels of private (from within and from outside the region) ownership and control.

A further implication of a tighter commercial focus in airlines' boards and managements will be a resistance to meeting obligations imposed by government, to provide particular services for example, without compensation. The immediate policy challenge is to design and implement systems of decision-making on the extent of support for network development in the region. Options for taking competitive bids on meeting these targets should also be explored. Techniques for subjecting the proposals to studies of their costs and benefits should also be developed.

Just as private participation in airport infrastructure requires consideration of complementary regulatory reform, so higher levels of private participation in airline operations require consideration of new ways to meet community expectations of service standards.

One of the more important aspects concerns operation of developmental and remote or low-density routes. Several of the routes that the South Pacific airlines fly are apparently loss-making and airlines cross-subsidise these from their profitable routes, such as those to the Pacific Rim countries. Private operators are much less likely to be willing to cross-subsidise chronic loss-making routes than publicly owned airlines; indeed, their ability to do so could be much reduced by competition from low-cost carriers on hitherto profitable routes. Governments that wish to continue to ensure that these community service routes be served will have to make alternative arrangements to subsidise them. This problem has been faced by many countries, such as Australia, and European regions, that have opened up their airline markets to competition. There is now a growing fund of experience on which the Pacific nations can draw (see ICAO 2005).

Mention has already been made of the opportunities emerging from the availability of new small jet aircraft. Questions remain about the corporate structure in which new services might be provided, and whether they are best installed through existing operators or whether (as evident in other markets) they are managed efficiently in separate corporate structures. If the latter, further questions emerge about the recognition of new operators under air services agreements in the region. Some structures for the adoption of this new technology hinge on access to various 'capacity sharing' models—for example, one suggestion is that aircraft operations be provided by a business which is separate from marketing (so each airline buys the capacity it requires from the operating company). Options such as this should be tested in the marketplace, and not adopted by regulation.

A complementary activity to both the assessment of support for community services, and to the examination of new corporate structures associated with technological change, could be the consolidation of data in the region on the existing networks. This would provide opportunities for various parties to undertake an assessment of the gaps in connectivity in the region. There are interests in this matter in both the public and private sectors.

AIRPORT INFRASTRUCTURE

The traditional approach to supply of airport and other aviation infrastructure has been for the government to provide and operate the infrastructure directly itself. This is usually, though not always on a cost-recovery basis. Ideally, when new investment to expand or improve capacity is proposed, the government will undertake an assessment, such as a cost–benefit analysis, and determine whether the benefits exceed the costs. If they do, it will proceed with the development, ensuring that infrastructure is neither inadequate nor excessive.

In reality, matters are often not so straightforward. Sometimes assessments will indicate that investments are well worthwhile, but funding limitations will delay or prohibit investment. Airports are often regarded as prestige projects, and governments will make investments that create too much capacity, and create facilities that are excessively lavish. Such investments will lead to the airport being costly to finance and operate and the government may later be faced with a funding crisis, or the airport may be forced to set high charges.

The emerging model in the provision of airport infrastructure is for greater participation by the private sector. This participation can happen in varying degrees. Airlines, for example, might operate, and own or lease, terminals. Non-airline firms, including other airports, may own and operate terminals. Alternatively, an airport might be corporatised—retained in public ownership, but required to operate under commercial principles. At the extreme, the airport as a whole might be privatised, either by sale to strategic investors or by floatation on the stock market.

There are several advantages in private involvement (these are similar to those noted above, in the context of airlines). Private investors will have a keen interest in cost efficiency, since their profitability depends on it. Some private investors may have more ready access to funds for investment—this is especially relevant for Pacific island countries, whose governments may have difficulty in funding large new investments. Private investors may also be more innovative—for example, they may be able to make more out of the airport's prospects in retail.

The disadvantage is that airports often possess considerable market power, and the private owners will have every incentive to use this power. They will set prices very high, since they will be unchecked by competition. Governments normally recognise this, and handle it by regulation. Thus, in the United Kingdom, when the London airports were privatised, the government set in operation a price-cap system of price regulation. The same happened when Australia privatised its airports, though Australia has since moved to a system of price monitoring with a threat of regulation should the airports be shown to be abusing their market power. New Zealand also has a system of imposing a threat of regulation on the airports, though there is no explicit monitoring.

While regulation can resolve the market power issue, it comes at a price. In particular, regulation tends to distort the incentives for investment. That is, regulation which is effectively cost-based will give rise to excessive investment—airport corporations will be willing to invest excessively, since they are able to pass on excess costs to their customers. Price-cap systems of regulation, which consist of specifying, for an extended period, a maximum price that the corporation can charge, can give rise to inadequate investment. Additional investment will result in higher costs for the airport, but will not yield any additional revenue, since prices are capped. Even when a rigid price cap is not imposed, inadequate investment may be the result of a slow regulatory process, with the regulator being unwilling to approve price increases proposed by the firm to fund investment because it is sceptical of the firm's need to invest or increase prices. Problems of inadequate investment in Australia's infrastructure have been blamed on the regulatory process (Exports and Infrastructure Taskforce 2005).

Whichever direction is chosen by the Pacific island countries, there will be issues to be resolved. If government access to funds for investment is not a problem, continued public ownership and operation is feasible. Governments that own airports will need to give attention to the incentives they are given to keep costs down, and the incentives they are given to assess potential investments rigorously, and only invest in worthwhile projects.

Alternatively, if countries go down the path of greater private involvement, they will have to come to an explicit resolution of the regulatory issues. The Pacific island countries do not have much by way of regulatory expertise or experience, and setting up extensive regulatory structures, such as those that exist in Australia or the United Kingdom is not likely to be feasible. It may be feasible to develop simple regulatory structures for airports and other aviation infrastructure that is privatised. Alternatively, when assets or whole airports are privatised, the government may be able to restrain the use of market power by imposing conditions in the contract of sale. Certainly, if airports or related assets are privatised without any attention to the market power issues, it is likely that private investors will press governments to accept excessive investment, since the greater the investment, the greater the profits. This will lead to higher user charges and damage to the country's tourism industry.

CONCLUSION

Geography and population conspire against airline development. There is a familiar list of problems which previous research has identified. That work has also made the point that regulation and policy have made the situation worse.

There are signs, however, of fundamental change in progress, including a lower tolerance for intervention and the financial burdens it creates. New options for doing business are emerging, and some economies, particularly the outer islands, have taken or look likely to take new options for designation of international operations. There are also new technological options, which might make a difference to the economics of high frequency operations, although uncertainties remain in that respect.

Developments of the system within the region are more difficult to anticipate, but progress to higher density and more competitive markets hinges on additions to capacity on the entry and exit routes to the region, and on increasing traffic coming into the region. The stage is already set for that development with the emergence of the low-cost carriers, the introduction of the Pacific Islands Air Services Agreement, plus the emergence of the model of Polynesian Blue.

The next breakthrough would be the entry of Fiji into an integrated regional market, with scope for accession to the arrangement by countries outside the foundation membership. Fiji has been resisting, but there are scenarios in which Fiji would find it advantageous to join the arrangement.

APPENDIX

PACIFIC ISLANDS FORUM
DRAFT DECLARATION OF PRINCIPLES ON REGIONAL
TRANSPORT SERVICES
APIA, 6 AUGUST 2004

Recognising that
- the provision and maintenance of regular, reliable and competitive air and shipping services is crucial to Forum island countries;
- changes in the transport sector, including an increasingly competitive market and new international safety and security requirements, have significant implications for aviation and shipping in the Pacific region; and
- Forum island countries have limited technical capacity;

Pacific Island Forum leaders declare the following principles as central to improving the efficiency, effectiveness and sustainability of air and shipping services:

1 Adherence to principles of good governance is crucial to the viability and sustainability of transport services. This includes, but is not limited to:
   a) accountability and transparency in financial management, strategic planning, investment decisions, awarding contracts, and board appointments;
   b) clear lines of responsibility for shareholders, boards and management; and
   c) accessing and acting upon professional advice, including in relation to decisions on infrastructure.

2 Transport services should, wherever possible, be run on a sustainable commercial basis.
   a) Where appropriate, this should include corporatisation and/or privatisation of government-owned services.
   b) Where transport entities remain in government ownership and are required to perform commercial activities, such entities should be adequately capitalised.
   c) Service levels should reflect demand and price should reflect the cost of delivery.

d) Where subsidies are judged to be necessary to fulfil declared social obligations, these should be open and transparent.

e) Where appropriate, legislated monopolies should be removed with a view to increasing competition.

3 A central responsibility of government in the transport sector should be in establishing and administering regulatory systems.

4 Increased efforts should be made to implement regional or sub-regional solutions to problems in the transport sector through, for example

a) strategic alliances

b) liberalisation of the economic regulatory environment

c) agreement by FICs to regional cabotage, where FICs could benefit from more services and greater competition

d) coordinated approaches to safety and security issues

e) better coordinated airline schedules

f) training and capacity building.

5 Forum member countries need to comply with internationally accepted standards on aviation and maritime security.

6 Donor support should be provided to Forum Island Countries to assist the implementation of transport sector reforms, conditional on a demonstrated commitment to good governance and economically sustainable solutions.

COMMENT

David Barber

Improvements in air transport are critical to further Pacific integration. With few exceptions, airline operations in the Pacific are marginal, mostly reliant on government funding and expatriate pilots, managers and engineers. The chapter by Findlay, Forsyth and King provides a useful summary of the intrinsic problems and governance constraints limiting reform of the aviation sector in the Pacific.

Many of these issues are long-standing and well-known. Some constraints are inherently difficult to address—such as remoteness, scale and thinness of routes—but constraints of distance and scale cannot alone explain the ongoing problems of Pacific aviation.

As the authors note, there have been examples of regional resource sharing through code share and other cooperative arrangements but often these have been reactive rather than proactive, or in some cases designed to curtail competition. To date, a regional airline has not been successful simply because of the conflict between commercial objectives and member states' expectations regarding the level of service delivery.

Improved technology (such as more appropriate jet aircrafts) is likely to have an impact on efficiency through a significant reduction in unit operating costs. But technology options are expensive and, realistically, available to only a few Pacific carriers.

Clearly broad issues of governance combined with policy inertia are major limitations to greater integration through reform of the aviation sector. The paper identifies a number of areas, including regional aviation agreements/ traffic rights, financial management and privatisation, where progress has been slow to occur. Indeed the level of government involvement in the sector is perhaps the most critical reform issue. Currently, in many island states, government has a role as both operator and as a regulator of aviation, creating a potential for conflict of interest.

If, as the authors indicate, there are opportunities for improvements in efficiency, why is there policy inertia and lack of commitment to genuine reform? Why is there not more regional integration or sharing of resources? Fundamentally, it seems many small island governments do not understand the industry well and/or obtain most of their advice from their airlines. Hence, there are deeply held concerns about the impact of reforms. While there have been many studies of the sector's problems there has been little quantitative analysis of potential winners and losers including in related sectors such as tourism. There are also legitimate concerns about adequacy of service and probably still some issues of nationalism.

The aviation industry is full of optimists. Despite the perennial problems, there is always a new entrant seeking to enter the market. Competition from low-cost carriers and pressures for rationalisation will continue. Most of the changes that have occurred in the sector have been market driven. Change can be managed. The least effective solution is to resist change.

11

PREFERENCE EROSION: THE CASE OF FIJI SUGAR

Satish Chand

Preference erosion refers to a situation where exporters with privileged access to specific markets lose their competitive advantage as barriers to trade in their export markets are lowered to third-country exporters. The case considered here is that of sugar exports from Fiji into the European Union under the Sugar Protocol. Exports of specified quantities of raw sugar from the African, Caribbean and Pacific (ACP) states to the European Community under the Cotonou Agreement enjoy guaranteed prices some two to three times the world market price. Preference erosion is a concern for the African, Caribbean and Pacific states given the impending liberalisation of the EU sugar regime. The decision in favour of the complainants, namely Australia, Brazil and Thailand, by the WTO panel on export subsidies to sugar by the EU could increase the pace of reform within the European Union and consequently accelerate the pace of preference erosion for the African, Caribbean and Pacific states.

Preference erosion is a serious issue for a number of developing countries. Yamazaki (1996), for example, notes that preferential imports into the European Union, United States, and Japan in 1992 accounted for 12 per cent of the total value of imports. The European Union as a destination and sugar as a product feature heavily in these discussions—the European Union, according to Yamazaki (1996), accounted for 73 per cent of the aggregate value of preferences, while sugar alone accounted for 46 per cent of the preference margin. Amongst the beneficiaries of preferential arrangements, Mauritius has consistently topped the list, with earnings from preferential access to its sugar exports into the European Union over the 2000–01 period amounting to 2.7 times what it would have earned if sold at the world market price; Fiji ranked eighth with earnings nearly double the value at world market prices (figures from Alexandria and Lankes 2004:Table 11.1).[1] A number of studies confirm that the benefits of preferences are highly concentrated within a relatively small group of economies, thus the problems of preference erosion are, therefore, likely to be equally concentrated (Hoekman and Ozden 2005). As a result, reforms to the European Union's sugar regime have the potential to draw significant interest from the WTO members who are likely to lose out in the process.

Fiji is particularly vulnerable to preference erosion. Sugar is a large sector that, as of 2001, accounted for some 7 per cent of GDP, 9 per cent of government revenues, 22 per cent of total exports, and the livelihood of nearly a quarter of the total population (Prasad and Narayan 2004). According to Page (2004), who draws on IMF estimates, a 40 per cent reduction in preference margins as a result of multilateral tariff reduction will result in a deterioration in the terms of trade of 8 percentage points for Fiji. An abrupt end to the sugar-preferences is likely to impose significant adjustment costs on the domestic economy, including a severe economic contraction, loss of government revenues, dislocation of households from rural to urban areas, and a worsening in the balance of payments position with consequences for the sustainability of the fixed exchange rate regime. These outcomes do not, as argued by Prasad and Akram-Lodhi (1998) and Oxfam (2002), constitute a case for continuation of the preferential arrangement, however. I argue here for assistance in the form of lump sum transfers equivalent in value to the rents implicit in the remaining life of the preferential arrangement to facilitate adjustment to a subsidy-free environment. The interventions considered here are specific to Fiji sugar but the principles have broader applicability.

This case study of Fiji sugar is illustrative of the issues and policy options in relation to preference erosion for six specific reasons.

- It concerns a commodity that is often claimed as one of the most distorted of internationally traded commodities (DFAT 2004; Oxfam 2002). The vast array of interventions in the global sugar market includes border tariffs, import quotas, and price guarantees.
- The study concerns the European Union, which is due to reform its sugar policy in the very near future, with ramifications for several African, Caribbean and Pacific countries.

- Sugar is a homogenous product, making it possible to compute preference margins without the need for quality adjustments—an issue that has plagued similar studies for clothing and bananas.
- An amicable solution to preference erosion between the African, Caribbean and Pacific states and the rest of the WTO membership is likely to dissipate opposition to the Doha round of negotiations. The African, Caribbean and Pacific sugar producing states,[2] for example, have joined a number of least developed economies to form the G-90 to block any further multilateral trade liberalisation that is likely to adversely affect their economies. Preference erosion was an issue of contention at the WTO ministerial meeting at Doha, particularly when the non-African, Caribbean and Pacific states objected to the request by the African, Caribbean and Pacific states for extension of the GATT waiver for their preferences. Panagariya (2003) contends that 'the fear on the part of the beneficiary countries that multilateral liberalisation would erode their preference margin has undercut their incentive to push harder for such liberalisation'.
- The small country assumption holds for Fiji in that changes in EU policies towards Fiji sugar are unlikely to have impacts beyond Fiji.

Table 11.1   Prices and quantities of sugar exports, 1990–2001

Year	$P^{EU(A)}$ (F$)	$P^{EU(B)}$ (F$)	P^{USA} (F$)	P^{WLD} (F$)	$Q^{EU(A)}$ (tons)	$Q^{EU(B)}$ (tons)	Q^{USA} (tons)	Total exports (tons)
1990	869.31	n.a.	621.95	351.08	157,891	n.a.	18,979	367,762
1991	896.53	n.a.	635.33	336.05	182,799	n.a.	14,800	355,146
1992	948.42	n.a.	532.92	333.19	197,740	n.a.	15,702	391,203
1993	856.04	n.a.	664.42	343.61	182,033	n.a.	8,403	400,919
1994	886.43	n.a.	615.97	362.85	169,055	n.a.	11,106	471,172
1995	875.21	778.89	631.84	368.73	191,420	55112	10,197	412,011
1996	902.66	771.87	935.79	364.10	137,554	30151	19,930	409,872
1997	911.32	697.99	656.83	374.37	145,566	33733	18,980	303,118
1998	1,110.20	881.57	n.a.	293.66	189,180	31932	-	253,058
1999	973.02	890.38	865.38	259.81	201,206	38448	18,513	336,437
2000	941.48	768.44	724.11	410.56	176,471	20331	9,083	308,283
2001	978.20	910.68	934.91	423.51	172,493	15700	9,065	243,873

Notes: P denotes per-ton price, in Fiji current price dollars, for sugar exports under preferential quotas A, B, and to the United States, respectively.
Source: Primary data sourced from Fiji Sugar Corporation, 2002.

- Finally, the study illustrates a case where rents have been dissipated through production inefficiencies. The withdrawal of EU sugar subsidies has been on the cards since 1986 when agriculture was first brought within the ambit of the GATT, and particularly since December 1994 following the European Union's commitment to limit the value of export subsidies (and the volume of subsidised sugar exports from the European Union) at the conclusion of the Uruguay Round. Preference erosion for African, Caribbean and Pacific sugar, therefore, is imminent.

The main findings of this chapter are that the rents from preferential access for sugar exports from Fiji have been large, amounting to nearly half the value of exports for the commodity and equal to some five per cent of GDP; the rents have been dissipated by inefficiencies in the growing of sugar cane and in the milling of the crop; a lump-sum transfer of the rents implicit in the remaining life of the preferential arrangement to sugar producers is likely to induce a rapid adjustment to a subsidy-free environment; and exposure of the domestic industry to world market prices is likely to improve resource allocation in the broader economy.

PREFERENTIAL ARRANGEMENT FOR SUGAR

Preferential access for Fiji sugar into the United Kingdom and subsequently into the European Union (after the United Kingdom joined the European Economic Community in 1974) has existed since the inception of the industry with indentured Indian labour in 1879. Sixty thousand workers, brought from India under the indenture scheme that lasted until 1916, subsequently formed the smallholder sector growing sugarcane on land leased from the indigenous population. Exports of sugar from Fiji to the European Union are governed by two trade agreements; namely, the Sugar Protocol and the Agreement on Special Preferential Sugar (SPS) between the African, Caribbean and Pacific states on the one hand and the European Union on the other. Article 1 of the Protocol states that

> the [European] Community undertakes for an indefinite period to purchase and import, at guaranteed prices, specific quantities of cane sugar, raw or white, which originate in the African, Caribbean and Pacific states and which these States undertake to deliver to it.

The price, according to Article 5 of the Protocol, is to be negotiated annually; Article 3 specifies the country quotas; and Article 7 states that the quota is to be divided amongst the remaining members should a member fail to meet its allocation. The Protocol does not have a sunset clause and the European Union has reiterated its commitment (via the Cotonou Agreement) to continue importing specified quantities of sugar from the African, Caribbean and Pacific states at agreed prices. The SPS Agreement was enacted in 1995 with an initial term of six years to meet the sugar deficit among Portuguese refineries following the accession of Portugal and Spain to the European Union in 1986. Sugar sold under the SPS agreement earns around 85 per cent of the price paid under the Protocol. The United States has also given preferential entry to approximately 10,000 tons of sugar annually from Fiji under the Generalised System of Preferences (GSP).

The preferential arrangements transfer significant rents to Fiji via its exports of sugar to the European Union and the United States. As shown in Figure 11.1 and Table 11.1, under the Protocol the price received—net of transport costs and importer margins—for exports of sugar to the preferential markets for the 10-year period to 2001 earned a premium that was 2.6 times the world market price (referred to in the table as A-sugar), 2.3 times the world market price under the SPS Agreement (referred to in the table as B-sugar), and 1.9 times the world market price under the GSP. The Protocol accounted

Figure 11.1   Price of sugar exports to the European Union, United States and world market, 1990–2001

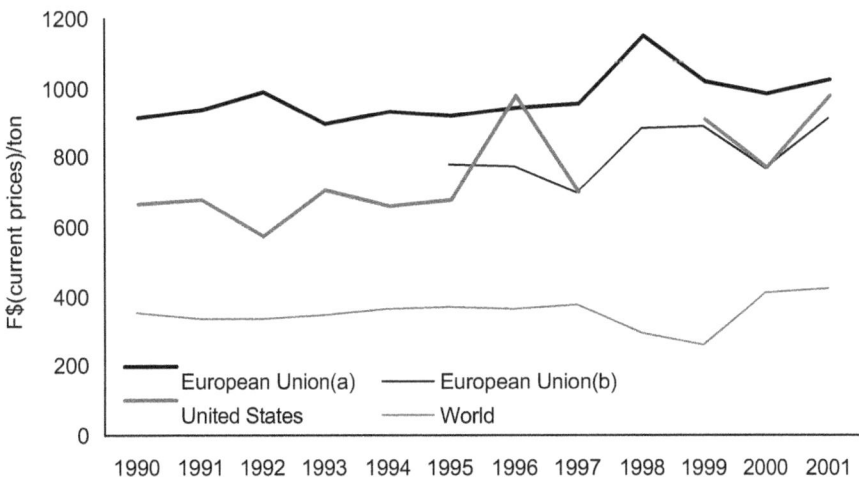

for some 90 per cent of the total quota rent-receipts, defined as the price premium multiplied by the preferential quota for the respective markets; SPS accounted for another six per cent, with the balance being accounted for by the GSP. For the 10 years to 2001, rents alone amounted to nearly half of the total value of exports of sugar; this equates to approximately five per cent of GDP (see Table 11.2).

The EU sugar regime has over the recent past come under attack on two specific grounds. First, while the European Union is self-sufficient in sugar, production within the European Union is alleged to entail large subsidies that in turn are claimed to disadvantage more competitive producers. Oxfam (2002:5), for example, reports that the production cost for a ton of white sugar in 2002 in Europe at €673 is nearly 2.4 times that of €286 for competitive producers such as Brazil, Colombia, Malawi, Guatemala and Zambia. Second, it is alleged the European Union has been dumping sugar on the world market. In 2002, for example, the European Union produced a total of 17 million tons of sugar and imported another 2.3 million tons, of which 1.5 million were imported from the African, Caribbean and Pacific states under preferential arrangements. Total consumption in the European Union in 2002 amounted to 12.7 million tons. Hence, some 7 million tons were exported.[3] The debate on the impact of protection on world sugar, however, goes back to the early

Table 11.2   Sugar rents by source, 1990–2001

Year	EEC (F$mn)	United States (F$mn)	Total rents (F$mn)	Rent/sugar exports (%)	Rent/GDP (%)
1990	81.83	5.14	86.96	n.a.	5
1991	102.46	4.43	106.88	n.a.	6
1992	121.66	3.14	124.79	56	6
1993	93.28	2.70	95.97	42	4
1994	88.51	2.81	91.32	36	4
1995	119.56	2.68	122.24	44	5
1996	86.38	11.39	97.77	32	4
1997	89.08	5.36	94.44	44	4
1998	173.25	-	173.25	71	6
1999	167.75	11.21	178.96	68	6
2000	100.97	2.85	103.82	44	3
2001	103.33	4.63	107.96	49	3

Notes: Calculated using data sourced from Fiji Sugar Corporation, 2002 and Reserve Bank of Fiji *Quarterly Review* (various issues).

1960s. Snape (1963) and Johnson (1964) were among the first to draw attention to the extent of protection, the ensuing rents to producers in the protected markets, and its impact on consumption and world market prices for the commodity. In his case for freer trade in sugar, Johnson (1966) argued that the ensuing efficiency gains could be used as foreign aid. He also pointed out that a deeper world market for sugar would reduce price variability.

Reforms leading to an erosion of the price premia within the Euroean Union have been long in coming. In its 1995 review of the sugar policy, the European Union clearly stated its intention to comply with its Uruguay Round commitments of 'substantial progressive reductions in agricultural support and protection'.[4] The impetus for withdrawal of EU sugar subsidies may have been hastened by a recent WTO ruling in favour of Australia, Brazil and Thailand that the EU sugar subsidies were in excess of the levels agreed to in the Uruguay Round Agreement.[5] The Cotonou Agreement lapses at the end of 2007, at which time preferential access to the EU market is due to be renegotiated. Any reforms of the EU sugar regime, including those arising from its commitment to WTO-sponsored rounds of multilateral trade liberalisation, will impact on the prices that African, Caribbean and Pacific states receive rather than market access for the guaranteed quantities of sugar into the European Union. African, Caribbean and Pacific states have received prices equal to those earned by sugar producers within the European Community; any liberalisation leading to a fall in the Community price of sugar will lead to preference erosion for the African, Caribbean and Pacific members.

A SYNOPSIS OF THE FIJI SUGAR INDUSTRY

Fiji sugar is produced from cane grown by a smallholder sector comprising some 21,000 farms with supply contracts to the Fiji Sugar Corporation (FSC).[6] The average farm is 4.6 hectares in area and produces around 160 tons of sugarcane (data from Kingi 2004). The farms are run predominantly with family labour and with animal draught power. Sixty-one per cent of the farms produce less than 150 tons of cane per year, with 25 per cent harvesting less than 50 tons (data from Prasad and Akram-Lodhi 1998). All of the farms are rain-fed, and production varies considerably between years as a consequence. In good years, characterised by rainfall evenly spread throughout the growing season, sugarcane production has surpassed 4 million tons.[7]

Sugar is produced with aged technology. The sugarcane is manually harvested—much like when the industry was established 125 years ago—by some 14,000 cutters operating in small gangs. The cane is transported to one of the four sugar mills operated by the FSC. Approximately equal quantities of cane are transported via the rail system operated by the FSC and on privately operated motor trucks (lorries); the latter have increased as sugarcane cultivation has expanded into areas without rail transport (Sugar Commission of Fiji 2002). Milling technology has changed little over the past half century. The mills are 68 per cent owned by the government, and employ around 3,000 workers—some only during the half-yearly harvesting season. Depending on milling efficiency and the volume of throughput, total sugar production has ranged from 264,000 (in 1975) to 517,000 tons (in 1994) (annual production data is given in Table 11.3).[8] The price paid to the growers for the cane is determined by a legislated formula, namely the Master Award, which apportions the average price received for the sugar produced between the Fiji Sugar Corporation and the grower.[9]

In spite of the favourable prices received for exports, the sugar industry has been in financial strife in the recent past. Fiji Sugar Corporation has recorded losses in each year from 1997 to 2002 achieving a record loss in 2001 of US$20.8 million. Independent financial auditors for 2001 noted that Fiji Sugar Corporation retained its status as a 'going concern' only because the Fiji government underwrote its operations. Another commentator has observed that the Fiji Sugar Corporation 'exists very much at the Governments' pleasure' and, given the prevailing cost structure, the equity of investors in FSC would be 'rapidly destroyed' with the suspension of preferential access to the EU market (White 2004).

The growers have been in similar strife. The average cost of producing a ton of sugarcane is estimated at around US$37 (Reddy 2004), but this figure varies considerably between farms. Rao (2004), using farm level data, shows that a farmer producing 160 tons of sugarcane earned an annual income gross of labour input of US$1,202 (data for 2001). This puts the farmer in poverty given that the rural-household 'basic needs poverty line' is US$115 per week (ADB 2003:9). This observation is consistent with an earlier study that suggested growers producing less than 200 tons of cane are likely to be in poverty (World Bank 1995).

If, as stipulated in the Master Award, 70 per cent of the total rents accruing from access to the preferential markets in 2001 were divided equally between the 22,000 growers, each grower would receive some US$4900. On the basis of this allocation, Fiji Sugar Corporation would receive US$32.4 million. Alternatively, each ton of sugarcane produced in 2001 earned US$38 in rents alone. On the 70:30 formula the grower (together with the landlord) received approximately US$27 per ton, while the balance of US$11 went to the Fiji Sugar Corporation. Neither the Fiji Sugar Corporation nor the growers are reported to have made super-normal profits. The large rents transferred via preferential prices paid for sugar exports from Fiji can only be reconciled with the poor financial state of the industry by noting the extent to which rents are

Table 11.3   Sugar production statistics, 1971–2002

Year	No. of contracts	Area harvested ('000ha)	Cane delivered ('000t)	Sugar produced ('000t)
1971	15,548	47	2,545	323
1972	15,612	44	2,238	303
1973	16,533	46	2,496	301
1974	16,546	45	2,151	272
1975	17,264	45	2,160	264
1976	17,667	47	2,283	286
1977	18,395	52	2,674	362
1978	18,456	54	2,853	347
1979	19,152	62	4,063	473
1980	19,700	66	3,360	396
1981	21,000	66	3,931	470
1982	21,574	69	4,075	487
1983	21,880	59	2,203	276
1984	22,130	69	4,290	480
1985	22,159	70	3,042	341
1986	22,182	69	4,109	502
1987	22,255	66	2,960	401
1988	22,127	64	3,185	363
1989	21,771	71	4,099	461
1990	21,334	70	4,016	408
1991	24,479	73	3,380	389
1992	23,334	73	3,533	426
1993	23,454	74	3,704	442
1994	23,264	74	4,064	517
1995	22,449	74	4,110	454
1996	22,304	74	4,380	454
1997	22,100	73	3,280	347
1998	22,146	57	2,098	266
1999	22,178	65	3,958	377
2000	22,179	63	3,786	341
2001	21,882	66	2,805	293
2002	21,246	65	3,423	330

Source: Fiji Bureau of Statistics, various issues. *Current Economic Statistics Bulletin*, FBS, Suva.

dissipated. This is the case of an industry that has moved up its average cost curve, exhausting all the rents through increased costs of production.

Fiji has strong incentives to ensure that the preferential quotas, particularly those to the European Union, are met. The substantial value of rents implicit in the preferential arrangement, together with the penalties in the form of loss of the preferential quota in the event of being unable to meet supply targets, induce production well above the preferential quota. Except for 1997, a record drought year, Fiji has always met its preferential quota. For the decade to 2001, production on average exceeded the preferential quota by around 60 per cent. While the European Union is the major market, accounting annually for 200,000 tons of sugar exports, another 10,000 tons is exported to the United States, and local consumption accounts for approximately 40,000 tons. Production in excess of the preferential quotas is sold at world market prices under bilateral access agreements with Canada, China, Japan, South Korea, Malaysia, Indonesia and New Zealand. Any remaining production is sold on the world market. There is no protection for sugar within the domestic market, thus the price paid at home reflects the world market price.

RENTS AND EFFICIENCY IN SUGAR PRODUCTION

The value of rents, V, implicit in a preferential arrangement can be estimated as the product of the preference margin, m, and the preferential quota, $\overline{Q}$ when the preference is fully utilised. That is

$$V = (P^{EU} - P^{W})\,\overline{Q} \equiv m\,\overline{Q}, \text{ for } Q^{X} \geq \overline{Q} \tag{11.1a}$$

$$V = (P^{EU} - P^{W})Q^{X} \text{ otherwise.} \tag{11.1b}$$

where $\overline{Q}$ is the level of the quota and Q^{X} is total exports. Since the marginal value of rents of production above the preferential quota is zero, a rent-maximising monopoly under conditions of certainty (as shown by Equation 11.1) will produce output just equal to the preferential quota. As noted above, this obviously has not been the case. The industry as a whole loses rents when aggregate output falls short of the preferential quota. Uncertainty with respect to realised output given unpredictable weather conditions (including tropical cyclones) during the growing season has encouraged above-quota production.

Rent dissipation takes place through the following four channels. First, the market structure in the form of a monopoly miller with a competitive smallholder farm sector has encouraged production in excess of the quota. Above-quota production, while raising unit production costs, has led to a fall in the average price received, given that production in excess of the preferential quota is sold at the much lower world market price. A monopoly miller that coordinates the growing and harvesting of sugarcane has an incentive to see that the preferential quota is fulfilled. The competitive nature of the smallholder sugarcane-growing sector encourages production in excess of the farm quota in the form of 'farm basic allotment'. The preferential rent forms a common pool that individual farmers access via their farm output. Where one farm's output in excess of the 'farm basic allotment' offsets that of another, as happens given the large variability in weather conditions across the sugarcane-growing regions, the 'lucky' farmer earns super-normal profits. The payment formula, based on averages, and without penalties for production in excess of the 'farm basic allotment' other than the lower price faced by all growers, encourages production beyond the farm allocations.[10]

Second, rents have been dissipated by milling inefficiencies. Technical milling efficiency, in terms of tons of sugarcane crushed to produce a ton of sugar (tcts), has deteriorated by approximately 30 per cent over the 30 years to 2002. This has happened as the (real) price of sugar, in 1995 prices, has fallen (see Figure 11.2). This observation is confirmed by regressing tcts on a time trend and the price of sugar. The estimates show that the number of tons of cane crushed to produce a ton of sugar, controlling for the price of sugar, increased at a rate of approximately one per cent per annum. This result, reported in Table A11.1 in the appendix, is robust to a number of alternate specifications. The Fiji Sugar Corporation, moreover, has an incentive to achieve the preferential quota but has little incentive to produce sugar in excess of the preferential quota. Anecdotal evidence supports this conclusion as the frequency of mill breakdowns has increased whenever throughput has been abnormally high.

Third, rents have been used to sustain favourable employment conditions within sugar manufacturing. Prasad and Akram-Lodhi (1998) report that high union densities and a well established industrial relations framework have ensured that FSC factory and field employees have benefited from both preferential prices and the sales security guaranteed by the Protocol.[11]

While Fiji Sugar Corporation is mandated to pay the minimum legislated wages, which for manufacturing sector workers for 1999 was US$97 per week,

Figure 11.2   Milling efficiency and price of sugar

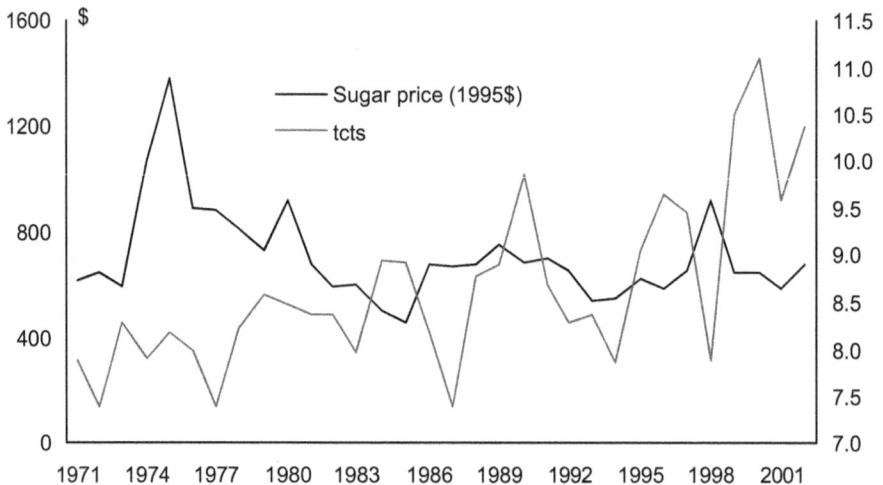

Source: Author's calculations based on data from *Current Economic Statistics* (various issues), Suva, Fiji.

the non-unionised cane cutters earned an average income of US$62 per week during the six-monthly harvesting season (wage data from Fiji Bureau of Statistics 2004 and Reddy 2004). As a large formal sector employer, the Fiji Sugar Corporation with its inflated wages would, moreover, draw the most productive workers whilst raising wage costs for the rest of the private sector. In 1999, payroll costs for the Fiji Sugar Corporation amounted to 55 per cent of total operating costs, a figure considered to be 'too high' by White (2004).

Fourth, rents have been dissipated via expansion of sugar cane production onto marginal land and/or those distant from the mills. Productivity within the Fiji sugar industry compares unfavourably with other sugar-producing nations. As an example, average cane output in Fiji at 19.6 tons per acre compares with a figure of 31.9 for Mauritius, 35.4 for Queensland, and 43.8 for Hawaii (data from Reddy 2004). The expansion of area under cultivation has meant that the average cost of delivering cane to the mills has risen over time, thus dissipating some of the rents. Land values within the sugarcane growing districts, moreover, have risen with the expansion of area under cultivation. With land rentals set at 6 per cent of the unimproved capital value, the landowners have shared in the rents from sugarcane farming.

The analysis thus far has been of a partial equilibrium nature. The general equilibrium effects, including the terms of trade effects, can be large if preference erosion leads to large dislocation of factors of production. Two studies that model the general equilibrium effects of trade liberalisation for Fiji show losses from preference erosion that are less than the value of the rents implicit in the subsidy. McDonald (1996) simulates the impact of Uruguay Round agricultural trade liberalisation; the results show a net welfare loss to Fiji equivalent to 2.52 per cent of GDP. Levantis et al. (2004) use a dynamic CGE model to simulate the impact of the removal of the subsidies implicit in the preference margin coming up with an annual loss of 1.1 per cent of GDP. Given that rents from the sugar preferences account for approximately 5 per cent of GDP and their loss is estimated to reduce welfare by a maximum of 2.5 per cent, the buy-out of the preferential arrangement will still deliver a net benefit equivalent to 2.5 per cent of GDP. At best, the preferences for Fiji sugar exports have played only a marginal role in assisting development,[12] a claim supported by the broad literature that shows that economic performance is determined principally by domestic policies (see Panagariya 2003). Access to preferential rents, moreover, may have impeded resource flows into the more dynamic sectors, thus constraining growth of aggregate output.

POLICY IMPLICATIONS

Given the evidence, it is doubtful whether preferential access for Fiji sugar into the European Union and the United States has helped create a viable industry. It may, however, have put off the death of an unviable one. It is also debatable whether the preferential arrangement has been good for Fiji's development. The dissipation of rents suggests that lump-sum transfers would have been a superior alternative in assisting development. Since the sugar preferences will erode, possibly rapidly, over the next decade, the question for policymakers is how to induce change to a subsidy free environment with minimal adjustment costs.

Given that rents from preferential access have been dissipated, their loss will reduce the rent-dissipating activities that have developed and thus improve economic efficiency. The gains, however, will materialise only after all the adjustments have taken place. In the interim, preference erosion will impose adjustment costs, particularly on immobile factors such as land currently being used for growing sugarcane and the labour and capital facing dislocation. A generation of sugarcane farmers with little in the way of transportable skills will face serious declines in their income from an already low level. The sugarcane cutter who now earns some US$62 per week in the harvesting season is, in the immediate term, likely to be left without a job. For many smallholders, expiring land leases are only going to compound these problems (see Reddy and Yanagida 1998; Levantis et al. 2003; Prasad and Narayan 2004). Many displaced farmers are reported to be moving into squatter settlements around the urban centres, and this social dislocation is creating its own problems.

Two studies have argued for more time in the withdrawal of preferences on the grounds of social and economic dislocation. Oxfam (2002:28) recommends that the European Union '[m]aintain quotas for the African, Caribbean and Pacific preferential sugar imports' while Prasad and Akram-Lodhi (1998:39) argue for the continuation of export subsidies through the sugar protocol claiming that, 'in the specific case of Fiji, trade is a more effective form of development cooperation'. The latter argues for a restriction on 'third country competition' for sugar exports to the European Union to allow farmers to improve efficiency and diversify into other products. I disagree with these recommendations. Such a program is likely to be counterproductive as it will prevent efficiency improvements, discourage diversification, and, most importantly, create incentives for lobbying for domestic subsidies when those from abroad expire. Grossman and Helpman (1996) provide a model that rationalises lobbying effort for protection by the incumbents in a sunset industry. Ozden and Reinhardt (2002) show that countries removed from GSP adopt more liberal trade policies than those remaining eligible and that greater utilisation of the preferences raises the resistance to trade liberalisation.

There is little doubt that the preferences will fall. The abolition of the preferential price arrangement is certain given the European Union's commitment to abiding by the WTO process. The loss of the subsidy, unless prepared for well in advance, will create serious adjustment pains for the economy as a whole. The incentives for managing the adjustment process are, therefore, strong. The EU Economic Partnership Arrangements contain measures to support adjustments to liberal trade as per WTO commitments (European Commission 2002). Article 68 of the Cotonou Agreement provides for '[a] system of additional support in order to mitigate the adverse effects of any instability in export earnings, including in the agricultural and mining sectors...within the financial envelope for support to long-term development', with island and land-locked economies identified as deserving favourable treatment.[13] Short-term respite from preference erosion can also be sought via the recently approved IMF Trade Integration Mechanism (see IMF 2004). Fiji could, at least in the short term, seek quota-free access to the EU market while the preference margin is lowered. Export income in this scenario would increase so long as the preferential price does not fall by more than 25 per cent,[14] but the relief provided will only be short term.

A permanent solution to preference erosion would involve measures that induce adjustment with compensation for the costs incurred. A self-funding mechanism, based on the value of rents implicit in each ton of sugar produced for the preferential market for the remaining life of the preferential arrangement could be developed as follows. Assume that the preferences would fall in two steps: first, by 40 per cent in three years' time followed by a complete withdrawal in another seven years. Furthermore, assume a preference margin of US$600 per ton and a discount rate of 5 per cent. These assumptions imply that the net present value of rents implicit in each ton of sugar produced over the remaining life of the preferential agreement is US$3,005. The preferential quota can be bought at this price; that is, the preferences can be bought out with rents implicit in the remaining life of the arrangement. The grower producing 160 tons of sugarcane, of which 100 tons are destined for the preferential market, would, on the basis of the 70 per cent share of rents, receive US$21,035. A rate of return of 5.7 per cent is all that is necessary for this sum to generate an income equal to the US$1,202 that the farmer earned, gross of labour input, from cane farming. On the assumption that 200,000 tons of sugar has access to the preferential market, the FSC would receive US$180 million. This amount could be used to fund the restructuring to a subsidy-free environment, or, if necessary, winding down of the industry.

It is possible that the Fiji sugar industry will become non-viable following the withdrawal of preferences. One commentator has suggested that

> a realistic evaluation of the industry's long term viability is needed. The most appropriate policy to pursue may well be one that enables the orderly winding down of the industry and its ultimate closure (White 2004:300).

Rather than spend further resources in evaluating the viability of the industry, the proposal put forward here allows industry itself to make this choice of its own volition. Market mechanisms are used to assess and decide the viability of the industry. The calculations made in this chapter suggest that whatever the outcome, the industry as a whole and the economy more generally benefit from the policy interventions suggested.

The upfront payment of rents implicit in the remaining life of preferential access has two major advantages over an extension of the current arrangements as suggested by Oxfam (2002) and Prasad and Akram-Lodhi (1998). First, the lump-sum payment creates an incentive for growers and the miller to adjust to a subsidy-free environment as early as possible. Waiting under this scenario is costly, particularly when preferential rents are dissipated. This is in sharp contrast to a push for extension of the deadline for withdrawal of preferences. Second, the market is used to induce adjustment with payments being fully funded from the remaining life of the preferential arrangement. The difficulty here will be in getting the European Union to pay the rents as a lump sum, but the Economic Partnership Agreements and Article 68 of the Cotonou Agreement do entertain such a possibility.

CONCLUSIONS

Preference erosion results when exporters with privileged access into industrial-country markets lose their competitive advantage as barriers to international trade are lowered under the Most-Favoured Nation (MFN) principle of the WTO. Active discrimination in favour of a select group of developing countries by their industrial country partners, permitted under 'Special and Differential Treatment' of GATT/WTO, is facing the closest scrutiny as the case against 'aid through trade' becomes increasingly convincing (see Panagariya 2003 and Hoekman and Ozden 2005). The African, Caribbean, and Pacific group of countries faces the prospect of losing preferential access to the EU market as the latter liberalises its trade under its WTO commitments. The case of Fiji sugar is used here to highlight both the challenges posed by preference erosion and policy options available to minimise the adverse consequences.

I show that rents from preferential access have been dissipated via inefficiencies in the growing of sugarcane, milling of the crop, and through higher wages for the unionised sector. Such dissipation is indeed not peculiar to the Fiji sugar industry but is a common phenomenon across industries and countries. Horstman and Markusen (1986), for example, have shown that subsidies and tariffs that lead to inefficient entry have negative welfare consequences. Snape (1963) and Johnson (1966) had made similar predictions with respect to interventions in the global sugar market. The erosion of the preferences, therefore, will be efficiency enhancing, as it will remove the rents that fund the inefficiencies in the first place. The aforementioned gains, however, will only accrue following adjustment to a subsidy-free environment; dislocation of capital, labour and land from sugar production in the interim will incur costs. Such costs can be contained with the provision of adjustment assistance. Resources for the assistance can be tapped from rents implicit in the remaining life of the preferential arrangement. Ozden and Reinhardt (2002) show that 'nonreciprocal preferences have the perverse effect of delaying trade liberalisation'; preference erosion, therefore, may induce unilateral liberalisation. Declining industries have a reputation for successfully playing the political system (see Grossman and Helpman 1996), so achieving the transformation above will not be easy.

The case of Fiji sugar has been used in this paper to address the specific problem of preference erosion. While the policies discussed here are particular to Fiji sugar, the principles have broader applicability. Fiji, for example, is facing preference erosion with respect to clothing exports to Australia and New Zealand under the South Pacific Regional Trade and Economic Cooperation Agreement (SPARTECA).[15] Sugar exports from Mauritius to the European Union are in a similar predicament to those of Fiji. The idea of trade adjustment funded with rents implicit in the remaining life of preferential access arrangements could be used more generally to fund costs of adjustment and induce restructuring to a subsidy-free environment.

ACKNOWLEDGMENTS

Helpful comments on an earlier draft of this paper from Malcolm Bosworth and Rod Duncan are gratefully acknowledged with the usual disclaimer.

NOTES

[1] The small country assumption has been invoked here. That is, it has been assumed that exports of sugar from Fiji and Mauritius have no impact on the world market price.

[2] African, Caribbean and Pacific states include Barbados, Belize, Congo, Cote d'Ivoire, Guyana, Fiji, Jamaica, Kenya, Madagascar, Malawi, Mauritius, St Kitts and Nevis, Swaziland, Tanzania, Trinidad and Tobago, Zambia and Zimbabwe.

[3]   Stocks of sugar held in Europe fell by 0.4 million tons, accounting for the balance between aggregate supply and demand (data from Oxfam 2002:8).

[4]   This was the Punta del Este Declaration of Ministers of Trade made in September 1986 (quoted from http://www.acpsugar.org/eusugar1995review.htm [accessed 18 October 2004]).

[5]   The EU appealed this decision on the grounds that the decision was based 'on an erroneous interpretation of the WTO provisions on agricultural export subsidies and inconsistent with the obligation of good faith'. The WTO's Appellate Body upheld an earlier Panel decision that the operation of the EU sugar regime was inconsistent with its obligations under the WTO Agreement on Agriculture.

[6]   The Fiji Sugar Corporation has small farms near its mills but they are used primarily for research.

[7]   In sharp contrast to Mauritius, irrigation has not been used in farming sugar cane. The difference could be explained by the fact that 55 per cent of sugarcane in Mauritius is produced by the sugar mills themselves on farms ranging in size from 700–5,500 hectares in size and that all land is privately owned.

[8]   By international standards, Fiji is a high-cost producer. The Fiji prime minister has publicly stated that cane yield per hectare in Fiji is the second lowest and sugar yield the worst amongst the 20 African, Caribbean, and Pacific (ACP) sugar-producing states (*FijiSUN*, 6 October 2004). The costs of producing a ton of sugar at the four mills, according to the prime minister, in Fiji dollars are 340, 320, 230, and 160 at the Penang, Lautoka, Labasa, and Rarawai mills, respectively.

[9]   The Master Award assigns 70 per cent of the proceeds from sugar exports of up to 325,000 tons to growers. This share rises to 72.5 per cent for exports between 325,000 and 350,000 tons, and to 75 per cent for exports greater than 350,000 tons (see Reddy 2004).

[10]   Alternative strategies for addressing the production uncertainty include buying insurance and building buffer stocks. Neither of these is realistic, however, as the first is not yet available, and the value of the second is questionable given the international experience with commodity marketing boards.

[11]   Establishing that mill workers appropriate some of the preferential rents requires the estimation of wage equations as in Krueger and Summers (1988) and Katz and Summers (1989). Data for such analysis, however, is absent. Workers hired on farms run by the Fiji Sugar Corporation earn wages well in excess of their counterparts in adjoining fields run by private operators. This has led to queuing for such opportunities.

[12]   This observation is consistent with international evidence that shows 'the track record of preferences to-date gives little reason to conclude that they will make a perceptible difference to growth and poverty reduction in the beneficiary countries' (Panagariya 2003). This same point was made much earlier by Whalley (1990).

[13] The quote is from: http://europa.eu.int/comm/development/body/cotonou/agreement/ agr30_en.htm [accessed 5 May, 2005].

[14] The price received under the Protocol is approximately $1000 per ton; the average price currently received for exports is F$750.

[15] SPARTECA is a non-reciprocal trade agreement where Australia and New Zealand offer duty-free and concessional access for several products from the developing island member countries of the South Pacific Forum. The agreement was signed in Kiribati on 14 July 1980 at the Eleventh Meeting of the Forum and came into effect from 1 January 1981. The current list of signatories to SPARTECA includes Cook Islands, the Federated States of Micronesia, Fiji, Kiribati, Marshall Islands, Nauru, Niue, Papua New Guinea, Solomon Islands, Tonga, Tuvalu, Vanuatu and Western Samoa.

APPENDIX

Table A11.1 Estimates of milling efficiency, 1971–2002

Variable name	Model 1	Model 2
Constant	2.17	2.20
	(4.94)**	(8.71)**
ln (sugar price)	−0.22	
	(−0.33)	
ln (cane price)		−0.041
		(−0.69)
Time	0.007	0.0069
	(4.62)**	(4.17)**
Number of observations	32	32
Adjusted R^2	0.43	0.44
Durbin Watson d-statistic	1.73	1.79

Notes: Dependent variable is tons of cane crushed to produce a ton of sugar (tcts), annual data from 1971–2002 used. Sugar and cane prices are in 1995 dollars; ** denotes significant at the 5 per cent level.

COMMENT

L. Alan Winters

This is a nice chapter continuing, as Satish Chand notes, a long and noble tradition of work on sugar trade policy. I have three sets of comments—on the domestic industry, the proposed redistribution scheme and the global context. First, however, I want to clarify the term 'rent'.

Consider Figure 1 below in which an industry has a rising marginal cost curve and faces given prices for its sales. The world price is P_W, but, because of preferences, the country actually receives P_P. Satish defines rent as $q^*(P_P-P_W)$, that is, area (a+b), but strictly this is 'quota rent'. Assuming no other distortions, Ricardian rent is (a+c)—the earnings in excess of those necessary to keep factors in their current employment. Relative to quota rent, this adds one area of rent for highly efficient firms even with free trade, and removes one as marginal costs increase through the policy-induced expansion of output.

The distinction between the two concepts is useful not only for interpreting this chapter but for several others in this volume. The answer to 'how much does supply fall as rents are reduced?' is zero for Ricardian rent (by definition), but not for quota rent. Similarly, does the payment of super-normal wages represent the 'dissipation' of rent? Maybe for quota rent, but on Ricardo's concept, it is merely the transfer of rent to a different part of society. Finally, will free trade eliminate rents? Yes for quota rents, but not for Ricardian rents. I don't wish to be prescriptive about which terminology is correct, but I do want us to be clear what it is we are analysing.

Figure C11.1 Rents in a model industry

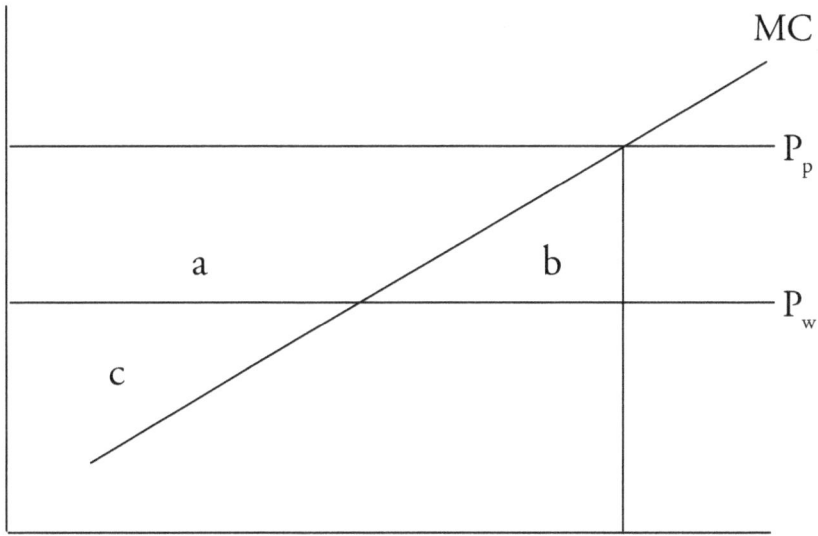

THE DOMESTIC INDUSTRY

Throughout the chapter, I found myself wondering about the role of the mills in the Fijian industry. According to the prime minister their costs diverge by a factor of greater than two. Why do the less efficient ones remain in business? Do they pay lower prices to farmers or receive higher prices for output? How is the Fijian quota in the European Union allocated between them? To the extent that prices are fixed and quotas allocated administratively, and if managers are not paid according to profits, there is little incentive for mills to be efficient, and their rising crush ratios are not surprising. Thus a good part of the rent dissipation Satish identifies probably arises from poor policy—the inefficient allocation of the quota. That is, Fiji could earn higher (Ricardian) rents merely by allowing efficient mills to expand at the expense of less efficient ones.

There is another policy distortion that appears to raise costs. Mills apparently pay an average price for any quantity of sugar delivered, so that, as Satish shows, farmers can increase their own share of the basically fixed revenue by producing and selling more. If the EU quota is Q^* and over-quota sales to the mills are Q', total farm revenue is $0.7^*(P_wQ^* + P_pQ^*)$ and price per unit

$0.7*(P_WQ'+ P_pQ*)/(Q'+Q*)$. This clearly exceeds P_W and so encourages production to a point where $M > P_W$ and, in this case, apparently leads output to exceed $Q*$. More rational would be to agree farm-level quotas, q_i, which would command price $0.7*P_p$ and for mills to purchase any additional units at a market clearing price. Because of the production uncertainty and the high costs of failing to supply $Q*$ to the European Union, the sum of the q_is would optimally exceed $Q*$, but beyond that safety margin the marginal incentives would be appropriately aligned. Whenever the sum of farmers' within-quota sales exceeded $Q*$, the over-quota market price would be $0.7*P_W$, but if ever the sum fell short, the price would rise above $0.7*P_p$ to reflect the value of meeting $Q*$ in order for Fiji to keep its overall quota in the European Union. Farmers could then make their own output decisions according to their risk aversion and the incentive for excess (and hence high-cost) production beyond the point where MC equalled expected MR (the price for marginal units) would be eliminated. This too would allow Fiji to make greater rents out of any given EU price/quota regime.

THE REDISTRIBUTION

Around one-quarter of Fiji's jobs stem for the sugar industry. From this I infer that a (perhaps the) major concern over preference erosion is social, and we need to ask whether Satish's scheme will satisfy social (distributional) objectives. This depends on details of its allocation. For example, what is the quantity base on which farmers' interests are to be bought out—a share of $Q*$, or, say, their actual q_i in a base year? If they are to sell their interest, it has to be well-defined. How does one ensure that some of the capital is transferred to the casual labourers who do the cutting—or, indeed, to any other labour. How do we ensure mill-owners compensate their workers, and does their 30 per cent share of the revenue cover that obligation?

There are also questions about whether all the capital sum that Fiji receives from the European Union should be redistributed or whether the government should hold some back to provide public goods or a steady flow of income through time. The latter issue is essentially that addressed by compulsory pensions. If individuals squander their capital compensation, they will suffer in future. But since a humane society will not let them starve, some of the burden of their profligacy will fall on society. Relatedly, if all the money is distributed, what ensures sugar producers/workers will not lobby for new support after a few years because of the adjustment costs they are still bearing? This time-consistency problem is a major issue for capital compensation schemes wherever policy is adjustable through time.

On the other side of the coin, of course, Fiji's rather blemished governance record has raised issues about the security of investments, either public or private. Moreover, whether the income flow is from private investments or a public pension, there is good reason to worry about the social health of a largely rentier or transfer-funded society.

THE GLOBAL CONTEXT

Finally, two small points. First, the Cotonou Agreement refers to additional support 'within the financial envelope'. I interpret this as implying that buying out the sugar quota will be at the expense of some other aid flow. This may not be desirable. Second, Satish analyses the erosion of Fiji's preferences in isolation, but in fact we are really talking about a regime change here. All sugar producers will be affected, so one really needs to conduct the exercise at a different P_w.

12

TOO YOUNG TO MARRY: ECONOMIC CONVERGENCE AND THE CASE AGAINST THE INTEGRATION OF PACIFIC STATES

Philip T. Powell

Transnational integration of state institutions in the Pacific islands is an active item on the regional agenda. In a recent Senate report, for example, Australia proposed the formation of a Pacific economic and political community (Commonwealth of Australia 2003). In theory, economic integration will raise the gains from trade, increase investment by reducing risk, and lower production costs by allowing the regional movement of resources to their most efficient use. In addition, political integration will relieve small island states of the fixed cost of managing and funding full-service independent governments. Bureaucracies can shrink and free skilled labour for employment in the private sector.

Scholars and policymakers assume that Pacific island integration is appropriate because regional cooperation via the Pacific Islands Forum has a history of success, transnational integration has benefited members of the European Union, and limited integration among developing economies has already occurred in Africa and the Caribbean. Always in search of ways to reverse the Pacific's growth paradox (that is, persistently low growth in spite of generous aid and natural resources), the policy community now sells integration as a fashionable solution to the region's economic problems. Lost in this exuberance over regional organisation is a robust analysis of where integration fits in the development trajectory of Pacific island economies. Global economic convergence establishes a theoretical growth path for island nations, and along this path, institutions must evolve at an optimal pace to support market activity. A mismatch between institutional complexity and level of development stalls further progress along the convergence path. Institutional evolution involves incremental community aggregation through establishment of new cooperative equilibria in society. In terms of convergence theory, transnational integration is successful only in an advanced stage of economic development and institutional evolution. In this context, integration of state institutions across Oceania is a misplaced endeavour that inefficiently consumes leadership focus and political energy.

A Pacific economic and political community as envisioned by Australia and other regionalists will achieve integration in form but not in substance. This insight becomes apparent when proposals for Pacific island integration are placed in comparative perspective with integration initiatives in Africa and the Caribbean. Current focus should instead be placed on integration at the national level. For a state to exercise legitimacy effectively (and non-coercively), the community it governs typically requires a strong sense of national identity. Policies designed to cement national identity and state legitimacy must rest upon a theory of how communities naturally aggregate themselves. Without stronger states, regional governance in the Pacific enjoys no firm foundation to ensure its sustainability and further development.

GLOBALISATION, ECONOMIC CONVERGENCE, AND STATE INSTITUTIONAL RESPONSE

Integration of Oceania implies erosion of the actual and potential role played by Pacific island states. At one extreme is a condition of economic and social autarky, where no communication, trade, or interaction occurs between Pacific island countries. In autarky, the state perfectly controls the inflow and outflow of information, goods, and inputs. The other extreme is full integration, where economic and demographic flows are not regulated, legal and constitutional provisions are fully standardised, and organs of government answer to one transnational state. Globalisation pushes states farther from autarky over time irrespective of those states' intentions. This migration does not necessarily change institutional architecture, but it changes the expectations placed on such architecture. Globalisation increases the payoff from comparative advantage, raises the opportunity cost of inefficient resource allocation, and sparks the convergence of economic preferences across communities. Unless the state willingly incurs heavy deadweight losses to preserve autarky (such as the case of North Korea), the flows of knowledge, technology, and people that drive these changes do not stop.

In this environment, state institutions remain relevant only if they evolve so that entrepreneurs can always capitalise on new market opportunities, and economically displaced individuals can always rely upon a social safety net. Globalisation causes social stress because it constantly redefines market 'winners' and 'losers' in a community. These shifts naturally occur as the geographic scope of market competition widens and the cycle of obsolescence of ideas, products, and technology quickens. The innovation of 'winners' generates economic growth, but the consternation of 'losers' generates political upheaval. 'Winners' must be taxed just enough to compensate 'losers' for their displacement and bribe them not to obstruct market activity (Sala-I-Martin 1997). In terms of traditional neoclassical theory, convergence of state institutions to a global norm reduces the fixed cost of entrepreneurship and innovation across markets. This maximises the surplus 'winners' generate for society and lessens the scarcity of resources available to the state for compensation of 'losers'.

While the endpoint of convergence achieved by globalisation is easily defined and identified in terms of theory, the optimal trajectory and pace of convergence is not. A central change agent within this evolutionary process is the state. If the institutions of state do not change and adapt quickly enough, a dangerous imbalance can occur. In one case, through an unexpected surge in power, the latest generation of 'winners' can co-opt the state to protect newly established monopoly positions. Economic cleavage widens in society because 'losers' receive no displacement compensation and the next wave of disruptive innovation cannot challenge the incumbency of the current 'winners'. Russia offers an example of this phenomenon. In 1992, President Boris Yeltsin removed market controls and state ownership requirements but did not equip institutions to support a transparent system of property rights and to privatise state assets at fair market value. Opportunities for massive arbitrage presented themselves and bore a new class of business élite known as the 'oligarchs'. The 'oligarchs' used violence (unchallenged by the state) to enforce their interpretation of contracts and rigged auctions of state assets to keep new competitors out of markets. As a result, by 1995, Russia's Gini coefficient (a measure of income inequality where zero is complete equality and one is complete inequality) had risen from 0.27 to 0.48 and the poverty rate had increased from two to 50 per cent of the population (Abdelal and Haddad 2001).

In an opposite case of imbalance, in response to new threats of economic dislocation, 'losers' can co-opt the state to reverse the gains of 'winners' through higher taxes and protect the bankruptcy of obsolete enterprises through subsidies and market controls. Equity in income is maintained, but returns to entrepreneurship are destroyed. The opportunity costs of economic insulation increase with globalisation. With no social surplus from innovation to fund transfer payments, the state must intensify market controls and incur higher levels of deadweight loss to maintain the industrial status quo. The gap between actual and potential per capita gross domestic product (GDP) widens. The United Kingdom provides a good example of this phenomenon. Global economic dominance in the United Kingdom, birthplace of the industrial revolution, created a new class of welathy business entrepreneurs. Upset with the wealth disparities this created, an aggressive and vocal labour movement motivated successive governments to implement and sustain generous social welfare policies after the First World War (Palmer and Goodman 1989). The standard rate of income tax increased from six per cent in 1913 to 50 per cent in 1947 and then progressively fell to 30 per cent in 1980 (Daunton 2002). The cumulative annual growth rate of real per capita GDP growth between 1913 and 1980 was 1.37 per cent in the United Kingdom compared with 1.75 per cent in the United States. By 1980, real per capita GDP in the United States was 69 per cent higher (Maddison 1983). In comparison, the effective individual income tax rate in the United States was 12 per cent in 1980 (Congressional Budget Office 1999).

State institutions in the United Kingdom and Russia did not correctly adapt to global shifts and the lag in both countries handicapped economic performance. If institutional change can inefficiently lag global convergence, then can it also inefficiently lead it? If so insistence on modern institutional design in countries not yet in economic takeoff could undermine a state's management of global change. For example, democracy is considered an institutional endpoint of economic convergence (Zak and Feng 2003), but early adoption of it might slow economic development. Democratic institutions sustain themselves only if competing parties find it in their self-interest to respect constitutional limits on power (Weingast 1997). The solution to this collective action problem takes time to achieve. If democracy pre-empts this process, rent-seeking opportunities suddenly expand and unrestrained political competition cannibalises state assets and hinders economic growth (Colombatto 1998). In this context, democracy is only a temporary vehicle for establishment of a new autocratic regime. Barro (1999) supports this empirically. In 1975, 10 African and two Pacific island countries enjoyed more democracy than could be explained by economic and demographic variables. Democratic institutions were inherited at independence despite low levels of economic development. By 1995, the level of democracy in six of these 12 countries had deteriorated to levels that did not meet statistical expectations.[1]

Another expected endpoint of economic convergence is monetary union (Sibert 1997). Adoption of a common currency theoretically increases investment because transaction costs fall, inflationary risk shrinks, and foreign exchange rate risk disappears. Membership is a positive net benefit—though only if there is a sufficient level of economic homogeneity and political collaboration among countries. If economies and national institutions have not converged enough to make this feasible, then premature monetary union can generate opportunity costs that overshadow any theoretical investment benefits. There is evidence that this has occurred in Africa. The East African Currency Board disbanded and the Rand Monetary Area was not able to adopt a common currency because member nations 'lacked the checks and balances in their political institutions...necessary for the credible conduct of monetary policy at the national level' (Guillaume and Stasavage 2000:1403). Countries within the West African Economic and Monetary Union and the Central African Economic and Monetary Community use the CFA franc, but interaction within the currency blocs remains problematic.[2] Variation in terms of national income sources (especially petroleum exports) prohibits a convergence in macroeconomic impact from currency area stabilisation measures. Because member countries surrender control of their monetary policy to the currency union, heterogeneity means that certain economic shocks at the national level go unsterilised (Fielding et al. 2004).

The success of currency unions in Africa is not only hampered by the lack of economic convergence, but also by a lack of common institutional independence and transparency. In a currency union, there is an incentive for member governments to run higher fiscal deficits—a regime can 'free ride' on other members' ability to protect the value of money in the face of its own inflationary policies. This prisoner's dilemma game dooms a monetary union's performance unless there is a strong transnational mechanism that enforces fiscal discipline (that is, coordinates a Pareto optimal solution that is not the Nash equilibrium). For example, a member of the Euro zone faces fines if deficits larger than three per cent of GDP and public debt larger than 60 per cent of GDP persist. Because no such rules are credible in the West African Economic and Monetary Union, member countries game the system and undermine the fiscal restraint required for optimal outcomes. Larger members are able to benefit at the expense of smaller members (Fielding 1996).

> The conclusion from comparison of the European Monetary Union and West Africa is that the danger of fiscal indiscipline as a result of forming a monetary union is much more likely in West Africa…given the region's history of central banks with limited independence and poor inflation records (Masson and Patillo 2002:409).

In the end, a lack of institutional development casts doubt on West Africa's readiness for a common currency.

As already stated, sustainable economic growth requires institutions that evolve to manage and respond to changes in consumer preferences, market opportunities, and the alignment of 'winners' and 'losers' from economic activity. Natural tendencies toward global economic convergence drive these changes and place pressure on uninsulated economies (Williamson 1996). Insights about optimal institutional evolution are best illustrated in Figure 12.1. Trajectory AZ is the development path of the theoretical 'average country' that evolves in an optimal pattern. Trajectory LZ is the development path of the most prosperous country. Over time, institutional architecture must change to enable continuous economic improvement along the trajectory. Thus, the architecture at point R must evolve to a different design by the time point S is achieved, and must morph yet again as point T is achieved. If the economy reaches point S but institutions have retained the architecture of point R, then performance stagnates as the disruption of market alignment at point S overtakes the ability of point R institutions to maintain Pareto optimal social cooperation (that is, to sustain a Pareto optimal solution in the game between economic 'winners' and 'losers'). In simple terms, this event mimics the United Kingdom's loss of global economic leadership after the First World War.

Trajectory UEZ is the development path of a developing country that encounters economic takeoff. The country begins with no performance improvement over time because of an underdevelopment bottleneck. Exogenous institutional change, though, occurs at point E and performance begins to converge to the average country. Just as with economic change in the most prosperous country, institutions must evolve through points F and G to sustain the trajectory. Two events can halt economic improvement. Momentum generated at point E can be short-lived and performance improvement can outpace capacity for institutional change. If point G performance is supported by point F institutions, then future performance stagnates because the country encounters the same misalignment described for trajectory LZ. This describes recent economic chaos in Russia. The rapid dissolution of communism suddenly enhanced Russia's investment potential (point E), but Yeltsin's government could not implement a system of property rights and transparent

Figure 12.1   Economic convergence and institutional evolution

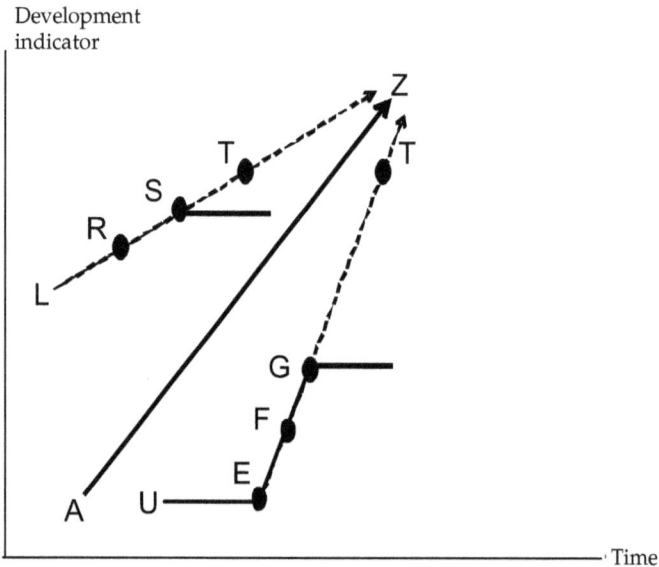

government fast enough to support higher levels of economic performance (point G). In contrast, momentum at point E might inspire too much confidence. In an effort to artificially speed development, policymakers would impose point T institutions (as observed in the most prosperous country) at point G performance. Paralysed by the unexpected complexity of point T institutions, society would no longer sustain cooperative equilibria in the games between market 'winners' and 'losers' and economic improvement would stop. This potentially describes a correlation between economic malaise and the failure of European-inspired unitary state parliamentary democracy in postcolonial Africa. It might also explain a link between worrisome inflation and monetary union in Africa. The impact of formal integration of government mechanisms across Pacific island states could mimic the failure encountered in these African examples of myopic institutional exuberance.

INSTITUTIONAL EVOLUTION AND INTEGRATION OF THE PACIFIC ISLAND STATES

For Pacific island policymakers, theory must guide practical decision making. Small domestic markets make Pacific island states more reliant on global economic opportunity to extend income than in other developing countries. With higher reliance comes greater vulnerability and an enhanced awareness of global institutional links. This explains early experiments in cooperation among Pacific island states. Momentum began with incorporation of the South Pacific Forum (now called the Pacific Islands Forum) in 1971 as an umbrella organisation for regional coordination. A search for common environmental and resource management strategies induced formation of the South Pacific Regional Environmental Program in 1974 and the Forum Fisheries Agency in 1979 (Rolfe 2000). Countries pooled public investments to create a regional airline, Air Pacific; a regional shipping company, the Forum Shipping Line; and a regional university, the University of the South Pacific (Chand 2003). Smallness and remoteness generated strong incentives for cooperation between island governments, and the region became a forerunner of transnational collective action in the developing world. While not all regional ventures met expectations— such as the failure of Air Pacific to be a regional instead of Fijian airline (see Shibuya 2003)—Oceania's 'network of cooperative institutions is unmatched elsewhere in developing economies in terms of effectiveness (Rolfe 2000).

Regionalism benefits the Pacific islands, but transnational coordination has not sparked the same type of economic takeoff witnessed in Europe. Real per capita GDP (measured in terms of year 2000 US dollars) averaged across the eight independent island states with populations over 90,000 residents (Federated States of Micronesia, Fiji, Kiribati, Papua New Guinea, Samoa, Solomon Islands, Tonga and Vanuatu) grew only 0.6 per cent on a cumulative annual basis between 1986 and 2002 from US$1,143 to US$1,257. Real per capita GDP actually fell in the Federated States of Micronesia and the Solomon Islands over this period (World Bank 2005). Concerned by a slow-growth equilibrium and the failure in state institutions it can generate, a new body of scholarship advocates economic integration to break the region's underdevelopment bottleneck. Scollay and Gilbert (1998) use a computable general equilibrium model to predict that a free trade pact with significant reductions in tariffs would increase employment and welfare in all island economies. Stoeckel and Davis (1998) argue that net benefits are even higher when Australia and New Zealand include themselves in the free trade zone. Results such as these fuel support for the Pacific Island Countries Trade Agreement (PICTA—an island nation free trade area), the Pacific Islands Agreement on Closer Economic Relations (CER—an Oceania free trade area including Australia and New Zealand), and Economic Partner Agreements with the European Union (EPAs—preferential trade access for island countries in Europe) (Narsey 2004). Brown and Ahlburg (1999) conclude that liberal allowance for emigration to Australia and New Zealand generates a significant source of income for Pacific island economies. Remittances fund investments that expand domestic production capacity and effectively substitute for foreign aid transfers. De Brouwer (2000) advocates adoption of the Australian dollar by the island states because political uncertainty, limited foreign exchange liquidity, and unexpected global currency shocks would have less impact on the domestic value of money. Duncan (2000) and Duncan and Xu (2002) favour it specifically for Papua New Guinea and the Solomon Islands because of institutional factors. The opportunity costs of funding and staffing a domestic central bank are inefficiently high and political pressure to monetise government debt is too intense.

Advocacy of economic integration by scholars feeds more ambitious arguments for political integration. Work toward a Pacific economic and political community has been proposed by the Australian government. The arrangement would include a common currency (most likely the Australian dollar), a common labour market, homogenous rules for fiscal policy, and standardised legal provisions related to crime, governance, and environmental protection (Commonwealth of Australia 2003). Chand (2003) sees the proposal as feasible if integration is incremental. Successful implementation of free labour, capital, goods, and services flows across national boundaries precedes establishment of a unified financial market, a common currency, and a standard for fiscal policy. Political unification then follows this achievement of a common market. As in the evolution of the European Union, participation by each Pacific island state would be voluntary. The idea of political integration is not new. Moore (1982) argued for a Pacific Parliament whose powers would evolve like that of the European Parliament. Under this scenario, island states incrementally surrender aspects of sovereignty to regional governance as the dialogue between national parliaments and the Pacific Parliament establishes institutional consensus. The benefit of political integration for island states is less financial overhead from government bureaucracy and easier implementation of modern governance tools. In theory, this means that full political independence was an inefficient strategy for Pacific island decolonisation. A recent paper from the Centre for Independent Studies states it bluntly: 'Had the colonial powers promoted a federation of Pacific states in the 1960s…instead of creating independent states in their own image, the Pacific could by now have been a prosperous region' (Hughes 2004:10).

A successful history of regional cooperation and potential gains from institutional economies of scale undergird the logic of Pacific island state integration. The purity of this logic, though, is dirtied by the realities of implementation. Free trade generates a net benefit for Pacific island economies in the long run, but new exposure to competition realigns labour, capital, and enterprises in the regional market and generates a new family of economic 'winners' and 'losers' in the short run. Narsey (2004) predicts that new free trade arrangements in the region will produce unacceptable job losses (especially in manufacturing) and reductions in public revenues. Unable to compensate 'losers' with opportunities for income restoration, weak island states will face pressure to backtrack on tariff reductions and market liberalisation. The new jumble of economic 'winners' and 'losers' could be exacerbated by unified adoption of the Australian dollar as the regional currency. Bowman (2004) shows that, because of intensified trade between East Asia and the Pacific islands, island currencies do not empirically track well with the Australian dollar. Adoption of the Australian dollar might require unwanted structural adjustment in macroeconomic terms. Analysis reveals that the US dollar is more appropriate for a regional currency, but adoption of it would tie island states to a central bank (such as the Federal Reserve) with no interest in the impact of policies on Pacific island communities.

In terms of political integration, a supra-national parliament with majority or super-majority requirements for legislation clashes with precedents of consensus construction and fluid agenda frameworks observed in the Pacific Islands Forum. The issue is one of culture.

> Harmony is the important concept here. Unanimous compromise has the underlying thought that nobody gets left out. … Voting on issues, in circumstances that in the West would be considered normal, is often taken to be offensive and the preference is for voting not to be used as a decision tool (Rolfe 2000:434).

Because decisions are reached in a manner consistent with cultural norms, the Forum enjoys legitimacy among islanders that enables efficacy in the implementation of regional policy. For example, as an explicitly transnational action sanctioned by the Forum through consensus, the stabilisation achieved by the Regional Assistance Mission to the Solomon Islands (RAMSI) earned widespread praise (Hegarty et al. 2004). In contrast, Australia's unilateral deployment of police to Papua New Guinea under the Enhanced Cooperation Program struggled to establish legitimacy. The Supreme Court's unwillingness to uphold legal immunity for Australian officers in Papua New Guinea and tension with the Royal PNG Constabulary hastened an early withdrawal of the police force (*Herald Sun*, 17 May 2005:8; Wakas and Tapakau 2005).

The issue of legitimacy highlights the difference between form and substance in terms of transnational institutions. Australia's proposal for regional integration is the latest in a series of initiatives by metropolitan countries (especially aid donors) that push Pacific islands to modernise state institutions and reform their interface with market activity. Island countries should hurry up and prepare themselves for globalisation to avoid further economic malaise and dependency on aid transfers. Through funding, donors have placed priority emphasis on efficient structures of governance and public administration as part of this preparation (Sutherland 2000). In theory, once the workflow and architecture of state institutions are modernised, transnational integration is easier and island countries benefit from the economies of scale of shared bureaucracy. This insistence on institutional form ignores the link between state effectiveness and legitimacy. Without a high level of coercion (and the public resources required to fund it), a professionally-staffed, modern, transparent state institution cannot implement policy if the relevant community does not accept it as legitimate. Institutions earn legitimacy if they successfully solve collective action problems indigenous to the community. As Larmour (2000) points out in the case of institutional performance in Melanesia, institutional designs imported under the guise of 'modernisation' typically lack legitimacy because they have not evolved enough to overcome the local idiosyncrasies of social coordination problems.

Transnational integration of institutions among Pacific islands is a concept intellectually imported from Europe where incremental surrender of sovereignty has benefited members of the Maastricht Treaty. While regional coordination has been a successful venture in Oceania, cooperation has not become integration—there is as yet no precedent for national sovereignty transfer to a regional supra-national body. In the Pacific Islands Forum, discussion of members' internal affairs of a member is taboo unless invited or approved by the country of focus (the Solomon Islands government's desire, for example, for intervention by RAMSI) (Rolfe 2000). Cooperation without integration, though, does not preclude future fusion of political institutions. Journey toward the 1992 Maastricht Treaty, for example, began in 1951 with the Treaty of Paris, which eliminated cross-boundary trade restrictions on coal, iron, and steel between France, West Germany, Italy, Belgium, Luxembourg and the Netherlands (Trumbull 2003). European Union members are just now voting on a transnational constitution (*New York Times*, 13 January 2005:15). For Oceania, timing is the important issue of integration. Successful political integration of Europe has taken 50 years, and the process started with countries at a much higher level of per capita GDP than the Pacific islands. A rush to integrate Oceania may therefore be an ill-timed institutional vault along the global convergence trajectory of economies in the region.

To underscore this argument, Oceania is compared to the Caribbean where another group of developing island countries is farther along in its integration efforts. Island states in the Caribbean established a free trade area in 1968. In 1973, this evolved into the Caribbean Community and Common Market (CARICOM) which added common external tariffs and tax harmonisation to free trade arrangements (Atkinson 1982). Considered successful, CARICOM enhanced the flow of goods and services between members and strengthened the region's position in global trade negotiations (Levitt 2004). A regional currency was formalised in 1983 with incorporation of the East Caribbean Central Bank to manage the supply of East Caribbean dollars (Worrell 2003). The macroeconomic impact of currency union, though, has not met theoretical expectations—especially since fiscal discipline has not been achieved. Kufa et al. (2003) argue that stability of the currency union is questionable because of the high level of public debt incurred by member governments. This along with a deficit in structural convergence among Caribbean economies implies little or no benefit from regional expansion of the currency union beyond its six current members—Antigua and Barbuda, Dominica, Grenada, St. Kitts and Nevis, St. Lucia, and St. Vincent and the Grenadines (Anthony and Hallett 2000). Efforts to form a West Indies federation were made shortly after Caribbean states won independence in the 1960s and 1970s, but political integration never occurred because benefits were not perceived to justify the surrender of national sovereignty (Padmore 1999). Before Caribbean political integration is possible, citizens of the region must develop a transnational West Indian identity that sparks indigenous solutions to development challenges and endows any supra-national Caribbean institutions with legitimacy to govern (Levitt 2004).

Table 12.1 reveals that the Pacific islands trail the Caribbean in terms of global economic convergence and evolutionary context. Between 1986 and 2002, real per capita GDP (measured in terms of year 2000 US dollars) averaged across 11 independent island states in the Caribbean grew only 1.4 per cent on a cumulative annual basis.[3] Over this period, real per capita GDP grew from US$4,697 to US$5,871 (World Bank 2005). Standard deviation across the country sample fell from US$4,286 in 1986 to US$4,231 in 2002. This result suggests some amount of economic convergence within the Caribbean. Comparatively, the Pacific islands experienced weaker growth (0.6 per cent cumulative annual growth rate) and a lower level of real per capita income (US$1,257 in 2002). In contrast, minor regional divergence occurred as standard deviation across the eight Pacific countries increased from US$541 in 1986 to US$634 in 2002. In terms of Figure 12.1, the Caribbean is closer to point Z than the South Pacific. In addition, aggregate growth performance indicates that, as a regional economy, the Caribbean is evolving in a manner more consistent with convergence theory. In the Caribbean's more advanced state, though, the stability of monetary integration is questionable and first steps toward political integration have not begun. If convergence theory is

Table 12.1   Convergence in the Caribbean and Pacific islands

Real per capita GDP (Year 2000 US$)	1986	1990	1994	1998	2002
Caribbean					
Antigua and Barbuda	6,313	7,618	8,657	9,012	9,157
Bahamas	15,747	15,832	14,510	14,928	15,338
Barbados	8,136	8,580	8,113	9,253	9,176
Dominica	2,519	3,132	3,308	3,722	3,476
Dominican Republic	1,524	1,576	1,724	2,103	2,458
Haiti	751	700	523	504	474
Jamaica	2,511	3,081	3,166	3,081	3,112
St. Kitts and Nevis	3,959	5,236	6,212	7,605	7,427
St. Lucia	2,702	3,933	4,226	4,376	4,143
St. Vincent and the Grenadines	2,069	2,574	2,624	2,878	3,136
Trinidad and Tobago	5,434	4,914	4,908	5,763	6,689
Caribbean average	4,697	5,198	5,271	5,748	5,871
Caribbean standard deviation	4,286	4,255	3,968	4,157	4,231
Pacific islands					
Fiji	1,851	1,867	1,999	2,055	2,253
Kiribati	439	431	461	543	564
Micronesia, FS of	1,916	1,965	2,169	1,837	1,818
Papua New Guinea	611	560	791	687	642
Samoa	1,227	1,185	1,144	1,310	1,485
Solomon Islands	766	788	855	855	585
Tonga	1,263	1,241	1,427	1,471	1,607
Vanuatu	1,071	1,050	1,299	1,239	1,100
Pacific islands average	1,143	1,136	1,268	1,250	1,257
Pacific islands standard deviation	541	559	590	537	634

valid, these observations from the Caribbean suggest that any discussion of currency union or political integration among Pacific island states is dangerously premature. A free trade pact may be the only form of integration worthy of consideration. Oceania's slow growth and economic divergence imply a continued underdevelopment bottleneck within the region (see the line segment UE in Figure 12.1). Breaking the bottleneck requires more internal focus on institutional development by Pacific island governments. Without internal strength, Pacific island states cannot effectively participate in transnational governance and current dreams of institutional integration are an academic distraction.

THEORETICAL FOUNDATIONS FOR SUSTAINABLE INSTITUTIONAL INTEGRATION

Opposition to integration of Pacific island states must rest upon a theory of institutional evolution. Such a theory can be grounded in cooperative game theory. If integration is sustainable, then the supra-national institutions formed from it successfully solve transnational collective action problems. Transnational integration can be considered a natural iteration in an evolutionary process of institutional aggregation that complements economic convergence and the pressure of globalisation that fuels it. Rubin (2001) argues that biological natural selection favoured humans who cooperated well in groups. The first phase of social aggregation was therefore a natural outcome of biology. The division of labour and scale economies achieved through cooperation generated a surplus that enhanced survivability and lengthened life. Early human cooperation occurred in small kin-based groups. This fact explains why family groups remain the fundamental unit of collective action in most societies. As human interaction widened and deepened through conflict, intermarriage, and trade, cooperation evolved across family units and formed hierarchies of group membership. For example, this type of evolution occurred in Fiji and leaves footprints in modern social structure and the native language. The fundamental unit of Fijian society is the *i tokatoka*, or extended family. Each *i tokatoka* belongs to a family group known as the *mataqali*. Multiple *mataqali* form a clan called a *yavusa*. A *vanua* aggregates *yavusa* groups for the purpose of political, economic and social interaction. An alliance among *vanua* forms a *matanitu* which is a Fijian tribal state (Lasaqa 1984). Although encouraged by the British colonial authority, the Council of Chiefs represents the latest iteration of community aggregation in Fiji. The council is now an 'apex of the Fijian administration' which 'had not previously existed in any form prior to colonisation because the Fijians had never organised themselves along national lines' (Lawson 1990:801).

The timing of the next level of aggregation is the important theoretical question. Conditions for stability and the time it takes to meet such conditions must be identified for policymakers who seek to manage the integration process. At a basic level, interaction between distinct units of society can be modelled as an infinitely-repeated prisoner's dilemma game (Rubin 2001). A unit can choose conflict or cooperation. Cooperation occurs naturally when the one-time payoff from conflict does not justify the loss of net gains from indefinite cooperation. To explain this dynamic, suppose two clans in a tribal society can interact. Either can raid the other's villages, extract resources, and enhance wealth through confiscation of the 'spoils of victory'. Conflict, though, prohibits an economic relationship that would generate gains from trade for each clan. If the expected present value of gains from trade is higher than the present value of the 'spoils of victory', then cooperation naturally occurs with no coercion. If cooperation is stable, then integration between clans occurs and a new level is added to society's hierarchy of group membership (Figure 12.2). Interaction of clans A and B forms AB and interaction of clans C and D forms CD, where AB and CD are the newest units of aggregation in society. In evolutionary terms, the next level of integration requires cooperation between AB and CD to form ABCD. As long as the stability of cooperation is guaranteed, the time it takes to evolve from one level of aggregation to the next is merely a function of how long it takes candidate integrants to communicate and appraise each other's comparative advantage.

Logically, ABCD only sustains itself if the AB and CD partnerships remain strong. Applied to the issue of Pacific integration, ABCD represents the

Figure 12.2   Hierarchy of community aggregation

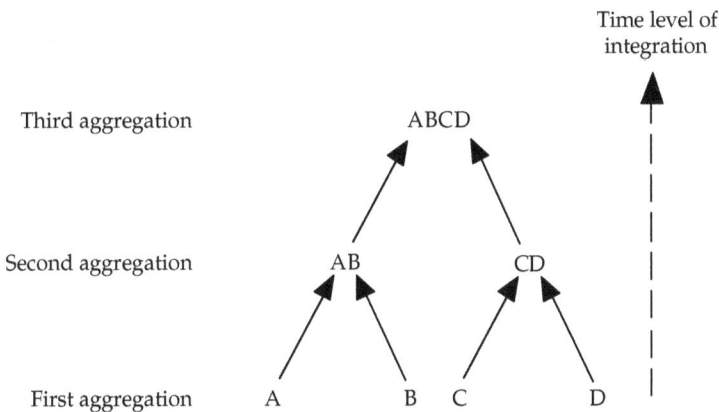

transnational institutions of regional governance and AB and CD each represent states that must cement the loyalty of their respective sub-national groups. Aid donors play an important role in the dynamics of this hierarchy because they typically fund an important share of state architecture in Pacific island nations. For example, grants from donors account for 20 per cent, 37 per cent, and 63 per cent of government revenue in Papua New Guinea, Samoa, and the Federated States of Micronesia respectively (Chamon et al. 2005; Komori et al. 2005; Sidgwick et al. 2004). In the context of Pacific integration, two traditional institutional development strategies by donors reveal themselves. A strategy of *regional transformation* initiates and funds the physical institutions of regional governance. Aid donors funding the construction of a Pacific Parliament by subsidising the salaries of Pacific island parliament members would exemplify this type of strategy. A strategy of *state transformation* financially supports modern institutions of state in Pacific island nations. Current examples include the allocation of A$10 million by AusAID to enhance the capacity of Fiji's courts, police, prisons, and Ministry of Justice and New Zealand's provision of a Solicitor-General for the Attorney General's Office of Kiribati (AusAID 2004; NZAid 2002).

A third strategy of *state evolution* is an alternative to the two *transformation* strategies previously mentioned. A *state evolution* strategy is different because it does not directly finance the organs of state. The focus is instead on investment in a national environment that naturally, but indirectly, hastens a state with more legitimacy. In many developing countries, state legitimacy must ultimately come from rural indigenous institutions that already enforce social norms and solve collective action problems. Kenny (1998) offers empirical support for this view with a case from Senegal, and Powell (2004) uses game theory to justify application of the hypothesis to Melanesia. The idea dictates policies that strengthen (or at a minimum do not threaten) the political role of traditional institutions and enable a natural evolution of civil and economic arrangements that consensually invite a stronger institutional role for the state. Projects that enhance the capacity of indigenous institutions and the rural economy to generate income, either directly through the provision of capital or indirectly through the generation of public goods, achieve this goal. Under these arrangements, indigenous institutions simultaneously enhance their wealth and call upon the state to facilitate a market environment that expands income-earning opportunities. The voluntary surrender of mineral rights to the state by indigenous tribes within Botswana in response to the discovery of diamonds provides an example of how this can occur (Alfaro et al. 2003). Although *state transformation* better characterises the aid strategies of Australia and New Zealand, both countries fund some projects that support *state evolution*. For example, AusAID contributes to the Ha'apai Development Fund in Tonga, which expands infrastructure in outer islands. The fund is governed by a committee that includes local decision-makers (AusAID 2003). This project simultaneously expands rural income potential, makes indigenous leaders stakeholders, and gives the state an obvious opportunity to add economic value and enhance its legitimacy.

Using the lexicon of Figure 12.2, an aid strategy of regional transformation funds the institutions of ABCD, a strategy of state transformation funds the institutions of AB and CD, and a strategy of state evolution separately targets the institutions of A, B, C, and D. The contrast between the transformation strategies and state evolution strategy is a classic tension between 'top-down' and 'bottom-up' development strategies. Certain logic behind the regional transformation and state transformation strategies has merit. Philosophically, their proponents believe that well-designed institutions naturally breed good governance. For example, as already mentioned, de Brouwer (2000), Duncan (2000), and Duncan and Xu (2002) advocate adoption of the Australian dollar by Pacific island states. This policy would enable Pacific island states to enjoy the instant anti-inflationary benefits of a credible Australian central bank and would remove the financial burden on domestic taxpayers of funding the overhead of a central bank. These points underscore two general arguments made in favour of transformation strategies. First, institutional changes can be made fairly quickly when shepherded by the money and technical expertise of donors. Results can be achieved much faster than the incremental nature of state evolution. Second, proposed changes are based on institutional trial-and-error that has already occurred in developed countries. Developing countries can avoid inefficiencies and adopt 'best practices' in terms of institutional design.

Critics of this institution-cum-governance view argue that it dangerously oversimplifies the issue of legitimacy. Kenny (1998:161) argues this in the context of Africa.

> The concentration on the importance of governance…is based on a view of the state as an independent actor rather than as imbedded in a social structure…New institutional structures will fail throughout most of Africa because it is not formal institutional structures which promote state legitimacy, but informal structures and beliefs.

An absence of legitimacy makes the purchase of institutional success expensive for aid donors. The success too is unsustainable because it disappears once aid transfers stop. If a donor is willing to subsidise institutional success *ad infinitum*, then a state transformation or regional transformation strategy might be the most efficient. In this case, however, assimilation, rather than integration, better describes the long-term goal. Integration is an incremental aggregation of pre-existing sovereign units whereas assimilation dissolves the sovereignty of one unit and subsumes its membership into another unit that strengthens its own sovereignty. For example, regional adoption of the Australian dollar will shut down central banks in the Pacific islands and transfer authority over monetary policy to the Reserve Bank of Australia. In theory, the maximum scope of a state's legitimacy correlates with the dimensions of policy that it can potentially control. When the conduct of monetary policy is transferred to a foreign central bank, the ceiling on legitimacy that a Pacific island state can achieve falls a degree. Whereas Australian dollarisation of the Pacific represents assimilation, adoption of the Euro by European Union members describes true integration. The states involved do not struggle to establish legitimacy and the new currency is an explicit expression of European aggregation rather than adoption of an already existent medium of exchange. The lesson for Pacific island aid donors is to be clear on long-term goals. If integration is the goal (at either the national or regional level), institutions that are a product of aggregation must have legitimacy before they will function without external subsidy and management. If assimilation is the goal, then donors must be prepared to assume a permanent financial and administrative burden that bribes the loyalty of the integrated Pacific island community. Failure to distinguish between these goals and align aid projects appropriately will generate another round of disappointment in the performance of foreign assistance in the Pacific.

CONCLUSION

As a region, the island states of Oceania are not ready for transnational integration of institutions. The success of integration in the European Union and the existence of free trade areas and currency unions in the Caribbean can spark misplaced exuberance for integration among Pacific scholars. Integration strategies should be grounded in application of global convergence theory. High levels of per capita income, economic homogeneity, and a strong sense of transnational identity have made the 50 year process of European integration a success. The Caribbean has not evolved to the same point as Europe. For this reason, the stability of the East Caribbean Currency Union is questionable, and no credible movement toward political integration is witnessed. The Pacific islands are one step behind the Caribbean. Many Pacific island states, especially in Melanesia, have failed to integrate communities within their own national boundaries. The legitimacy of the state as a national actor must first be established before transnational integration becomes an initiative worthy of pursuit.

Convergence theory is an imperfect but useful theoretical tool for framing the Pacific islands' development trajectory. Through growth in real per capita GDP, economic convergence speeds a developing economy toward the prosperity enjoyed by countries that exercise global economic leadership. The growth path is supported by a process of institutional evolution that incrementally integrates units of society through establishment of new cooperative equilibria among larger and larger groups. At this time, integration of state institutions in the Pacific would be an artificial and unsustainable leapfrog in the process of community aggregation. Imposition of a relatively advanced institution upon only partially evolved Pacific island economies would generate inefficient complexity and impede the region's ability to break its underdevelopment bottleneck. A 2003 Senate Report suggests a leadership role for Australia in spearheading the construction of institutions for regional governance (Commonwealth of Australia 2003). Australian policymakers should not confuse integration with assimilation. Integration requires patience because Pacific island states must first gain legitimacy among their own polities. Regional institutions of governance will have no chance of sustainability unless this first occurs. An alternative goal for Australia would be assimilation. Adoption of the Australian dollar in the region would be a first step in this direction. A newfound willingness among troubled Pacific states to allow Australian public servants to fill positions in their own government hints at potential acceptance of assimilation if the economic benefits generously compensate for the transfer of administration or sovereignty to Canberra. The charge to the Australian taxpayer of assimilation, though, will be much higher and the commitment much longer than if Canberra chooses a more patient approach of integration and state legitimacy enhancement.

Assuming that assimilation is not a preferred choice, analysis reveals the following takeaways for regional policymakers. The Pacific Islands Forum should continue its tradition of reaching decisions through consensus based on a fluid agenda of discussion. Because this process is consistent with the cultural norms of islanders, the execution of decisions by the Forum carry a needed level of legitimacy. As this legitimacy strengthens itself through iterations of successful cooperative ventures, a stronger foundation for regional integration will develop in the long run. Australian efforts to rush regional integration and make the Forum more aggressive simply reverse the Forum's legitimacy and make it less effective as an agent of collective action. In the short run, the Forum should not waste energy on proposals for currency union or transnational merger of governance and public administration. Discussion of integration should limit itself to free trade pact implementation as envisioned by PICTA and CER. The trade success of CARICOM suggests a hopeful future for these two initiatives.

If foreign donors desire regional integration, they should replace explicit discussion of integration with a domestic focus on changes that endow Pacific island states with more legitimacy among their citizens. These changes likely require constitutional reform that decentralises power and weakens the unitary nature of parliamentary democracies in the region. Transfer of limited constitutional sovereignty to federalised jurisdictions achieves two desirable outcomes. First, the distribution of state spending will be better equalised in geographical terms. This better allocates public good production and theoretically speeds rural income growth. Decentralisation of public finance also reduces the spoils of corruption within the parliament and among bureaucrats in the capital city. Second, transfer of power to local units politically dominated by traditional decision-makers forces the state to cooperate with indigenous institutions. This benefits the state in the long run because policies will be a product of partnership with indigenous institutions that already command the loyalty of local polities. In the end, domestic legitimacy of Pacific island states is a necessary condition for successful transnational integration of Pacific island governance. Island governments and aid donors should sequence their policy initiatives and political energy in a logical way that recognises this fact.

NOTES

[1]   See Table 5 of Barro (1999). The six countries that performed below expectations in 1995 in terms of democracy were Cameroon, Fiji, Gambia, Kenya, Lesotho and Liberia. The six countries that maintained democracy at or above the expected level were Botswana, Mauritius, Senegal, Tanzania, Zambia, and Papua New Guinea.

[2]   The East African Currency Board comprised Kenya, Uganda, and Tanzania. It started in 1960 and disbanded in 1972. The Rand Monetary Area consists of South Africa, Namibia, Lesotho and Swaziland. Botswana was an original member but left (Guillaume and Stasavage 2000). The West African Economic and Monetary Union includes Benin, Burkina Faso, Côte d'Ivoire, Guinea-Bissau, Mali, Niger, Senegal and Togo. Cameroon, Central African Republic, Chad, Republic of Congo (Brazzaville), Equatorial Guinea and Gabon make up the Central African Economic and Monetary Community (Fielding et al 2004). The CFA BCEAO Franc is the official currency in the West African Union and the CFA BEAC Franc is the official currency in the Central African Community.

[3]   Because 1986 is the first year for which data are available for the Federated States of Micronesia, it was chosen as the beginning of the sample period for comparison purposes. Since the island states are the focus of comparison, non-island countries in Central or South America were deliberately excluded from the Caribbean sample. Grenada was excluded because of incomplete World Bank data during the 1986–2002 period. Cuba was excluded because of its position as an institutional outlier and its lack of membership in CARICOM.

COMMENT

Theodore Levantis

Powell has taken an issue which, in his words has become a fashionable solution to the Pacific region's economic problems, and turned it on its head. He is convincing in his opinion that regional integration is misconceived and inappropriate, and his arguments are backed with sound reasoning and a well informed understanding of international parallels. However, the modelling and economic theorising presented appear to be peripheral to the paper—their purpose is to explain principles rather than prove Powell's arguments—so I would have preferred to see this aspect downplayed.

I am convinced that Powell is correct in his conclusions, however, the 'policy community', as Powell describes it, is riding a wave and this quality work is likely to leave little impression in these circles. It will not be until regional integration fails that policy direction will change and a new fashion is embraced.

But will regional integration fail? So long as the Australian government finances the concept, the process will continue. I agree with Powell that it is likely to fail to bring anything to development in the Pacific, and it will do little if anything to improve institutions and lower costs. Instead, the process will divert attention and resources away from priority needs within the Pacific nations.

For example, a free trade pact will do little, if anything, for economic prosperity in the region. The nations of the Pacific have similar economic structures—in particular import/export structures—and do not have the depth and diversity to take advantage of reductions in trade barriers. Exports are dominated by commodities and international tourism, and imports are dominated by manufactures, the bulk of which have no competing industries in the region. Are the small gains in a free trade pact worth diverting scarce resources and scarce skilled public sector labour in these countries to pursuing this objective?

A currency union, for the reasons that Powell outlined, could be disastrous. Moreover, if a Pacific currency is established and then allowed to float, there will be similar consequences of extreme exchange volatility that Papua New Guinea has suffered since the float of the kina in 1995—with devastating consequences for business and investment in that country (see Levantis and Manning 2002). Alternatively, if the Pacific nations were to adopt the Australian dollar, it would enable these nations to maintain the exchange stability that they already enjoy (all countries other than Papua New Guinea peg their exchange rate) but with long-term certainty. However, regional integration is not needed for individual Pacific nations to adopt the Australian dollar.

Pacific nations are separated by thousands of kilometres of ocean and travel between them is difficult, costly, and irregular. Under these conditions it is unbelievable that people in policy circles would consider a common labour market could contribute in any way to development. Only the very top echelon of the labour market would have the means to travel in countries like Solomon Islands, Papua New Guinea and Vanuatu. Most other nations in the Pacific have a community focus of exporting their labour to developed nations, particularly Australia, New Zealand, the United States and Canada. This has been highly successful for Tonga and Samoa in particular and has underpinned their success in human development indicators—despite the absence of a production base, or a potential production base. The export of labour from these nations is not going to divert to poorer neighbouring Pacific countries.

I agree with Powell that transnational public administration will fail to bring benefits for the reasons he has outlined. The Pacific is not like the Caribbean nations, which are in the vicinity of each other, or the European nations, for which international travel can be achieved by car, bus or rail. Having institutional bodies with responsibility across thousand of kilometres of ocean, where travel is so difficult and costly, makes no sense. There are proven exceptions to this—the University of South Pacific is a good example—but to be an exception, the institutions need to be free or relatively free of domestic functions. For example, there cannot ever be central Pacific institutions operating health services, law and order functions, tax collections or primary and secondary education. Statistical collection is one area where it may be worthwhile investigating the merits of integration. However, it is hard to imagine that, in view of the isolation of these nations, integration would be better than direct institutional support in each country from, say, the Australian Bureau of Statistics.

As Powell says, we should first focus on building and strengthening the institutions in Pacific nations before entertaining ideas of integration. The priorities need to be put in order. The best approach for the Australian government to take for assisting the building and strengthening of institutions is to establish supportive alliances with the corresponding institutions in Australia (statistic collections is a good example). It is to the merit of Australian policymakers that some progress has been made in pursuing this path in recent years.

REFERENCES

Abbott D. and Pollard, S., 2004. *Hardship and Poverty in the Pacific*, Asian Development Bank, Manila.

ABC Online, 2003. AM—Fiji's Foreign Minister Talks about Pooled Regional Governance, 23 July. Available from http://www.abc.net.au/am/content/2003/s908328.htm (accessed 20 April 2005).

Abdelal, R. and Haddad, K., 2001. *Russia: the end of a time of troubles?*, Havard Business School Case 9-701-076, Harvard Business School Publishing, Boston.

Alesina, A. and Spolaore, E., 2003. *The Size of Nations*, MIT Press, Cambridge, Massachusetts.

Alesina, A. and Wacziarg, R., 1997. *Openness, Country Size and the Government*, NBER Working Paper No. 6024, National Bureau of Economic Research, Cambridge, Massachusetts.

Alfaro, L., Spar, D., Allibhoy, F. and Dev, V., 2003. *Bostwana: a diamond in the rough*, Harvard Business School Case 9-703-027, Harvard Business School Publishing, Boston.

Andriamananjara, S. and Schiff, M., 2001. 'Regional cooperation among microstates', *Review of International Economics*, 9(1):42–51.

Anthony, M.L. and Hallett, A.H., 2000. 'Is the case for economic and monetary union in the Caribbean realistic?', *World Economy*, 23(1):119–45.

Asian Development Bank (ADB) and Ministry of Finance and Planning Fiji, 2003. *Fiji: Poverty Status,* Discussion Paper, TA 6047, Asian Development Bank, Manila.

Atkins, J., Mazzi, S. and Easter, C., 2000. *A Commonwealth Vulnerability Index for Developing Countries: the position of small states*, Economic Paper 40, Commonwealth Secretariat, London.

Atkinson, G.W., 1982. 'Economic integration in the Caribbean Community: a problem of institutional adjustment', *Journal of Economic Issues*, 16(2):507–13.

AusAID, 2004. *Pacific Program Profiles 2003–04*, AusAID, Canberra.

——, 2005. *Country Programmes: Pacific*, AusAID, Canberra. Available from http://www.ausaid.gov.au/country/southpacific.cfm (linkaccessed).

Auty, R.M., 2001. *Resource Abundance and Economic Development*, Oxford University Press, Oxford.

Banerjee A., Dolado, J.J., Galbraith, J.W. and Hendry, D.F., 1993. *Co-integration, Error Correction, and the Econometric Analysis of Non-stationary Data: advanced text in econometrics*, Oxford University Press, Oxford.

Banerjee, A., Hendry, D.F., and Smith, G.W., 1986. 'Exploring equilibrium relationships in econometrics through static models: some Monte Carlo evidence', *Oxford Bulletin of Economics and Statistics*, 48(3):253–77.

Barclay, K. and Yoshikazu, W., 2000. 'Solomon Taiyo Ltd—tuna dreams realised?', *Pacific Economic Bulletin*, 15(1):34–47.

Barro, R.J., 1999. 'Determinants of democracy', *Journal of Political Economy*, 107(6):S158–S183.

Bertignac, M., Campbell, H.F., Hampton, J. and Hand, A., 2000, 'Maximizing resource rent from the Western and Central Pacific Tuna Fisheries', *Marine Resource Economics*, 15(3):151–77.

Bhagwati, J., 2004. *In Defense of Globalization*, Oxford University Press, Oxford.

Bowman, C., 2004. 'Pacific Island countries and dollarisation', *Pacific Economic Bulletin*, 19(3):115–32.

Briguglio, L., 1995. 'Small island developing states and their economic vulnerabilities', *World Development*, 23(9):1615–32.

——, 1997. *Alternative Economic Vulnerability Indicators for Developing Countries*, Report to the Expert Group on Vulnerability Indices UN-DESA, Rome 17–19 December.

——, 2002. 'The economic vulnerability of small island developing states', in Hsin-Huang Michael Hsiao, Chao-Han Liu, and Huei-Min Tsai (eds), *Sustainable Development for Island Societies: Taiwan and the world*, Asia-Pacific Research Program, Academia Sinica and SARCS Secretariat Publication, Taiwan:73–89.

——, 2003. The Vulnerability Index and Small Island Developing States: a review of conceptual and methodological issues, Paper prepared for the AIMS Regional Preparatory Meeting on the BPoA+10 Review, Praia, Cape Verde, 1–5 September.

——, 2004. 'Economic vulnerability and resilience: concepts and measurements', in L. Briguglio and E.J. Kisanga (eds), *Economic Vulnerability and Resilience of Small States*, Islands and Small States Institute, Malta and Commonwealth Secretariat, London:43–53.

—— and Galea, W., 2003. *Updating the Economic Vulnerability Index*, Occasional Papers on Islands and Small States 2003–4, Islands and Small States Institute, Malta.

Briguglio, L., Pesseud, B. and Stern, R., 2005. Towards an Outward-Oriented Development Strategy for Small States: issues, opportunities and resilience building, mimeo, World Bank, Washington, D.C.

Brown, R.P.C. and Ahlburg, D.A., 1999. 'Remittances in the South Pacific', *International Journal of Social Economics*, 26(1/2/3):325–44.

Bureau of Transport and Regional Economics, 2003. *International city pairs time series 1999–current.* Department of Transport and Regional Services, Canberra. Available from http://www.btre.gov.au/statistics/aviation/international_time_series_downloads.aspx (accessed 6 June 2005).

Caton, A. and McLoughlin, K. (eds), 2004. *Fishery Status Reports 2004: status of fish stocks managed by the Australian Government*, Bureau of Rural Sciences, Canberra.

Central Intelligence Agency (CIA), 2005. *The World Fact Book 2005*, Central Intelligence Agency, Washington, DC. Available from http://www.cia.gov/cia/publications/factbook/index.html (accessed 6 June 2005).

Chamon, M., Semblat, R., and Morant, A., 2005. *Samoa: selected issues and statistical appendix*, IMF Country Report 05/221, International Monetary Fund, Washington, DC.

Chand, S., 2003. 'An assessment of the proposal for a Pacific economic and political community,' *Pacific Economic Bulletin*, 18(2):117–24.

——, Grafton, R.Q. and Petersen, E., 2003. 'Multilateral governance of fisheries: management and cooperation in the Western and Central Pacific tuna fisheries', *Marine Resource Economics*, 18(4):329–44.

Chanda, R., 2003. Linkages between Mode 4 and Other Forms of Services Trade, Paper presented at the OECD–World Bank–IOM seminar on Trade and Migration, Geneva, 12–14 November.

Collier, P., 1995. 'The marginalization of Africa', *International Labor Review*, 134(4–5):541–57.

Colombatto, E., 1998. 'An institutional view of LDC failure', *Journal of Policy Modeling*, 20(5):631–48.

Commonwealth of Australia, 2003. *Pacific Engaged: Australia's relations with Papua New Guinea and the island states of the south-west Pacific*, Senate Foreign Affairs, Defence and Trade References Committee, Commonwealth of Australia, Canberra.

Commonwealth Secretariat, various years. *Small States: economic review and basic statistics*, Annual Series, Commonwealth Secretariat, London.

Congressional Budget Office, 1999. *Preliminary Estimates of Effective Tax Rates*, Congressional Budget Office, Washington, DC.

Cordina, G., 2004a. 'Economic vulnerability, resilience and capital formation', in L. Briguglio and E.J. Kisanga (eds), *Economic Vulnerability and Resilience of Small States*, Islands and Small States Institute, Malta and Commonwealth Secretariat, London:104–112.

——, 2004b. 'Economic vulnerability and economic growth: some results from a neo-Classical growth modelling approach', *Journal of Economic Development*, 29(2):21–39

Crocombe, R. and Neemia, U., 1983. 'Options in university education for the Pacific islands', *Pacific Perspective* 12(1):5–17.

—— and Meleisea, M., 1988. 'Achievements, problems and prospects: the future of university education in the South Pacific' in R. Crocombe and M. Meleisea (eds), *Pacific Universities: achievements, problems and prospects*, Institute of Pacific Studies, University of the South Pacific, Suva:20–34.

Crowards, T., 2000. *An Index of Inherent Economic Vulnerability for Developing Countries*, Staff Working Paper 6/00, Caribbean Development Bank, Barbados.

Daunton, M., 2002. *Just Taxes: The politics of taxation in Britain, 1914–1979*, Cambridge University Press, Cambridge.

de Vries, B.A., 1975. 'Development aid to small countries', in P. Selwyn (ed.), *Development Policy in Small States*, Croom Helm Ltd, London.

Department of Foreign Affairs and Trade (DFAT), 2004. *Closing Statement on DS 265 Made to the Dispute Settlement Panel of the WTO*, Asutralian Department of Foreign Affairs and Trade, Canberra. Available from http://www.dfat.gov.au/trade/negotiations/disputes/040101_first_panel_hearing_closing_statement_sugar.html (accessed 28 February 2005.)

——, 2005. *Country, Economy and Regional Information*, Australian Department of Foreign Affairs and Trade, Canberra. Available from www.dfat.gov.au/geo/ (accessed 3 May 2005).

Docquier, F. and Marfouk, A., 2005. *Measuring the International Mobility of Skilled Workers (1990–2000)*, Policy Research Working Paper 3381, World Bank, Washington, D.C.

Downes, A.S., 1988. 'On the statistical measurement of smallness: a principal component measure of size', *Social and Economic Studies* 37(3):75–96.

Duncan, R.C., 1994. 'On achieving sound and stable economic policies in the Pacific Islands', *Pacific Economic Bulletin*, 9(1):21–26.

——, 2002. 'Dollarising the Solomon Islands economy', *Pacific Economic Bulletin*, 17(2):143–46.

——, Cuthbertson, S., and Bosworth, M., 1999. *Pursuing Economic Reform in the Pacific*, Asian Development Bank, Manila.

Duncan, R. and Temu, I., 1997. 'Trade, investment and sustainable development of natural resources in the Pacific: the case of fish and timber' in *Enhancing Cooperation in Trade and Investment between Pacific Island Countries and Economies of East and South-East Asia*, Development Research and Policy Analysis Division (DRPAD), United Nations, New York:175–211.

Encontre, P., 1999. 'The vulnerability and resilience of small island developing states in the context of globalization', *Natural Resources Forum*, 23(3):261–70.

Ergas, H. and Findlay, C., 2003. 'New directions in Australian air transport', *Agenda*, 10(1):27–42.

——, 2004. Value Based Airlines, Paper presented at the ANU/NECG Conference on the Performance of Air Transport Markets, Canberra, 24–25 June.

Esty, D.C., Levy, M., Srebotnjak, T. and de Sherbinin, A., 2005. *Environmental Sustainability Index: benchmarking national environmental stewardship*, Yale Center for Environmental Law Policy, New Haven.

European Commission, 2002. *Economic Partnership Agreements: a new approach in the relations between the European Union and the African, Caribbean and Pacific countries*, European Commission, Belgium.

Exports and Infrastructure Taskforce, 2005. *Australia's Export Infrastructure: Report to the Prime Minister*, Canberra, May.

Falkland Islands Government, 2005. 'Fisheries', Falkland Islands Government, Falkland Islands. Available from http://www.falklandislands.com/business/fisheries.asp (accessed 8 June 2005).

Food and Agriculture Organisation, 1999a. Sustainable Production, Intensification and Diversification of Agriculture, Forestry and Fisheries in Small Island Developing States, Special Ministerial Conference on Agriculture in Small Island Developing States, Rome.

——, 1999b. Trade Issues Facing Small Island Developing States, Special Ministerial Conference on Agriculture in Small Island Developing States, Rome.

——, 2005. *Total Production 1950–2003*, Fishstat Dataset, FAO, Rome. Available from http://www.fao.org/fi/statist/fisoft/FISHPLUS.asp (accessed 8 April, 2005).

Farrugia, N., 2004. Economic Vulnerability: developing a new conceptual framework and empirically assessing its relationship with economic growth, MA Thesis, University of Malta, Malta.

Field, M., 2004. 'Fiji sugar turns sour: time has run out for country's sugar industry', *Pacific Magazine*, March 2004. Available online at http://www.pacificislands.cc/pm32004/pmdefault.php?urlarticleid=0005 (accessed 27 Septmeber 2004)

Fielding, D., 1996. 'Asymmetries in the behaviour of members of a monetary union: a game-theoretic model with an application to West Africa', *Journal of African Economies*, 5(3):343–65.

——, Lee, K., and Shields, K., 2004. 'The characteristics of macroeconomic shocks in the CFA Franc Zone', *Journal of African Economies*, 13(4):488–517.

Fiji Islands Bureau of Statistics, 1999. *Annual Employment Survey: 1999*, Fiji Islands Bureau of Statistics, Suva.

Fischer, S., Hernandez-Cata, E. and Khan, M.S., 1998. *Africa: is this the turning point?*, IMF Paper on Policy Analysis and Assessment 98/6, International Monetary Fund, Washington, DC.

Forsyth, D.,1998. 'Labour markets and economic growth in the PDMCs', in R. Duncan, R. Crocombe, D. Forsyth, S. Chand, and N. Vousden, *Improving Growth Prospects in the Pacific*, Pacific Studies Series, Asian Development Bank, Manila:69–100.

——, 2003. Framework for EPA Negotiations with the European Union: investment study, Report for Pacific Islands Forum Secretariat, Suva

Forsyth, P and King, J. 1996. 'Cooperation, competition and financial performance in South Pacific aviation', in G. Hufbauer and C. Findlay (eds), *Flying High: liberalising civil aviation in the Asia Pacific*, Washington Institute for International Economics, Washington:99–118.

Fry, G., 1994. 'Climbing back onto the map? The South Pacific Forum and the new development orthodoxy', *Journal of Pacific History*, 29(3):64–72.

——, 2005. Pooled Governance in the Island Pacific: lessons from history, Paper presented at the International Workshop on Pacific Integration and Regional Governance, Canberra, 8–9 June.

Gillett, R., McCoy, M., Rodwell, L. and Tamate, J., 2001. Tuna: a key economic resource in the Pacific, Report prepared for the Asian Development Bank and the Forum Fisheries Agency, Asian Development Bank, Manila.

Grafton, R.Q., Arnason, R., Bjørndal, T., Campbell, D., Campbell, H.F., Clark, C.W., Connor, R., Dupont, D.P., Hannesson, R. Hilborn, R., Kirkley, J.E., Kompas, T., Lane, D.E., Munro, G.R., Pascoe, S., Squires, D., Steinshamn, S.I., Turris, B.R. and Weninger, Q., 2005. *Incentive-based Approaches to Sustainable Fisheries*, Economics and Environment Network Working Paper EEN 0501, Australian National University, Canberra.

Gregan, T. and Johnson, M., 1999. *Impacts of Competition Enhancing Air Services Agreements: a network modelling approach*, Productivity Commission Staff Research Paper, AusInfo, Canberra.

Grossman, G. and Helpman, E., 1996. 'Rent dissipation, free riding, and trade policy', *European Economic Review*, 40(3–5):795–803.

Guillaume, D. M. and Stasavage, D., 2000. 'Improving policy credibility: is there a case for African monetary union?', *World Development*, 28(8):1391–407.

Gwartney, J. and Lawson, R. with Samida, D., 2000. *Economic Freedom of the World: 2000 Annual Report*, The Fraser Institute, Vancouver.

Gwartney, J. and Lawson, R., with Park, W. and Skipton, C., 2001. *Economic Freedom of the World: 2001 Annual Report*, The Fraser Institute, Vancouver.

Gwartney, J. and Lawson, R., with Park, W., Wagh, S., Edwards, C. and de Rugy, V., 2002. *Economic Freedom of the World: 2002 Annual Report*, The Fraser Institute, Vancouver.

Hampton, J., Sibert, J.R., Kleiber, P., Maunder, M.N. and Harley, S.J., 2005. 'Decline of Pacific tuna populations exaggerated?', *Nature*, 434(7037):E1.

Hegarty, D., May, R., Regan, A., Dinnen, S., Nelson, H., and Duncan, R., 2004. *Rebuilding State and Nation in Solomon Islands: policy options for the regional assistance mission*, State, Society, and Governance in Melanesia Discussion Paper 2004/2, Research School of Pacific and Asian Studies, The Australian National University, Canberra.

Hinds, L., 2003. 'Oceans governance and the implementation gap', *Marine Policy*, 27(4):349–56.

Hoekman, B. and Ozden, C., 2005. *Trade Preferences and Differential Treatment of Developing Countries: a selective survey*, World Bank Policy Research Working Paper 3566, World Bank, Washington DC.

Horstmann, I.J. and Markusen, J.R., 1986. 'Up the average cost curve: inefficient entry and the new protectionism', *Journal of International Economics*, 20(3–4):225–47.

Hughes, H., 2003. *Aid has Failed in the Pacific*, Issue Analysis 33, The Centre for Independent Studies, Sydney.

——, 2004. *The Pacific is Viable!*, The Centre for Independent Studies, Issue Analysis 53, St. Leonards, Australia.

Ihedru, O.C., 1995. 'The political economy of Euro-African fishing agreements', *Journal of Developing Areas*, 30(1):63–90.

Inder, S., 1974. 'Up front with the editor', *Pacific Islands Monthly*, 45(6):3.

International Civil Aviation Organization (ICAO), 2005. *A Study of an Essential Service and Tourism Development Route Scheme*, International Civil Aviation Organization, Montreal.

International Monetary Fund, 2004. *Fund Support for Trade-related Balance of Payments Adjustments*, Policy and Development Review Department, International Monetary Fund, Washington DC. Available from http://www.imf.org/external/np/pdr/tim/2004/eng/022704.pdf (accessed 7 February 2005).

Jayaraman, T.K., 2001. 'Prospects for a currency union in the Pacific: a preliminary study', *Journal of Pacific Studies*, 25(2):173–202.

——, 2003. 'Is there a case for a single currency for the South Pacific islands', *Pacific Economic Bulletin*, 18(1):41–53.

——, 2005. *Dollarisation of the South Pacific Island Countries: results of a preliminary study*, USPEC Working Paper 2005/1, Department of Economics, University of the South Pacific, Suva.

——, Ward, B.D. and Xu, Z.L., 2005. *Are the Pacific Islands Ready for a Currency Union? An empirical study of degree of economic convergence*, USPEC Working Paper 2005/2, Department of Economics, University of the South Pacific, Suva.

Johnson, H.G., 1966. 'Sugar protectionism and the export earnings of less developed countries: variations on a theme by R.H. Snape', *Economica*, 33(129):34–42.

Katz, L. and Summers, L., 1989. 'Industry rents: evidence and implications', in M.N. Baily and C. Winston (eds), *Brookings Papers on Economic Activity, Microeconomics 1989*, Brookings Institute Press, Washington:209–90.

Kaufmann, D., Kraay, A. and Mastruzzi, M., 2005. 'Governance matters IV: governance indicators for 1996–2005', *World Bank Economic Review*, 18(2):253–87.

Kenny, C., 1998. 'Senegal and the entropy theory of development', *European Journal of Development Research*, 10(1):160–88.

Komori, T., Gunting, E., and Christensen, B., 2005. *Federated States of Micronesia: selected issues and statistical appendix*, IMF Country Report 05/13, International Monetary Fund, Asia and Pacific Department, Washington, DC.

Krueger, A.B. and Summers, L., 1988. 'Efficiency wages and the inter-industry wage structure', *Econometrica*, 56(2):269–93.

Kufa, P., Pellechio, A., and Rizavi, S., 2003. *Fiscal Sustainability and Policy Issues in the Eastern Caribbean Currency Union*, International Monetary Fund Working Paper 03/162, Western Hemisphere Department, Washington, DC.

Langley, A., Hampton, J., Williams, P. and Lehodey, P., 2005. *The Western and Central Pacific Tuna Fishery, 2003: overview and status of stocks*, Tuna Fisheries Assessment Report 6, Secretariat of the Pacific Community, Noumea.

Larmour, P., 2000. 'Explaining institutional failure in Melanesia', *Pacific Economic Bulletin*, 15(2):143–48.

Lasaqa, I., 1984. *The Fijian People*, Australian National University Press, Canberra.

Lawson, S.L., 1990. 'The myth of cultural homogeneity and its implications for chiefly power and politics in Fiji', *Comparative Studies in Society and History*, 32(4):795–821.

Levantis, T. and Manning, M., 2002. *The Business and Investment Environment in PNG: the private sector perspective*, Institute of National Affairs, Port Moresby.

Levantis, T., Jotzo, F. and Tulpule, V., 2004. 'Sweetening the transition in EU sugar preferences—the case of Fiji', *The World Economy*, 28(6):893–915.

Levitt, K.P., 2004. 'Independent thought and Caribbean community,' *Canadian Journal of Development Studies*, 25(2):225–37.

Lewis, K., 1995. *What Can Explain the Apparent Lack of International Consumption Risk Sharing?*, NBER Working Papers 5203, National Bureau of Economic Research, Cambridge, Massachusetts.

Lindert, P. and Williamson, J., 2001. *Does Globalization Make the World More Unequal?*, NBER Working Paper 8228, National Bureau of Economic Research, Cambridge, Massachusetts.

MacKinnon, J.G., 1991. 'Critical values for co-integration tests in long run economic relationships' in R.F. Engle and C.W.J. Granger (eds), *Readings in Co-integration*, Oxford University Press, Oxford.

Maddison, A., 1983. 'A comparison of levels of GDP per capita in developed and developing countries, 1700–1980', *The Journal of Economic History*, 43(1):27–41.

Masson, P., 2001. *Globalization: facts and figures*, IMF Policy Discussion Paper PDP/01/4, International Monetary Fund, Washington, DC.

—— and Patillo, C., 2002. 'Monetary union in West Africa: an agency of restraint for fiscal policies?', *Journal of African Economies*, 11(3):387–412.

Mawuli, A., 2005. 'A macro-appraisal of the Kina float', *Pacific Economic Bulletin*, 20(1):44–55.

McDonald, S., 1996. 'Reform of the EU's sugar policies and the African, Caribbean and Pacific countries', *Development Policy Review*, 14(2):918–41.

McKinnon, R.I., 1963. 'Optimum currency areas', *American Economic Review*, 53(1963):717–24.

McLoughlin, R. and Findlay, V., 2005. Implementation of Effective Fisheries Management, Paper presented at ABARE Outlook 05, 2 March, Canberra.

Micco, A. and Serebrisky, T., 2004. *Infrastructure, Competition Regimes and Air Transport Costs: cross-country evidence*, Working Paper 510, Inter-American Development Bank, Washington, DC.

Moore, M., 1982. *A Pacific Parliament: a political and economic community for the South Pacific*, Asia Pacific Books, Wellington.

Munro, G.R., 1979. 'The optimal management of transboundary renewable resources', *Canadian Journal of Economics*, 12(3):355–76.

——, Van Houtte, A. and Willmann, R., 2004. *The Conservation and Management of Shared Fish Stocks: legal and economic aspects*, Fisheries Technical Paper 465, Food and Agriculture Organization (FAO), Rome.

Myers, R.A. and Worm, B., 2005. 'Fisheries: decline of Pacific tuna populations exaggerated? Meyers and Worm reply', *Nature*, 434(7037):E2.

Narsey, W., 2004. 'PICTA, PACER, and EPAs: weaknesses in Pacific island countries' trade policies', *Pacific Economic Bulletin*, 19(3):74–101.

Neemia, U., 1986. *Cooperation and Conflict: costs, benefits and national interests in Pacific regional cooperation*, Institute of Pacific Studies, University of the South Pacific, Suva.

New Zealand Agency for International Development (NZAid), 2004. *Strategy for the New Zealand Development Cooperation Programme with Kiribati, 2002–2007*, NZAid, Wellington.

New Zealand Ministry of Foreign Affairs and Trade (MFAT), 2004. 'Pacific Cooperation: Voices of the Region', The Eminent Persons' Group Review of the Pacific Islands Forum, MFAT, Auckland.

New Zealand Ministry of Transport and New Zealand Ministry of Foreign Affairs, 2001. Multilateral Agreement on the Liberalization of International Air Transportation and Trade, New Zealand Ministry of Transport and New Zealand Ministry of Foreign Affairs, Wellington. Available from www.maliat.govt.nz.

Organisation for Economic Cooperation and Development (OECD), 2005. *Aid statistics, Aid Recipient Charts*, OECD, Paris. Available from www.oecd.org/dac/stats/recipientcharts (accessed 2 June 2005).

Oxfam, 2002. *The Great EU Sugar Scam: how Europe's sugar regime is devastating livelihoods in the developing world*, Oxfam Briefing Paper Number 27, Oxfam, Oxford.

Özden, C. and Reinhardt, E., 2003. *The Perversity of Preferences: GSP and developing country trade policies, 1976–2000*, World Bank Policy Research Paper 2955, World Bank, Washington, DC.

Pacific Islands Forum Fisheries Agency, 2005. 'US$11 million to support fisheries management in the Pacific', Pacific Islands Forum Fisheries Agency, Honiara. Available from http://www.ffa.int/node/512 (accessed 10 June 2005).

Pacific Islands Forum Secretariat, 2004. *Pacific Regional Transport Study*, Final Report Volume 1, Pacific Islands Forum Secretariat, Suva, Fiji.

Padmore, O.R., 1999. 'Federation: the demise of an idea', *Social and Economic Studies*, 48(4):21–63.

Page, S., 2004. *Preference Erosion: helping countries to adjust*, The Doha Development Agenda: Impacts on Trade and Poverty Briefing Paper 5, Overseas Development Institute, London.

Palmer, D. and Goodman, J.B., 1989. *Great Britain: decline or renewal?*, Havard Business School Case 9-389-011, Harvard Business School Publishing, Boston.

Panagariya, A., 2000. 'Preferential trade liberalization: the traditional theory and new developments', *Journal of Economic Literature*, 38(20):287–331.

——, 2003. *Aid Through Trade: an effective option*, Economics Working Paper Archive at WUSTL, International Trade Paper 0403006. Available from http://www.columbia.edu/~ap2231/Policy%20Papers/ayres-cgd-panagariya-rev_Aug_03.pdf (accessed 18 November 2005).

Parris, H. and Grafton, R.Q., 2005. Fishing for a Future: sustaining development in the western and central Pacific island countries, Paper presented at the International Workshop on Pacific Integration and Regional Governance, 8–9 June, Canberra. [REF AS CHAPTER NO?]

Petersen, E.H., 2002. 'Economic policy, institutions and fisheries development in the Pacific', *Marine Policy*, 26(5):315–24.

——, 2005. *Institutional Economics and Fishery Management*, Edward Elgar, Cheltenham (in press).

Powell, P.T., 2004. 'A theory of atomistic federalism for Melanesia', *Pacific Economic Bulletin*, 19(3):49–63.

Prasad, S. and Akram-Lodhi, A., 1998. 'Fiji and the Sugar Protocol: a case for trade-based development cooperation', *Development Policy Review*, 16(1):39–60.

Rao, G., 2004. 'Lending trends in the sugar cane sector', *Fijian Studies*, 1(2):301–14.

Reddy, M., 2004a. "Farm productivity, efficiency and profitability in Fiji's sugar industry", *Fijian Studies*, 1(2):225–41.

——, 2004b. 'Survival strategies for the Fiji sugar industry', *Fijian Studies*, 1(2):265–85.

Rodrik, D., 1996. *Why Do More Open Economies Have Bigger Governments?*, NBER Working Paper 5537, National Bureau of Economic Research, Cambridge, Massachusetts.

Rolfe, J., 2000. 'The Pacific Way: where "non-traditional" is the norm', *International Negotiation*, 5(3):427–48.

Rubin, P.H., 2001. 'The state of nature and the evolution of political preferences', *American Law and Economics Review*, 3(1):50–81.

Sachs, J.D. and Warner, A.M., 2001. 'The curse of natural resources', *European Economic Review*, 45(4–6):827–38.

Sala-I-Martin, X., 1997. 'Transfers, social safety nets, and economic growth', *IMF Staff Papers*, 44(1):81–102.

Saldhana, C., 2004. 'Strategies for good governance in the Pacific', *Asia Pacific Economic Literature*, 18(2):30–43.

Schiff, M., 2001. 'Will the real "natural trading partner" please stand up', *Journal of Economic Integration*, 16(2):245–61.

—— and Winters, L.A., 2003. *Regional Integration and Development*, World Bank, Washington, DC, and Oxford University Press, Oxford and New York.

Schrank, W.E., Arnason, R. and Hannesson, R., 2003. *The Cost of Fisheries Management*, Ashgate, Aldershot.

Schurman, R.A., 1998. 'Tuna dreams: resource nationalism and the Pacific Islands' tuna industry', *Development and Change*, 29(1):107–36.

Scollay, R., 1998. Free Trade Options for the Forum Island Countries, Report prepared for South Pacific Forum Secretariat, Suva (assisted by John Gilbert and Darryl Collins).

——, 2003. SPARTECA Rules of Origin and the Development of the Fijian TCF Industry, Report for Commonwealth Secretariat, London.

—— and Gilbert, J., 1998. 'Free trade among Forum island countries', *Pacific Economic Bulletin*, 13(2):118–25.

Secretariat of the Pacific Community (SPC), 2000. *Tuna Fishery Yearbook*, Secretariat of the Pacific Community, Noumea.

Sharer, R., 1998. 'Trade liberalization in Sub-Saharan Africa', in Z. Iqbal and M.S. Khan (eds), *Trade Reform and Regional Integration in Africa*, International Monetary Fund, Washington, DC.

Shibuya, E., 2003. The Problems and Potential of the Pacific Islands Forum, Paper presented at Island State Security 2003: 'Oceania at the Crossroads' Conference, Asia-Pacific Center for Security Studies, Honolulu, 15–17 July.

Sibert, A., 1999. 'Monetary integration and economic reform', *The Economic Journal*, 109(452):78–92.

Sidgwick, E., Kojo, N., and Tareen, M., 2004. *Papua New Guinea: selected issues and statistical appendix*, IMF Country Report 04/356. International Monetary Fund, Washington, DC.

Snape, R., 1963. 'Some effects of protection in the world sugar industry', *Economica*, 30(117):63–73.

South Pacific Forum, 1972. Final Communiqué, Second South Pacific Forum Meeting, Canberra, 23–25 February.

South Pacific Forum, 1971. Final Communiqué, First South Pacific Forum Meeting, Wellington, 5–7 August.

Srinivasan, T.N. and Bhagwati, J., 1999, *Outward Orientation and Development: are the revisionists right?*, Economic Growth Center Discussion Paper No. 806, Yale University, New Haven.

Stoeckel, A. and Davis, L., 1998. 'Costs and benefits of a free trade area between forum island countries and Australia and New Zealand', *Pacific Economic Bulletin*, 13(2):126–32.

Streeten, P., 1993. 'The special problems of small countries', *World Development*, 21(2):197–202.

Sugar Commission of Fiji, 2002. The Fiji Sugar Industry, Briefing notes for Mr Poul Nielson, European Union Commissioner for Development & Humanitarian Affairs, 18 September (unpublished).

Sutherland, P., 2002. 'Why we should embrace globalization', *Finance and Development*, 39(3):n.p. Available from http://www.imf.org/external/pubs/ft/fandd/2002/09/sutherla.htm (accessed 3 April 2005).

Sutherland, W., 2000. 'Global imperatives and economic reform in the Pacific island states', *Development and Change*, 31(2):459–80.

Taylor, A.M. and Obstfeld, M., 2004. *Global Capital Markets: integration, crisis, and growth*, Cambridge University Press, Cambridge.

Thomas, J., 2002. 'The squid that saved the Falkland Islands', *The Slate*, 18 March. Available from http://slate.msn.com/id/2063325/ (accessed 4 June 2005).

Transparency International, 2001. *National Integrity Systems: Transparency International Country Study Report—Fiji*, Report prepared by Olaks Consulting Services for Transparency International, Melbourne, Australia.

——, 2004. *National Integrity Systems: Cook Islands 2004*, Report prepared by Dr Takiora Ingram and Mathilde Urhle for Transparency International, Melbourne, Australia.

—— and Asia Pacific School of Economics and Government, 2003. *National Integrity Systems: Transparency International Country Study Report—Papua New Guinea*, Report prepared for Transparency International, Melbourne, Australia.

——, 2004a. *National Integrity Systems: Transparency International Country Study Report—Kiribati*, Report prepared by Ueantabo Neemia Mackenzie for Transparency International, Melbourne, Australia.

——, 2004b. *National Integrity Systems: Transparency International Country Study Report—Marshall Islands*, Report prepared by Nancy Pollock for Transparency International, Melbourne, Australia.

——, 2004c. *National Integrity Systems: Transparency International Country Study Report—Nauru*, Report prepared by Ruben Kun, Roland Kun and Whitlam Togomae for Transparency International, Melbourne, Australia.

——, 2004d. *National Integrity Systems: Transparency International Country Study Report—Palau*, Report prepared by Donald Schuster for Transparency International, Melbourne, Australia.

——, 2004e. *National Integrity Systems: Transparency International Country Study Report—Samoa*, Report prepared by L. Asofou, R. Sinclair, U. Va'a and S. Lameta for Transparency International, Melbourne, Australia.

——, 2004f. *National Integrity Systems: Transparency International Country Study Report—Solomon Islands*. Report prepared by Paul Roughan for Transparency International, Melbourne, Australia.

——, 2004g. *National Integrity Systems: Transparency International Country Study Report—Tonga*, Report prepared by Kerry James and Taniela Tufui for Transparency International, Melbourne, Australia.

——, 2004h. *National Integrity Systems: Transparency International Country Study Report—Tuvalu*, Report prepared by Tauaasa Taafaki for Transparency International, Melbourne, Australia.

——, 2004i. *National Integrity Systems: Transparency International Country Study Report—Vanuatu*, Report prepared by Tess Cain and Anita Jowitt for Transparency International, Melbourne, Australia.

Trumbull, G., 2003. *The Creation of the European Union*, Havard Business School Case 9-703-032, Harvard Business School Publishing, Boston.

UNCTAD, 1997. The Vulnerability of Small Island Development States in the Context of Globalisation: common issues and remedies, Background Paper for Expert Group Meeting on Vulnerability Indexes for Small Island Developing States, New York, 17–19 December.

——, 2002. *Handbook on the UNCTAD Agricultural Trade Policy Simulation Model (ATPSM)*. Version 2.2, UNCTAD, New York, Available online at http://www.unctad.org/tab (accessed 17 September 2003).

——, 2003. *Handbook of Statistics*, UNCTAD, New York.

United Nations Development Programme (UNDP), 2004. *Human Development Report 2004: cultural liberty in today's diverse world*, UNDP, New York.

Van Santen, G. and Müller, P., 2000. *Working Apart or Together: the case for a common approach to management of the tuna resources in exclusive economic zones of Pacific island countries*, Pacific Islands Discussion Paper 10, East Asia Pacific Region, Papua New Guinea and Pacific Islands Country Management Unit, World Bank, Washington, DC.

Vanzetti, D. and Peters, R., 2003. Making sense of agricultural trade policy reform, Paper presented to the 25th International Conference of IAAE, Durban, South Africa, 16–22 August.

Wakas, W. and Tapakau, E., 2005. 'ECP ultimatum', *PNG Post-Courier*, Port Moresby, May 5, p. 1.

Weingast, B.R., 1997. 'The political foundations of democracy and the rule of law', *American Political Science Review*, 91(2):245–63.

Wells, J., 1996. *Composite Vulnerability Index: a preliminary report*, Commonwealth Secretariat, London.

——, 1997. *Composite Vulnerability Index: a revised report*, Commonwealth Secretariat, London.

Western and Central Pacific Fisheries Commission, 2004. Proposed Budget for the Commission for its First financial Period from 1 January 2005 to 31 December 2005, Western and Central Pacific Fisheries Commission, Pohnpei, Federated States of Micronesia.

Whalley, J., 1990. 'Non-discriminatory discrimination: special and differential treatment under GATT for developing countries', *Economic Journal*, 100(403):1318–28.

White, M., 2004. 'The financial viability of the Fiji Sugar Corporation: an assessment from the corporation's annual financial reports', *Fijian Studies*, 1(2):287–300.

Williamson, J. G., 1996. 'Globalization, convergence, and history', *Journal of Economic History*, 56(2):277–306.

Winters, L.A., 2000. 'The EU's preferential trade agreements: objectives and outcomes', in P. van Dijck and G. Faber (eds), *The External Economic Dimension of the European Union*, Kluwer Law International, The Hague:195–222.

—— and Martins, P.M.G., 2004. 'When comparative advantage is not enough: business costs in small remote economies', *World Trade Review*, 3(3):347–83.

——, 2005. *Beautiful but costly: business costs in small remote economies*, Economic Paper Series 67, Commonwealth Secretariat, London.

Winters, L.A., Walmsley, T., Wang, Z and Grynberg, R., 2003a. 'Negotiating the temporary movement of natural persons: an agenda for the development round', *The World Economy*, 26(8):1137–62.

——, 2003b. *Liberalising Labour Mobility under the GATS*, Economic Paper Series 53, Commonwealth Secretariat, London.

World Bank, 1993. *Pacific Island Transport Sector Study—Vol. 1 Transport Issues: a regional perspective*, Report 10543-EAP, World Bank, Washington, DC..

——, 1995. *Fiji: restoring growth in a changing global environment*, World Bank Economic Report 13862, World Bank, Washington, DC.

——, 2000a. *Small States: meeting challenges in the global economy*, Commonwealth Secretariat/World Bank Joint Task Force report, Washington DC and London.

——, 2000b. *Pacific Regional Strategy,* East Asia and Pacific Regional Office Report 20370-EAP, World Bank, Washington, DC.

——, 2001. *Globalization, growth and poverty: facts, fears and an agenda for action*, Policy Research Report **NO?**, World Bank, Washington, DC.

——, 2003. *Sustainable Development in a Dynamic World: transforming institutions, growth, and quality of life*, Oxford University Press, New York.

——, 2004. *Doing Business: understanding regulation*, World Bank, Washington, DC.

——, 2005. *World Development Indicators Online*, World Bank, Washington, DC. Available at http://publications.w_-_orldbank.org/WDI/ (accessed 13 April 2005).

Worrell, D., 2003. *A Currency Union of the Caribbean*, International Monetary Fund Working Paper 03/35, Money and Exchange Affairs Department, Washington, DC.

Xu, Xinpeng, 1999. 'The exchange rate regime in Papua New Guinea—getting it right', *Pacific Economic Bulletin*, 14(2):48–60.

Yeats, A.J., Amjadi, A., Reincke, U. and Ng., F. 1996. 'What caused sub-Saharan Africa's marginalization in world trade', *Finance and Development*, 33(4):38–41.

Zak, P.J. and Feng, Y., 2003. 'A dynamic theory of the transition to democracy', *Journal of Economic Behavior & Organization*, 52(1):1–25.

INDEX

www.ingramcontent.com/pod-product-compliance
Lightning Source LLC
Chambersburg PA
CBHW040151270326
41926CB00071B/4617